MW01484576

Composers on Composing for Band
Volume Two

Also available from GIA Publications, Inc.:

Composers on Composing for Band

Edited by Mark Camphouse

James Barnes

Timothy Broege

Mark Camphouse

David Gillingham

David R. Holsinger

Karel Husa

Timothy Mahr

W. Francis McBeth

Robert Sheldon

Jack Stamp

Frank Ticheli

Composers
on Composing
for Band

volume Two

edited by **Mark Camphouse**

james **Curnow**
johan **de Meij**
julie **Giroux**
donald **Grantham**
robert **Jager**
pierre **La Plante**
david **Maslanka**
philip **Sparke**
eric **Whitacre**
dana **Wilson**

with a foreword by **Gary D. Green**

GIA Publications, Inc.
Chicago

G-5920
© 2004 GIA Publications, Inc.
7404 S. Mason Ave., Chicago, IL 60638
www.giamusic.com

Chapter 3 "Johan de Meij" is adapted from an interview
by Anthony Fiumara and translated from the Dutch
by Lisa de Vries.

ISBN: 1-57999-385-0
Cover design: Yolanda Durán
Book layout: Robert Sacha
All rights reserved. No portion of this book may be
reproduced, stored in a retrieval system, or transmitted in
any form or means—electronic, mechanical, photocopying,
recording, or other, without prior written permission of
GIA Publications, Inc.

Printed in the United States of America

The intuitve mind is a sacred gift and the rational mind is a
faithful servant. We have created a society that honors
the servant and has forgotten the gift.

—Albert Einstein

On the occasion of his 90th year, this volume is respectfully and affectionately dedicated to the legendary Frederick Fennell, founding father of the modern wind band/ensemble and unceasing composer's advocate.

Table of Contents

Foreword

by Gary D. Green

Volume Two of *Composers on Composing for Band* is a welcome addition to this distinguished series. Having read and studied the collection of writings in both volumes, I am pleased to report that each contains valuable insights into the creative process that until now have been available to only a small number of conductors. By conceiving the concept of inviting these composers to write and by organizing their thoughts into a meaningful foundation, Mark Camphouse has provided us with an essential look into the life and mind of the artist-composer.

Inspiration is the most vital aspiration of musical experience. Without inspiration, our study of music and consequently our teaching of it become tedious, directionless, and ultimately meaningless. The music we choose to study and teach our students becomes an "open window" into the depths of our musical being. By sharing their thoughts and their compositional concepts, the composers enable us to be better prepared in bringing more thoughtful and sensitive re-creative interpretations to our music making.

It is my firm belief that we, as teacher-conductors, act simply as conduits through which the composer's spirit (intent) flows. It is a humbling responsibility to know that we must appreciate and comprehend everything we can about the music that we are to teach. Issues of technique, pitch, tempi, phrasing, and dynamics, to name a few, are important but can leave us without the satisfaction of a true musical feeling. The great Pablo Casals stated, "Technique and wonderful sound can sometimes be astonishing . . . but it is not enough!" In my mind, the question becomes "Then what is enough?" By reading and careful study, and by entering into the dream world of the composer, we are better prepared to understand the beauty and the humanity that he or she expresses within the limitations of musical notation.

In matters of the spirit, we make our personal decisions as to where we may stand in the area of spiritual theology. However, in matters of the spirit in music, we must pay close attention to the musical details that are so important to the success of any performance. These details include pitch, technique, pulse, dynamics, line, and other matters of musical preparation. It becomes clear that if we accomplish those details, we are then ready to step effortlessly into the realm of the spirit. It is that selfless step that we must take in order to pay respect to the composer. **Technique provides clarity – the spirit provides inspiration**.

This collection of writings by these well-established composers provides for us a door through which we may enter and make new discoveries. As with their compositions, these writings ask us to look more closely into the being of the person and the artist. And by doing so, we may then make the decision to either look beyond that door or to walk away. Should we enter (and they encourage us to do so) we are changed in a way that is unique to each of us, and we never return to the way we once were. The goal of the composer is to inspire and to change the world in which we live. It is our responsibility to seek those things that change us into becoming better teachers, musicians, and human beings. By choosing great literature to perform with our ensembles and by seeking to better understand the creative process, we inspire greatness in ourselves and in our students. And that is the primary goal of all art!

We now have in our possession a book that will inspire us to look beyond the façade of the notes and the score. The notes written by the composer are mere symbols and do not contain the meaning or the feeling of the music. In reading these pages, I believe that you, like me, will find greater understanding and ability to become a composer's advocate. And in doing so and by pledging ourselves selflessly to that unique responsibility, we will always remain students of music and of composers. I have worked closely with many of these wonderful artists and have found them to be grateful when we seek the truth in their music. *Composers on Composing for Band* is an inspirational series that will guide us all toward a better understanding of the magic of music.

It is my hope that you will be as inspired to know these wonderful people and their work as I have. I am so grateful to have been alive during this exciting time of new and important musical creativity and look forward to more years of service to the greatness of composition through the performance of inspired works. Thank you, Mark Camphouse and all of the composers associated with this project. You have made our lives richer through your sacrifices and your gifts.

—Gary D. Green, director of bands
University of Miami, Coral Gables, Florida

Introduction

by Mark Camphouse

While valuable for composition, music education, and applied music performance students, the *Composers on Composing for Band* series is primarily intended for wind band conductors at all levels who are interested in gaining fresh insights and perspectives from the ultimate source of musical creativity – the composer.

As with Volume One, the ten co-authoring composers of this book come from widely varied backgrounds. Their life experiences, professional careers, artistic and educational philosophies, and their approaches to the compositional process contrast as vividly as do their distinct creative voices. But the reader will also discover some important shared values, goals, and principles among the composers, most notably:

- A desire to bring closer the creative and re-creative realms of music and music-making, thereby promoting greater understanding and a more meaningful and mutually beneficial partnership between the composer and the conductor;

- A commitment to leave a legacy of high-quality wind band repertoire to enlighten, enrich, and entertain audiences of future generations;

- A passion for teaching and inspiring tomorrow's composers, conductors, and performers.

Compared to Volume One, there is an even greater breadth and variety of composers in this volume, including the important creative contributions of two leading European colleagues. The geographical range of American composers spans from Montana to Mississippi, New York to California. Their music ranges from some of the finest and most enriching repertoire for middle and high school bands to some of the most challenging and complex works, which require the musical maturity of leading college, university, adult/community, and professional military bands. The ten composers in this volume are splendid musical citizens and possess the highest standards of artistic and personal integrity. Each is able to see the "big picture" of our profession and is influential in shaping its future.

The format from Volume One to Volume Two remains essentially the same. The 12 topics addressed by each composer in his or her respective chapter include:

A. Biography
B. The Creative Process
C. The Approach to Orchestration
D. Views from the Composer to the Conductor Pertaining to Score Study and Preparation
E. The Relationship Between the Composer and the Commissioning Party
F. Views on the Teaching of Composition and How to Mentor the Young Composer
G. Individuals Who Have Been Especially Influential on My Development and Career
H. Ten Works I Believe All Band Conductors at All Levels Should Study

I. Ten Composers Whose Music Overall Speaks to Me in Especially Meaningful Ways

J. The Future of the Wind Band

K. Other Facets of My Everyday Life (family, leisure time, and hobbies)

L. Comprehensive List of Works for Band

The ten composers in Volume Two share my view that there is an ongoing need for a book series of this kind that enables all wind band conductors at all levels to have a rare, unique, and fascinating glimpse into the composer's world. I hope this exchange will foster more stimulating dialog, meaningful interaction, and mutual understanding among composers, conductors, performers (and ultimately audiences!) of both today and tomorrow.

—Mark Camphouse

Fall 2004,

Radford, Virginia

chapter **1**

james
Curnow

The opportunities afforded all participants through involvement in the band movement are incredible. Where else can a performer, composer, conductor, and, yes, sometimes even a vocal soloist, go to find such immediate musical acceptance, individual accomplishment, and personal expressive satisfaction than in a band?

A. Biography

James Curnow was born in Port Huron, Michigan, in 1943 and raised in Royal Oak, Michigan, where he received his initial musical training in the public schools and The Salvation Army Instrumental Programs. He lives in Nicholasville, Kentucky, where he is president, composer, and educational consultant for Curnow Music Press, Inc., publisher of significant music for concert band and brass band. Curnow is also composer-in-residence (Emeritus) on the faculty of Asbury College in Wilmore, Kentucky, and editor of all music publications for The Salvation Army in Atlanta, Georgia.

For his formal training, Curnow earned a bachelor of music from Wayne State University in Detroit, Michigan, and a master of music from Michigan State University in East Lansing, where he studied euphonium with Leonard Falcone and conducting with Dr. Harry Begian. His studies in composition and arranging were with F. Maxwell Wood, James Gibb, Jere Hutchinson, and Irwin Fischer.

Curnow has taught in all areas of instrumental music, both in the public schools (five years), and at the college and university level (thirty-two years). He is a member of several professional organizations, including the American Bandmasters Association, College Band Directors National Association, National Band Association, and the American Society of Composers, Authors and Publishers (ASCAP). In 1980 Curnow received the National Band Association's Citation of Excellence. In 1985, while a tenured associate professor at the University of Illinois at Champaign-Urbana, he was honored as an outstanding faculty member. Among his most recent honors are inclusion in Who's Who in America, Who's Who in the South and Southwest, and Composer of the Year by the Kentucky Music Teachers Association and the National Music Teachers Association in 1997. Curnow has received annual ASCAP standard awards since 1979.

As a conductor, composer and clinician, he has traveled throughout the United States, Canada, Australia, Japan, and Europe where his music has received wide acclaim. Among his awards for band composition are: the ASBDA/Volkwein Composition Award in 1977 (*Symphonic Triptych*) and 1979 (*Collage for Band*), the ABA/Ostwald Award in 1980 (*Mutanza*) and 1984 (*Symphonic Variants for Euphonium and Band*), the 1985 Sixth International Competition of Original Compositions for Band (*Australian Variants Suite*), the 1994 Coup de Vents Composition Competition of Le Havre, France (*Lochinvar*), a commission through recognition of the KMTNA in 1997 (*On Poems of John Keats for String Quartet*), and second place in the 2001 International Trumpet Guild Composition Competition (*Three Episodes for Trumpet and Piano*).

Curnow has been commissioned to write more than 200 works for concert band, brass band, orchestra, choir, and various vocal and instrumental ensembles. His published works now number well over 400. His most recent commissions include those by the Tokyo Symphony Orchestra (*Symphonic Variants for Euphonium and Orchestra*), the United States Army Band "Pershing's Own" (*Lochinvar*, Symphonic Poem for Winds and Percussion), Roger Behrend and the DEG Music Products, Inc., with Willson Band Instrument Companies (Concerto for Euphonium and Orchestra), the 1996 Atlanta Committee for the Olympic Games (*Olympic Fanfare and Theme for the Olympic Flag*), the Kentucky Music Teachers Association/National Music Teachers Association in 1997 (*On Poems of John Keats for String Quartet*), the University of North Carolina at Greensboro, Focus On Piano Literature 2000 (*Three Episodes for Trumpet and Piano*), John Whitwell, director of bands at Michigan State University, (*Ode And Epinicion*), and the Capitol Quartet (*Dialogues for Saxophone Quartet, Winds and Percussion*).

B. The Creative Process

I am a great lover of poetry and non-fiction, and I spend much of what free time I have reading. Many of my works are based on ideas gleaned from literature I have read that has inspired me.

During the first 25 years of my full-time teaching career, much of my creative time came during early morning hours, weekends, and school breaks. I have always felt blessed that I never seemed to require much sleep and was able to channel early morning hours into writing time. Most mornings I was up by 3:00 a.m. and would write until leaving for my teaching duties.

I have always had an unquenchable desire to compose and a continuous drive to improve my skills by listening, studying the works of great composers, and practicing composition daily. Because my pianistic skills are extremely limited (i.e., non-existent), I very early developed the ability to hear and sing written music regardless of the form or medium. This skill was reinforced by an early teacher who required me to sing and understand my assignments before I could play them on my euphonium.

The years spent growing up in a strong church music program in The Salvation Army were another wonderful source for developing my aural skills. The hours spent singing in various vocal ensembles and playing in instrumental groups forced my ear to become "tuned" to listening, to tone, intonation, harmonic structures, melodic construction, and development. This training was absolutely free, but priceless!

Consequently, all of my composing is done without the use of the keyboard, though I generally sit at my piano (using two to eight, never ten fingers) to occasionally check my work. I do not consider this anything special; it is just the way I work.

I write everything (as do my students) in short score form. This is sometimes expanded to three, four, or five staves depending on the complexity of the work. I am a composer who writes by color, and because of this, I make notes on my short score during the writing process.

I guess I would be considered an "old-fashioned" composer in that I do not use a computer program during the creative process and prefer pencil and paper. In order for me to "hear" the colors of the entire ensemble as I work on the full score, I need to have the full score visible at all times. A computer screen just does not work for me. Over the years, I have always been fortunate enough to have copyists available to do all the laborious "nitty-gritty" work of score and part preparation. I do, however, especially in the last few years, use the computer as a listening tool for proofing and editing my writing before signing off on the final score.

C. The Approach to Orchestration

One of the most frequently asked questions (after "How much money do you make?") is: What orchestration book(s) did you study to learn how to create all the beautiful sounds in your music? While there are numerous excellent orchestration and band arranging books available, I have never discovered one that is able to actually "teach" the creation of sounds of instrumental combinations or musical colors. All music involves aural skills, and the art of instrumental colorization must be learned through listening experiences. However, I do not mean to minimize the importance of learning the basics of instrumental ranges, registrations, timbre, and technical capabilities.

Being a euphonium player, with sometimes uninteresting parts to play (the 20th-century composer has done little to encourage players of one of the most beautiful-sounding, expressive instruments in the band) and generally placed inconspicuously near the back of the band, I was able to do a great deal of listening to the color combinations of earlier composers and to develop a helpful repertoire of visual and aural combinations (i.e., how various combinations of instruments work together to establish a vast variety of colors).

Consequently, when I compose, I write a short score very similar to a piano score (larger for more expansive, difficult works). As I write, I make copious notes as to which instruments I actually hear in each passage. When I eventually write the full score, the task basically is a technical one of getting the notes on the paper. One potential drawback to orchestrating by color is the fact that a computer program is almost useless because only a few instruments can be seen at one time. Besides, I can't smell the graphite when using one!

For me, one of the most satisfying and greatest thrills of composing is to be able to see the music come "alive" on the score.

D. Views from the Composer to the Conductor Pertaining to Score Study and Preparation

Score study and analysis, for me, comes under the heading: Pre-rehearsal Planning—Diagnosis. I have had the occasion over the years to talk with many great conductors, and not one of them when asked about his or her process of preparing a score prior to a rehearsal has ever shown me an unmarked score. Interpreting and teaching a score is impossible without detailed score analysis and an in-depth understanding of all aspects of the piece.

Some teachers espouse that a conductor should listen to a recording of a piece before beginning the actual score study process. I think just the opposite is true. My advice would be to never listen to a recording of a work until you have spent hours immersing yourself in all the various aspects of the score and can "sing" it in your mind over and over again. In this way, the conductor develops such an aural sense of what the composer has written that he can begin to add his own interpretation and love of the music, not another conductor's.

Here are some basic aspects of the score that I feel conductors must understand before they can even begin to think about "making music" with the score.

1. *Historical placement:* This includes pertinent information for developing a knowledge of the context of the composition. The circumstances surrounding the creation of the work also include cultural and social aspects of the music. The historical or stylistic period can be anything from nationalism, impressionism, expressionism, and neo-classicism to 12-tone, serial, aleatoric, and jazz. If the piece was a commission or a premiere, ask yourself who, what, where, when, and why it was written. Is the composition programmatic, whether based on poetry, a story, a painting, or a play? Or is it absolute music? All of these considerations are important to the stylistic interpretation of the score.

2. *Key signatures and key changes:* Although the conductor is not required to be able to negotiate the key signatures and key changes, he must be aware of all the implications for his performers (i.e., relationship of keys to registers, ranges, and intonation).

3. *Meters:* The conductor must be aware of all aspects of the time signatures including the basic pulse changes, if any; the problems they present to the player; and how to negotiate

these changes. Here is where practice, practice, practice of "stick technique" becomes necessary.

4. *Tempi:* Be aware of various tempi in the score. Know all that they involve and how to conduct through tempo changes.

5. *Melodic lines:* Be able to locate, identify, and mark impor- tant melodic and motivic material such as main themes, secondary themes, motifs, and countermelodies, and be able to sing, if necessary, in the proper key, pitch, and rhythm. Developing an accurate system of marking or highlighting all important melodic material is crucial to a thorough understanding and interpretation of the score.

6. *Harmonic scheme:* Analyze, as much as possible, the harmonic layout, the pitch centers of movements or large sections, and harmony as related to scales and keys.

7. *Rhythmic scheme:* Identify rhythmic devices such as syncopation, hemiola, diminution, augmentation, polyrhythms, and ostinati. Be able to sing and demonstrate all of the above.

8. *Dynamic plan:* This should include an overall dynamic scheme (mark or highlight major dynamic contrasts), large section climaxes, phrase climaxes, dynamic effects such as terraced dynamics and extremes (*ff-pp, fp, sfz*), and the use of percussion to heighten effects and subtle nuances.

9. *Articulations:* Know where they are and what problems they may present.

10. *Interpretation–phrasing and style:* Directives or expression marks (upper left-hand corner of the first page of the score) will dictate style, tempo, and mood.

11. *Form:* Analyze external forms including sectional forms (binary, ternary, rondo), variation forms (theme and

variation, passacaglia, chaconne), developmental forms (sonata allegro), imitative forms (fugue, canon, canzona), and dance forms (minuet, gigue, gavotte). Also examine internal forms such as periods (a complete musical thought), sections (a short division of one or more periods of a composition), and phrases (short passages, complete in themselves).

Now that the score is completely learned and understood, musical expression and personal interpretation begins.

E. The Relationship Between the Composer and the Commissioning Party

I have had the privilege of being commissioned to write more than 200 works for vocal organizations, bands, orchestras, solos, and duets for just about any combination of instruments and voices possible. My first commission was in 1969, and since then the commissioning process has always been a varied and most enjoyable undertaking. A number of years ago, I organized my commissioning fee and contract materials in a computer file, and I have it available whenever necessary. Commissions come directly from the commissioning party via personal contact at conventions, clinics, and guest conducting engagements as well as by fax, phone, and through the Internet.

My fees for a commissioned work are based on a set fee per grade level up through grade four. After grade four, the amounts per grade level increase considerably because of the time and creative energy it takes to compose and score long, advanced works.

Because I still enjoy working with pencil and paper, I have never taken the time away from writing to immerse myself in a music engraving program. I include the cost of hiring a copyist in my commission fees because it frees me for the "creative" part of the commission and allows me to make better use of my time.

For me one of the joys of the commissioning process is the opportunity to conduct the premiere. It is important for me to not only conduct the ensemble but to meet and express appreciation to the performers, and, in the case of a school commission, to meet the teachers, administrators, and the people who have financially contributed to the commission.

Every commission is accompanied by hours of hard work and commitment to raising funds to pay composer fees. I always appreciate this commitment, and I am always grateful for being selected to compose the music.

All commissions should be a partnership between the composer and the commissioning party. I always begin the process by asking for the following:

1. *Level of difficulty:* I never want to over- or under-estimate the abilities of an organization.
2. *Soloists:* When writing for an educational organization, I sometimes write sparsely scored pieces, which feature small ensembles and more proficient players within the larger ensemble. I feel it is impossible to teach the necessary tools of good, confident solo playing if there are no solos in the music.
3. *Size of the ensemble:* This is of great importance when approaching the full score for approximating balance and blend.

4. *Instrumentation:* What instruments do they have available, particularly double reeds, low woodwinds, and percussion? Although I try to accommodate the commissioning party's ensemble as much as possible, I always score what I actually hear in my composer's ear and then adjust when necessary through the use of cross-cueing (not indiscriminate doubling).

5. *Style:* What type or style of piece would they prefer? (i.e., march, overture, suite, variations, etc.) Often the commissioning party has performed some of my works and has a general concept in mind regarding the style of piece they would like to have me compose.

These are all factors that I consider when beginning a newly commissioned work, however, I never let any or all of these factors dictate what I write. The creative process must be unlimited and unqualified.

F. Views on the Teaching of Composition and How to Mentor the Young Composer

One of the joys of my teaching career (37 years at the public school, college, and university levels) has been the opportunity to teach one-on-one composition. It has been my experience that the fundamentals of composition (music theory, counterpoint, form and analysis, orchestration, and even music history) can, through an in-depth, continuous process, be taught with great effectiveness. However, the creative and intuitive compositional gift cannot be taught but only guided by the teacher.

Also the all-important drive and desire to compose must come naturally from within the developing composer. I always tell my students that to become a composer one must practice composing as often as an instrumentalist or vocalist who wishes to become a professional performer must practice. Only a daily regimen of practicing the art of composition and furthering the creative process will bring success.

G. Individuals Who Have Been Especially Influential in My Development and Career

I believe that people's entire lives are shaped by the people who cross their path. The two most important and influential people were my parents, Clyde and Kathryn Curnow. They were (and my mother still is) wonderful, godly role models in every aspect of my life: spiritual, social, and, of course, musical. They were both amateur church musicians and continuously modeled commitment, dedication, and excellence in all of their endeavors.

My two brothers, Clyde (an amazing amateur tuba player) and Paul (an outstanding conductor, composer, and an incredible tuba player), are a continuous source of inspiration and encouragement through all of our music making together.

I must pay special tribute to my wife, Margaret (Marge), who has given selflessly during our 40 years of marriage, and our three children, Jeff, Lisa, and Amy, for their unending support and encouragement of my career. They all are wonderful!

My high school band directors, Russell J. Peters and Joseph D. Parker, though diverse in their approach to teaching, were always available to encourage and direct my developing musical abilities. Perhaps one of the most influential people in my life has been a little known and unheralded music teacher and dedicated Salvation Army bandmaster, Max Wood. He is a master teacher, conductor, and composer with whom I had the privilege of studying conducting, composing and arranging, euphonium, and, yes, musical and spiritual commitment, from the age of 14 through my undergraduate degree in music. He is now retired (so he says), but he continues to conduct a wonderful Salvation Army brass band in Florida.

Last, though there were many more along the way, my two major mentors during my college and teaching years were Leonard Falcone (euphonium) and Dr. Harry Begian (conducting). Mr. Falcone taught me to go beyond the written page as a soloist (funny how that also applies to conductors), and Dr. Begian (I still have a hard time calling him Harry) showed me a love for music, commitment to the discipline of music making, music history, music theory, form and analysis, and rehearsal technique in *every* rehearsal. He will always be my teacher!

H. Ten Works I Believe All Band Conductors at All Levels Should Study

An impossible task, but here are some thoughts on a few of my many favorites.

1. The six Brandenburg Concertos by Johann Sebastian Bach. These works lead to an understanding of how to handle virtuosic passages for the entire orchestra.

2. Symphony no. 2 by Johannes Brahms is notable for its sheer beauty and melodic structure.

3. The Octet for Wind Instruments by Igor Stravinsky provides insight into composing for smaller ensembles.

4. Serenade in B-flat Major for 13 Wind Instruments, K. 361 by Wolfgang Amadeus Mozart. All seven movements are superb demonstrations of writing for winds and a great study in form.

5. *Don Juan* by Richard Strauss is exceptional programmatic music and has unparalleled orchestration.

6. Concerto for Orchestra by Béla Bartók. Orchestration, orchestration, orchestration!

7. Symphony for Band by Vincent Persichetti is a unique, unequalled approach to scoring for winds and percussion.

8. Symphony in B-flat by Paul Hindemith is excellent for the study of symphonic form and counterpoint.

9. *Mathis der Maler* by Paul Hindemith is notable for the confluence of spiritual thought and the creative process.

10. *Chichester Psalms* by Leonard Bernstein. Voices and instruments combine in an incredible array of color and texture, demonstrating the concept of text painting.

I. Ten Composers Whose Music Overall Speaks to Me in Especially Meaningful Ways

If you will permit me to do so, I would prefer to think in terms of the musical influences on my compositions (for all mediums) and the composers who, through score study and listening, have had a profound influence on me as a composer:

1. *Melodic inclinations*: **Robert Schumann**, **Felix Mendelssohn**, **Eric Ball** (Salvation Army brass band composer), **Sir Dean Goffin** (Salvation Army brass band

composer), **Paul Creston**, **Paul Hindemith**, **John Ireland**, and **Ralph Vaughan Williams**.

2. *Harmonic inclinations*: **Aaron Copland**, **Claude Debussy**, **Paul Hindemith**, **Samuel Barber**, **Charles Ives**, **Eric Ball**, **Ray Steadman-Allen** (Salvation Army brass band composer), **Paul Creston**, **Carl Orff**, **Leonard Bernstein**, **Norman Dello Joio**, and **Percy Grainger**.

3. *Counterpoint*: **Johann S. Bach**, **Wolfgang Amadeus Mozart**, **Ludwig van Beethoven**, **Paul Hindemith**, **Vincent Persichetti**, and **Leonard Bernstein**.

4. *Form*: **Wolfgang Amadeus Mozart**, Ludwig van Beethoven, Sir Dean Goffin, Felix Mendelssohn, Franz Schubert, **Norman Dello Joio**, and **Paul Hindemith**.

5. *Orchestration*: **Richard Strauss**, **Maurice Ravel**, **Sergei Rachmaninoff**, **Ottorino Respighi**, **Aaron Copland**, **Igor Stravinsky**, **Samuel Barber**, and **Leonard Bernstein**.

6. *Scoring for Band*: **Percy Grainger**, **Alfred Reed**, **Paul Creston**, **Robert Russell Bennett**, **Erik Leidzen**, **Clifton Williams**, and **John Barnes Chance**.

J. The Future of the Wind Band

I guess the fact that I have been involved with bands and band music since I was eight years old speaks volumes about my love for and commitment to bands. I also feel that my 37 years as a music educator, principally in the instrumental area, and the establishment of Curnow Music Press, Inc., ten years ago for the publication of band music and educational materials show my commitment to the future of the wind band.

At one time in my education, I had to make a decision regarding continuing my studies in a vocal (I did a great deal of singing and choral writing in my early years.) or instrumental track. There has never been a doubt in my mind that I made the correct decision, and I have never looked back.

The opportunities afforded all participants through involvement in the band movement are incredible. Where else can a performer, composer, conductor, and, yes, sometimes even a vocal soloist, go to find such immediate musical acceptance, individual accomplishment, and personal expressive satisfaction than in a band—particularly a band committed to serving the needs of the community?

As one who has had the good fortune to travel as a composer and conductor, I am enamored with the community band movement worldwide. In my opinion, it is the best thing going in amateur music making today, and it certainly is an important indicator as to whether or not our music education system is working. If students continue to play throughout their lives, we have done a great job as educators. If they drop out after high school or college, we have failed them miserably.

Therefore, if the large number of strong community band programs throughout the world is any indicator of the future of the band movement, I am truly excited about things to come. Bring it on.

K. Other Facets of My Everyday Life

My life has always centered on family, church (The Salvation Army), and music.

My wife, Marge, and I recently celebrated 40 years of marriage. Marge is an oil and watercolor painter, and though she graciously puts my music, our children, and the church ahead of her own desire to be creative, she has still managed to turn out quite a wealth of work. You should also know that she finished her college degree (*cum laude*) after the birth of our three children and taught public school art in Kentucky and Illinois. She likes to say that she is now the head of a very selective art school and is content to have only our three grandchildren as pupils.

We have three delightful children who have all enjoyed making music over the years. (Jeff—San Pedro, California: bass trombone, Lisa—Estes Park, Colorado: percussion, and Amy—Dallas, Texas: voice). We never pushed them to select music as a career but simply encouraged them to enjoy it. Amy has chosen music as a profession, and if you listen to the music on television and radio jingles, you have probably heard her sing. We have three wonderful grandchildren whom we enjoy immensely. Much of what free time we have is spent traveling to visit children and grandchildren.

I enjoy reading, especially history (biographies and Revolutionary and Civil War stories) as well as poetry. I find that there is a terrific correlation between my joy of reading and writing music, and that is inspiration. Many of my compositions (75-80%) have sprung from an especially poignant poem or a sense of "place" described in a favorite novel.

Marge and I (and our children) have always enjoyed traveling and have had the privilege of journeying worldwide because of the opportunities afforded us through music. We are very blessed.

L. Comprehensive List of Works for Band

Grade 0.5

Great Composers. (2000, Curnow Music Press, Inc.)

Jamaican Holiday, Suite of Jamaican Folk Songs. (2:00, 2004, Curnow Music Press, Inc.)

Meet the Great Composers. (2000, Curnow Music Press, Inc.)

Grade 1

Cantigas España. (3:10, 1996, Curnow Music Press, Inc.)

The Centurions. (2:05, Curnow Music Press, Inc.)

Chorale and Caprice. (3:00, 2003, Curnow Music Press, Inc.)

El Niño. (2:30, Curnow Music Press, Inc.)

Festivo Fantastico. (2:20, 1999, Curnow Music Press, Inc.)

Grandfather's Clock. (2:05, 1987, Jenson)

Infinity Concert March. (2:10, 1992, Hal Leonard)

Jolly Old Sleigh Ride. (2:00, 1996, Curnow Music Press, Inc.)

Legion of Merit. (2:15, 2004, Curnow Music Press, Inc.)

Megaforce. (2:00, 1997, Curnow Music Press, Inc.)

The Mighty Nile. (3:15, 2001, Curnow Music Press, Inc.)

Suncatcher. (2:00, 2000, Curnow Music Press, Inc.)

An Unfinished Symphony. (2:20, 1997, Curnow Music Press, Inc.)

Viva Espanole. (2:49, 1984, Hal Leonard)

Grade 1.5

Ancient Castle. (3:55, 2002, Curnow Music Press, Inc.)

Blazon. (2:00, 1997, Curnow Music Press, Inc.)

Canadian Sketches. Dedicated to all my Canadian friends. (2:50, 1996, Curnow Music Press, Inc.)

El Camino Real. (2:10, 2001, Curnow Music Press, Inc.)

Energy! (2:00, 2001, Curnow Music Press, Inc.)

Flashpoint. (2:00, 2000, Curnow Music Press, Inc.)

Pathfinder. (2:20, 1999, Curnow Music Press, Inc.)

Taddington Square. (3:20, 1996, Curnow Music Press, Inc.)

The Three Drummers. Percussion trio feature. (2:00, 2004, Curnow Music Press, Inc.)

Variations on a French Carol. (2:20, 1996, Curnow Music Press, Inc.)

Grade 2

African Sketches. (1:50, 1992, Hal Leonard)

The Argonauts–Overture. (2:00, 1986, Jenson)

Away In the Manger. (2:02, 1990, Music Works, Jenson)

Bach Variants. Commissioned by the Paul R. Haas Middle School Band, Philip A. Cole, director, Corpus Christi, Texas, and dedicated to Paul and Mary Haas. (4:10, 1999, Curnow Music Press, Inc.)

Baroque Suite for Piano and Band–Three movements. (2:55, 1997, Curnow Music Press, Inc.)

Bingo for Percussion and Band. (2:01, 1979, Studio P/R)

Blockbuster Percussion. (2:35, 2002, Curnow Music Press, Inc.)

Brookside Festival. Commissioned for the Brookside School Senior Band, Allendale, New Jersey, by David and Melissa Marion as well as Collette Rumpeltin-Mather, band director. (3:15, 2002, Curnow Music Press, Inc.)

Canterbury Coronation. (2:10, 1996, Curnow Music Press, Inc.)

Canticum. (2:40, 1988, Music Works, Jenson)

The Carolers–Fanfare for Christmas. (2:10, 1997, Curnow Music Press, Inc.)

The Cavaliers. (2:42, 1990, Jenson)

Christmas Angels. (3:00, 2002, Curnow Music Press, Inc.)

A Christmas Celebration–Eight separate carol settings. Includes four parts with optional fifth part and may be adapted to full-band instrumentation; for grades 2, 3, and 4. (1998, Curnow Music Press, Inc.)

Christmas Echo Hymn. (2:05, 1977, Studio P/R)

Christmas Nocturne, "Stille Nacht." (2:43, 1991, Music Works, Jenson)

Christmas Tidings. (2:50, 1985, Jenson)

Crusaders Overture. (2:10, 1985, Jenson)

Down Under. (2:15, 1993, Hal Leonard)

English Carol Fantasy. (2:40, 2001, Curnow Music Press, Inc.)

Excursions. (2:20, 2001, Curnow Music Press, Inc.)

Fanfare and Flourishes–grade-2 version. (2:00, 1998, Curnow Music Press, Inc.)

Firebrook Prelude. Commissioned by and dedicated to the members of the Hedrick Middle School Band, Medford, Oregon. (4:25, 1995, Curnow Music Press, Inc.)

Flute Fancy–Flute Feature. (2:24, 1985, Jenson)

French Christmas Carol Fantasy. (2:08, 1989, Jenson)

The General–Concert march. (2:40, 1983, Jenson)

I Love A Parade. (2:00, 1983, Jenson)

International Christmas Salute. (3:00, 1996, Curnow Music Press, Inc.)

Irish Legends. (2:00, 1991, Jenson)

Introduction and Beguine –Trumpet solo accompanied by band or piano. Dedicated to our daughter, Amy Elizabeth Curnow. (2:10, available from the composer)

Jingle Bells. (1:50, 1990, Jenson)

Jolly Jingle Holiday. (2:00, 1987, Jenson)

Korean Folk Rhapsody. (2:10, 1988, Jenson)

Kum Ba Yah. (1:58, 1990, Jenson)

Land of Shining Waters. Written for and dedicated to Cal Smith and the teachers and students of the Peterborough County Board of Education, Peterborough, Ontario, Canada. (2:33, 1991, Jenson)

Monticello Montage. Commissioned by and dedicated to the 1993 Albermarle County Middle School Honors Band, Charlotte, Virginia. (3:00, 1994, Hal Leonard)

Theme from *Moorside Suite* by Holst, arranged by Curnow. (2:40, 1984, Jenson)

Music Shall Live–Vocal, band, optional strings, or piano. Commissioned by the North Chicago Community Unit School District 187. (7:30, 1998, Curnow Music Press, Inc.)

Northlake Festival Overture. (3:10, 1993, Hal Leonard)

Norwegian Wood. (2:10, 1992, Jenson)

Now the Day is Over. (3:15, 1986, Jenson)

Polly Wolly Doodlin' –Flute section feature. (2:00, 1984, Jenson)

Prelude and Scherzo. (3:08, 1991, Jenson)

Prima Vista. (3:10, 1989, Music Works, Jenson)

Puccini Fantasy–Flute solo. (2:02, 1993, Jenson)

Quantum Variations. (2:56, 1991, Music Works, Jenson)

Rockbridge Overture. (2:02, 1993, Jenson)

Rogue's March–Percussion feature. For our daughter, Lisa Anne Curnow. (3:10, 1981, Jenson)

Seafarer–Overture. (2:57, 1989, Jenson)

Sea Odyssey. (3:00, 1989, Jenson)

Shenandoah–Concert march. (3:00, 1989, Jenson)

Shepherd's Song – "Come, All Ye Shepherds." (2:10, 1991, Jenson)

Sojourner 2000. (2:35, 1999, Curnow Music Press, Inc.)

Song for the Earth–Terra Beata. (3:00, 1991, Jenson, Hal Leonard)

Spirit of '76–Concert march. (3:00, 1976, Studio P/R)

Spitfire Overture. (3:29, 1990, Music Works, Jenson)

S.S. Titanic–Concert march. (3:00, 1985, Jenson)

Stonehenge Overture. (2:20, 1992, Hal Leonard)

Sugar Creek Saga. (2:00, 1995, Curnow Music Press, Inc.)

Symphonic Chorale for Band. (2:05, 1987, Jenson)

Tambourine Mountain Overture. (2:30, 1988, Jenson)

Tribute to America. (2:42, Jenson)

Two Moods for Trombone and Band. Available from the composer and dedicated to our son, Jeffrey S. Curnow. (3:00, 1980, Studio P/R)

Trumpeter's Winter Holiday– Trumpet Solo with Band. (3:40, 2003, Curnow Music Press, Inc.)

Vanguard. (2:40, 2003, Curnow Music Press, Inc.)

Variations on a Theme by Thomas Tallis by Ralph Vaughan Williams, arranged by Curnow. (3:45, 1984, Jenson)

With Sweet Jubilation–Christmas. (3:25, 2000, Curnow Music Press, Inc.)

Grade 2.5

A Day at the Circus–Suite. (7:30, 1998, Curnow Music Press, Inc.)

A Day at the Museum–Suite. (9:00, 1997, Curnow Music Press, Inc.)

A Day at the Zoo–Suite. (9:10, 1996, Curnow Music Press, Inc.)

A Day At The Fair–Suite. (5:00, 2003, Curnow Music Press, Inc.)

Echo Carol. (2:00, 2004, Curnow Music Press, Inc.)

Olympic Fanfare and Theme–grade-2.5 version. (3:10, 1996, Curnow Music Press, Inc.)

Sandcastles–Suite. (5:40, 2000, Curnow Music Press, Inc.)

Snapshots from the Great Lakes–Suite. Commissioned by the Thunder Bay Junior High School Eighth Grade Symphonic Band of Alpena, Michigan, Raymond R. Reynolds, Conductor. (6:40, 2001, Curnow Music Press, Inc.)

Unlimited Praise. Sacred collection for various ensembles with four parts and optional fifth part, useable by full band or orchestra, grades 2, 3, and 4. (2001, Curnow Music Press, Inc.)

Grade 3

A Night at the Ballet. (3:00, 1998, Jenson)

Acclamation, based on the hymn "All Glory, Laud, and Honor." Commissioned by the 1996-1997 J. Frank Faust Junior High School Band, Chambersburg, PA, Patrick and Dina Carter-Ishler, directors. (7:10, 1998, Curnow Music Press, Inc.)

Aevia. (2:56, 1988, Music Works, Jenson)

Amber Waves of Grain, Rhapsody on "America the Beautiful." (3:30, 1994, Jenson)

American Folk Suite. (3:10, 1989, Jenson)

Apple Island Legend–A Native American Saga. Commissioned by the Orchard Lake, Michigan, Middle School Symphony Band, Douglas Blackwell, conductor. (6:00, 1997, Curnow Music Press, Inc.)

Ballad and Scherzo for Trumpet/Saxophone and Band. (3:00, 1987, Jenson)

Bell Carol Fantasy. (2:00, 1986, Jenson)

Black Is the Color of My True Love's Hair. (2:20, 1985, Jenson)

Camptown Sketches–Suite for Band. (2:42, 1989, Jenson)

Canterbury Tales–Suite for Band. (3:00, 1991, Music Works, Jenson)

Canticle for Clarinet and Band–Clarinet solo. (2:19, 1992, Jenson)

Canticles for Band. Commissioned by the Bernese Cantonal Music Association for the 20th Bernese Cantonal Music Festival in Huttwil, Switzerland, June 1999. (6:50, 1999, Curnow Music Press, Inc.)

Chant and Capriccio. Commissioned by the Iowa Bandmasters Association for the 1997 All Iowa Middle School Honor Band. (3:40, 1997, Curnow Music Press, Inc.)

Christmas Carillon. For the Asbury College Concert Band, Wilmore, Kentucky, Dr. Lynn Cooper, conductor. (2:50, 1998, Curnow Music Press, Inc.)

A Christmas Celebration. Eight separate carol settings with four parts and an optional fifth part, useable by full band or orchestra, grades 2, 3, and 4. (1998, Curnow Music Press, Inc.)

Christmas Classics. (3:00, 1993, Jenson)

A Christmas Flourish. (1:50, 1998, Curnow Music Press, Inc.)

Christmas Party. (2:00, 2001, Curnow Music Press, Inc.)

Christmas Past. (2005, 1984, Hal Leonard)

Christmas Tidings–March. (3:00, 1986, Jenson)

Constellations. (4:30, 1996, Curnow Music Press, Inc.)

Deck the Halls. (2:02, 1991, Jenson)

Edgewood Festival –Suite for Band. Commissioned by the Buckeye Music Boosters for the 1984-1985 Wallace H. Brandon Junior High School Eighth Grade Band, Ashtabula, Ohio, Laurie Lafferty, director. (7:43, 1984, Jenson)

Fanfare and Hymn For All Nations, "Ode to Joy." (2:52, 1990, Jenson)

Fanfare for a New Era. (2:26, 1992, Jenson)

Fanfare for Christmas. (2:01, 1992, Jenson)

Fanfare Prelude on *Finlandia.* (3:02, 1985, Jenson)

Fanfare Prelude on "Joy to the World." (2:58, 1985, Jenson)

Fanfare Prelude on "Ode to Joy." (2:33, 1984, Jenson)

Fanfare Prelude on "Westminster Carol." (2:40, 1986, Jenson)

Fantasy on an English Christmas Carol. (2:30, 1987, Jenson)

Festia–Concert opener. (2:10, 1986, Jenson)

Finale from Symphony no. 3–Organ by Saint-Saëns, arranged by Curnow. Commissioned by the Cedarville, Michigan, High School Band, Alan Jacobus, conductor. (3:00, 2002, Curnow Music Press, Inc.)

Flirtations for Flute–Flute solo or section feature. (2:00, 2002, Curnow Music Press, Inc.)

Heavy Artillery–Percussion section feature. (3:00, 1986, Jenson)

Introduction and Beguine–Trumpet solo with band. (2:55, 1979, Studio P/R)

Introduction and Capriccio. (2:30, 1999, Curnow Music Press, Inc.)

Jessamine Station Overture. Commissioned by the Jessamine County High School Band, Alan Jacobus, director. (3:00, 1975, Studio P/R)

J.F.K. in Memoriam with optional narration. (10:10, 1995, Curnow Music Press, Inc.)

Journey to Centaurus–Concert march. To the Jessamine County, Kentucky, Junior High School Band, Larry Hostetler, director. (2:56, 1980, TRN)

Joyous Celebration –"Joy to the World." (3:02, 1990, Music Works, Jenson)

Joyous Tidings. (2:50, 1988, Jenson)

Jubilee!–Spirituals for Band. (4:00, 1986, Jenson)

Lion of Lucerne. (5:06, 1986, Jenson)

Logos I. (3:52, 1990, Music Works, Jenson)

Lone Star Celebration. Commissioned by the Association of Texas Small School Bands for the 1995 All-State Band in San Antonio, Texas. (6:10, 1995, Curnow Music Press, Inc.)

The Minuteman–Concert march. (3:04, 1989, Jenson)

The Music-Makers. For SATB chorus with orchestra, band or piano accompaniment. Commissioned for the dedication of the Clayton County Schools Performing Arts Center, Clayton County, Georgia. (6:15, 2000, Curnow Music Press, Inc.)

Mid-West Golden Jubilee Overture. Written for the 1996 celebration of the 50 years of success of the Midwest International Band and Orchestra Clinic and dedicated to John P. Paynter, past president, for his tireless devotion to the Clinic. (5:25, 1996, Curnow Music Press, Inc.)

Nathan Hale Trilogy. Commissioned by and dedicated to the students of the Nathan Hale Middle School Concert Band, Theodora Sotiropulos, conductor. (5:10, 1990, Music Works, Jenson)

Northern Legend. Commissioned by the Sault Area Junior/Senior High School Bands, Sault Ste. Marie, Michigan, Alan Jacobus, director. (4:35, 1991, Hal Leonard)

Of Courage and Patriotism. Commissioned by the Perrysburg Band and Orchestra Boosters, Perrysburg, Ohio, for the dedication of the new Perrysburg High School. (6:20, 2002, Curnow Music Press, Inc.)

The Old Man of the Mountain–Based on Native American Folk Lore. Commissioned by The New Hampshire Band Directors Association. (6:00, 1998, Curnow Music Press, Inc.)

An Oriental Portrait. (2:00, 1993, Hal Leonard)

Phoenix Overture, A Legend for Band. Commissioned by the Hoopston-East Lynn Junior High School Band, Hoopston-East Lynn, Illinois, Joseph D. Goble, director. (3:00, 1982, Jenson)

The Pioneers. Commissioned for the Gordon Gregory Middle School Wind Ensemble, Nancy Plantinga, conductor, in 1990 for their prestigious performance at the Midwest International Band and Orchestra Clinic in Chicago. (2:55, 1990, Music Works, Jenson)

Psalm Tune Variations. Commissioned by Shenandoah Valley Academy Composer's Festival, New Market, Virginia, Bruce Wilson, director. (6:06, 1986, Jenson)

Quintessence. (4:05, 1994, Jenson)

Renaissance Suite. (4:15, 1983, Jenson)

Russian Folk Song Rhapsody. (3:25, 1992, Hal Leonard)

Saxophone Ragtime. (3:00, 1990, Jenson)

Seacliffe Overture. Commissioned by Model Laboratory School Band of Eastern Kentucky University, Richmond, Kentucky, Ken Schubert, band director. Dedicated to George Hurst. (4:52, 1982, Jenson)

Silver Ribbon Chanteys–Folk Song Suite. Commissioned by the Lancaster Band Boosters for the Lancaster City (Ohio) Schools Instrumental Department for the 2001 All-City Band Program. (6:05, 2001, Curnow Music Press, Inc.)

Songs from the Orient. (2:01, 1987, Hal Leonard)

Sovereign Variants. Commissioned by and dedicated to the students of the King City Secondary School Senior Concert Band, King City, Ontario, Canada, Jim Corbett, conductor. (5:10, 1992, Hal Leonard)

The Spirit Soars. Commissioned by and dedicated to the 15th annual Festival of Bands for the following southern Indiana high school bands: Barr-Reeve, Loogotee, Mitchell, North Knox and South Knox. (4:45, 2003, Curnow Music Press, Inc.)

Spoon River Saga Overture. Commissioned by the Edison Junior High School Band, Macomb, Illinois, Joseph D. Goble, director of bands. Dedicated to the memory of Roscoe P. Linder. (4:05, 1989, Jenson)

Stille, Stille, Stille. (3:10, 1994, Jenson)

Superstition Mountain Overture. Commissioned by Gary Sauerbrunn and family in memory of Deanna Marie Sauerbrunn, Mesa, Arizona. (4:00, 1984, Jenson)

Symphonic Prelude and Dance. (3:20, 1993, Music Works, Jenson)

Three Colonial Ballads–Suite for Band. (4:02, 1994, Jenson)

Trilogy for Concert Band. Commissioned by the Baleland Hills High School Band, Pontiac, Michigan. Jeff Evans, conductor. (3:00, 1983, Studio P/R)

Time Excursion. (2:32, 1986, Jenson)

Under Three Flags. Commissioned by the Robert W. Woodruff Band of Woodward Academy, College Park, Georgia, Charles Brodie, director. (3:35, 1994, Curnow Music Press, Inc.)

Variations on a Burgundian Carol. (3:18, 1988, Music Works, Jenson)

Variations on a Ninth. Commissioned by the Ovid-Elsie Area High School Band Boosters for the Ovid-Elsie High School Band, Roger and Nadine Weyersburg, band directors. (4:52, 1989, Jenson)

Variants on an Early American Hymn Tune, "Holy Manna." Commissioned by the Jessamine County High School Band, Jessamine County, Kentucky, Alan Jacobus, director. (5:00, 1981, Jenson)

Voluntary on "Old Hundreth," by Purcell, arranged by Curnow. Transcribed for the Asbury College Concert Band, Wilmore, Kentucky, Dr. Lynn Cooper, conductor, for the Asbury College Reunion Concert Band. (2:45, 2000, Curnow Music Press, Inc.)

What Child Is This? "Greensleeves." (2:04, 1990, Jenson)

When The Morning Stars Sang. Commissioned for the East Shore Honors Band, Port Huron, Michigan, by David and Barbara Teeple; Scott Teeple, conductor. (6:00, 2003, Curnow Music Press, Inc.)

When Time Will Be No More–In Memoriam. Commissioned in memory of Peter J. Swanson, 1983-1998, trumpet, Thomas Worthington Symphonic Band, Worthington, Ohio. (5:45, 2000, Curnow Music Press, Inc.)

Where Mythical Beings Play. Commissioned by the American School Band Directors Association Education Foundation, Inc. Dedicated to the school bands of America. (5:45, Curnow Music Press, Inc.)

Grade 4

American Triptych. Commissioned by the Eastern Hills League Schools Honors Band of the Eastern Cincinnati, Ohio Area. (6:00, 1984, Jenson)

Appalachian Sketches Commissioned by the George Rogers High School Band, Lexington, Kentucky, Chuck Campbell, conductor. (6:30, 1977, Studio PR)

Canadian Folk Song Rhapsody. Commissioned by Susan Jaffee in honor of her brother and her sister-in-law, Morrie and Mary Backun, Vancouver, British Columbia, Canada. (4:04, 1991, Jenson)

Canticle of the Creatures–Symphonic Suite. Commissioned by the North Hills High School Band, Pittsburgh, PA, Warren Mercer, director. (12:00, 1983, Jenson)

Capriccio and Cavatina. Commissioned by John New. (5:07, Jenson)

Capriccio for Trombone and Band. (5:00, Studio P/R)

Celebration Variations, based on the shape note melody, *Pizgah.* Commissioned for the 20th Anniversary Celebration by the Birmingham, Michigan Concert Band, Grant M. Hoemke, director. (7:20, 1998, Curnow Music Press, Inc.)

Celestial Celebration, Promised Land. Commissioned by Asbury College on the occasion of the Centennial Celebration, 1890-1990, and dedicated to the Asbury College Concert Band, Dr. Lynn Cooper, conductor. (8:04, 1990, Jenson)

Christmas Concert March. (3:07, 1979, Studio P/R)

Christmas Fancies. Dedicated to the Asbury College Concert Band, Wilmore, Kentucky, Dr. Lynn Cooper, director. (2:45, 2000, Curnow Music Press, Inc.)

Christmas Prelude. (7:04, 1989, Jenson)

Christmas Triptych. (6:06, 1978, Studio P/R)

Collage for Band. Winner, 1979 ASBDA-Volkwein Award dedicated to the Asbury College Concert Band, Dr. Joseph D. Parker, conductor, 1977. (8:00, 1977, Volkwein)

James Curnow

Concertpiece for Trumpet and Band or Piano. Concert Band Version Commissioned by Woody English, soloist, The United States Army Band, Washington, D.C. (7:05, 1998, Curnow Music Press, Inc.)

Dublin Sketches–Variations on "Slane." Commissioned by the Stevens Point Area Public School, Stevens Point, Wisconsin, Dr. Dwight Stevens, superintendent, Russell Mikkelson, director of bands, 1985. (7:08, 1985, Jenson)

Exaltation, "Guide me, O Thou Great Jehovah." Commissioned by the Seventh-day Adventist Intercollegiate Band Festival at Union College in Lincoln, Nebraska. (7:21, 1990, Jenson)

Fanfare and Flourishes–grade-4 version. Concert Band version commissioned by the Alfred M. Barbe High School Band, St. Charles, Missouri, Steve Hand, director. (2:25, 1994, Curnow Music Press, Inc.)

Fanfare Prelude on "God of Our Fathers." Commissioned by the Chicago Christian, Illiana Christian, and Timothy Christian High Schools, Directors Michael A. Katterjohn, Alan Bileu, and Richard Landman. (3:24, 1983, Jenson)

Fanfare Prelude on "Hanover." Commissioned by the University of Wisconsin–Eau Claire, Donald George, conductor. (3:00, 1970, Studio P/R)

Fanfare Prelude on "The Italian Hymn." (2:20, 1995, Curnow Music Press, Inc.)

Fanfare Prelude on "Lancashire." (3:15, 1981, Jenson)

Fanfare Prelude on "Lobe den Herren" or "Praise To The Lord The Almighty." Commissioned by and written for the West Shore Christian Academy, Muskegon, Michigan, Alan Jacobus, director. (3:00, 1982, Jenson)

Fanfare Prelude on "O God Our Help in Ages Past." Commissioned for the Centennial of Friends University in Wichita, Kansas, for the University Band, Dr. John W. Taylor, conductor. (4:00, 1999, Curnow Music Press, Inc.)

29

Fanfare and Jubiloso. Commissioned by the Wheaton Illinois Municipal Band, Dr. Bruce Moss, conductor, in commemoration of their 70th anniversary and dedicated to Dr. Harry Begian, in appreciation of his musical inspiration and dedication to excellence. (2:40, 2001, Curnow Music Press, Inc.)

Fantasia for Tuba and Band–soloist grade 5, band grade 4. Commissioned by the Roanoke Rapids Band Boosters, North Carolina, David L. Hawks, director and David G. Lewis, tuba soloist, of the North Carolina Symphony. (8:15, 2002, Curnow Music Press, Inc.)

Fantasia on a Southern Folk Hymn, "Wondrous Love." Commissioned by the Loma Linda Academy Symphonic Band, Loma Linda, California, Philip Binkly, conductor. (7:50, 1988, Jenson)

Fantasy for Christmas. (3:09, 1976, Studio P/R)

Fantasy on a Sea Chantey–Mallet percussion trio. (2:06, 1988, Jenson)

Festivity–A Celebration for Band. Commissioned for the 20th anniversary of The Worlds of Fun Festivals of Music in Kansas City, Missouri, Dr. Russell Coleman, bandmaster. (5:24, 1993, Jenson)

Fiddle Tunes from the American Revolution –Two Movement Suite. Commissioned by the New York State Band Director's Association for its 20th Anniversary Symposium and dedicated to the memory of Richard H. Snook. (8:05, 2001, Curnow Music Press, Inc.)

Freedom Road–Spiritual. Commissioned by the Edgewood High School Band, Ashtabula, Ohio, Gene Milford and Laurie Lafferty, directors. (9:00, 1994, Curnow Music Press, Inc.)

Finale for a Winter Festival. Written for the Asbury College Concert Band, Wilmore, Kentucky, Dr. Lynn Cooper, director of bands. (5:25, 2004, Curnow Music Press, Inc.)

Four Symphonic Chorales. (2:00, Jenson)

Fox River Festival–Overture. Commissioned by and dedicated to the students of the band program at James B. Conant High School, Hoffman Estates, Illinois, Steve Hoernemann, director. (4:31, 1983, Jenson)

Heritage of Freedom, variations on "God of Our Fathers" with optional narration. Commissioned by the Rushmore Music Camp on its 20th Anniversary, Paul and Lois Hedge, founders and directors. (6:00, 1990, Jenson)

High Bridge Concert March. Commissioned by the Jessamine, Kentucky, County High School Band, Alan Jacobus, director. (3:20, 1976, Studio P/R)

Hymn and Alleluia. Commissioned by the Laurel County, Kentucky, High School Band, Jack Walker, director. (3:50, 1977, Studio P/R)

Intrada Americana. Commissioned by the Jessamine County, Kentucky, High School Band for their European Tour, Alan Jacobus, director. (2:22, 1979, Studio P/R)

Jubilate–Variations on "Prospect." Commissioned for the Third Annual Columbia College All-Female High School Band Clinic, January 25-27, 1991, by Columbia College, Columbia, South Carolina, Dr. Randolph Love, conductor. (6:04, 1991, Jenson)

The Last Spring by Grieg, arranged by Curnow. Transcribed for the Asbury College Concert Band, Wilmore, Kentucky, Dr. Lynn Cooper, director. (4:30, 1999, Curnow Music Press, Inc.)

Legend and Sundance–Native American. Commissioned by the South Dakota Bandmasters Association for the 1986 All State Band, Sioux Falls, South Dakota. (8:00, 1986, Jenson)

Let Creation Praise! for SATB Chorus, Winds and Percussion. Commissioned and Premiered by the St. Norbert College Music Department, Dr. Sharon Huff, director of bands, in Commemoration of the Centennial Celebration of St. Norbert College, 1898-1998. (7:50, 2000, Curnow Music Press, Inc.)

None But the Lonely Heart by Tchaikovsky, arranged by Curnow. Dedicated to the members of the American Concert Band, Sioux City, Iowa, Mike Hogan, conductor. (7:30, 2002, Curnow Music Press, Inc.)

Northwest Passage. Commissioned by the St. George's School Senior Concert Band, Marko Rnic, and Marc Compton, conductors, Vancouver, Canada. (8:30, 1996, Curnow Music Press, Inc.)

Ode and Epinicion. Commissioned by Michigan State University Bands honoring David L. Catron with affection and gratitude for his 27 years of dedication, leadership, and service. (5:00, 2002, Curnow Music Press, Inc.)

Olympic Fanfare and Theme for the Olympic Flag. Commissioned by the 1996 Atlantic Olympic Committee. (4:10, 1996, Curnow Music Press, Inc.)

Overture to a Winter Festival. Commissioned by the Concord Band, Concord, Massachusetts, William Toland, conductor. (7:35, 1995, Curnow Music Press, Inc.)

Partita for Band. Commissioned by and for the students and directors of the 29th annual Northwest Iowa Band Festival. (2:10, 1984, Jenson)

Prayer ("O Divine Redeemer") by Gounod, arranged by Curnow. Euphonium solo with band or piano accompaniment. Commissioned by Dr. Grady Hallman. (7:00, 2000, Curnow Music Press, Inc.)

Prelude and Celebration. Commissioned by Eastern Illinois University Bands in Commemoration of the Centennial Celebration of Eastern University, Dr. Joseph Manfredo, director of bands. (7:30, 1996, Curnow Music Press, Inc.)

Prelude on a Hymn of Praise. Commissioned by Howard Lehman for his students in the concert bands at North High School, Eau Claire, Wisconsin. (4:40, 1996, Curnow Music Press, Inc.)

Proclamation–Sacred. Commissioned in honor of the 100th anniversary of Camp-of-the-Woods, Speculator, New York. (5:30, 2000, Curnow Music Press, Inc.)

Rejouissance–Fantasia on "Ein Feste Burg." Commissioned by the St. Joseph, Michigan, Municipal Band, in honor of and lovingly dedicated to John E. N. Howard to celebrate 40 years as conductor. (6:02, 1987, Jenson)

Rhapsody on American Shaped Note Melodies. Commissioned in memory of William Harold (Bill) Baden by the Band Directors of Kershaw County, South Carolina. (5:20, 1996, Curnow Music Press, Inc.)

Rhapsody for Euphonium and Band. Dedicated to my teacher, Leonard Falcone. (6:10, 1978, Studio P/R)

Sinfonia Americana–Suite. Commissioned by the Ottumwa High School Band and Orchestra Boosters for the Ottumwa High School Symphonic Wind Ensemble, directed by William M. Cornelius. (7:40, 1988, Jenson)

Silver Celebration–Concert march. Commissioned by the Lansing, Michigan, Community Band, Richard Suddendorf, director. (4:00, 1992, Jenson)

Sou-gan, A Welsh Folk Song Setting. (4:50, 2003, Curnow Music Press, Inc.)

The Spirit of the Guard–Concert march. Commissioned by the Missouri Air National Guard in St. Louis, Missouri, in honor of the 60th Anniversary of "Lindbergh's Own" 110th Tactical Fighter Squadron for the 571st Air Force Band, Capt. Steve Aubuchon, conductor. (4:00, 1982, Jenson)

Symphonic Triptych. Winner of the 1977 Volkwein Award, Commissioned by the Conneaut, Ohio, High School Band, George Voytek, director. (7:50, 1976, Jenson)

Tates Creek Overture. Commissioned by the Tates Creek High School Band, Lexington, Kentucky, Leslie Anderson, director. (5:16, 1980, Studio P/R)

Three Irish Dances. Commissioned by the Portage Central High School Band, Portage, Michigan, Patrick W. Flynn, director of bands, and the Portage Education Foundation. (4:10, 1991, Jenson)

To Fly Without Wings. Commissioned by the Paris, Kentucky, High School Band, Philip Grigson, conductor for their 1997 European concert tour. (6:30, 1997, Curnow Music Press, Inc.)

Variations in Memoriam. Commissioned by the Fraser High School Band Council, Fraser, Michigan, Seymour Okun, director, in memory of Mac Carr. (8:40, 1977, Studio P/R)

Welcome Yule–Holiday SATB or SSA Chorus with Band or Orchestra by Emily Crocker, arranged by Curnow. Commissioned by the Music Department of Lampeter-Strasburg High School, Lampeter,

Pennsylvania, Jay Butterfield and D. Scott Loose, conductors. (3:50, 1993, Jenson)

Winds of Change–Three movement symphonic suite. Dedicated to Adlai E. Stevenson High School, Lincolnshire, Illinois, and commissioned by the Stevenson High School Bands, Jeff Slepak and Debbie Durham, directors. (11:30, 1997, Curnow Music Press, Inc.)

Grade 5

Australian Variant Suite. Commissioned by the Western Michigan University Bands, Kalamazoo, Michigan, Richard Suddendorf, director. (10:10, 1984, Jenson)

Celebration on a Theme by Saint-Saëns. Commissioned by the Norcross High School Band, Norcross, Georgia, William J. Pharris, director, and dedicated to the memory of Mark Nanney. (9:31, 1993, Hal Leonard)

Centennial Spirit. Commissioned by and dedicated to the Auburn University Band, Dr. Johnnie Vinson, conductor, in honor of its centennial anniversary. (3:40, 1997, Curnow Music Press, Inc.)

Ceremonial Flourishes. Commissioned by the United States Army Ground Forces Band, Fort McPherson, Georgia, Capt. Tony Cason, commander. (5:20, 1987, Jenson)

Concerto for Euphonium and Wind Ensemble or Orchestra–Solo, grade 6. Commissioned by the DEG Music Products, Inc., and the Willson Band Instrument companies for Roger Behrend, euphonium soloist, United States Navy Band. (12:10, Curnow Music Press, Inc.)

Concertino for Solo Percussionist and Symphonic Band. Commissioned for Robert Snider and the United States Navy Band. (14:30, 1994, Curnow Music Press, Inc.)

Concertino for Tuba and Band or Piano. Commissioned by Barton Cummings. (6:00, 2001, Curnow Music Press, Inc.)

Concertpiece for Clarinet, Winds and Percussion. Commissioned by the University of Illinois Symphonic Band, James Keene, director, for Howard Klug, clarinet soloist. (7:10, 1987, Jenson Composer's Editions)

Daystar-Variations for Symphonic Winds and Percussion. Commissioned by Kappa Kappa Psi National Band Fraternity and Tau Beta Sigma National Band Sorority and premiered by the National Intercollegiate Band. (7:50, 1993, Hal Leonard)

Down from the Shimmering Sky–Symphonic Suite. Commissioned for the 1999 Indiana All-State Band. Based on Native North American ceremonial masks. (15:00, 1999, Curnow Music Press, Inc.)

The Eagle's Flight–Variations on *Melita*. Commissioned for the 25th Anniversary of Mr. Jeffrey Greene, director of bands, Greece Olympia High School Band Teacher, New York. (10:00, 2003, Curnow Music Press, Inc.)

Fanfare for Spartacus. Commissioned by the Michigan State University Bands for the 125th Anniversary Celebration of the Band Program, Dr. John Whitwell, director of bands. (4:00, 1995, Curnow Music Press, Inc.)

Fantasy on a Colonial Air "Chester." Commissioned by the Lassiter High School Band, Marietta, Georgia, Alfred L. Watkins, conductor and dedicated to all past and present members of the symphonic band. Premiered on December 15, 1989, at the Midwest Band and Orchestra Clinic, Chicago. (7:06, 1989, Jenson)

Finale from *Andrea Chenier* by Gierodano, arranged by Curnow. This transcription of Act IV was commissioned by Dr. Harry Begian, in memory of Leonard Falcone. (12:00, 1999, Curnow Music Press, Inc.)

Five Concord Diversions for Brass Quintet, Symphonic Winds and Percussion Commissioned by the Concord Band of Concord, Massachusetts, William Toland, in commemoration of his 25th year as music director of the band. (10:15, 1988, Jenson)

Four Colonial Country Dances–Suite on American Colonial Country Dances. Commissioned by the Metropolitan Wind Symphony of Boston, Massachusetts, David J. Martins, conductor. (9:45, 1996, Curnow Music Press, Inc.)

Inventions from the Sacred Harp–Based on *Resignation*. Commissioned by the East Mecklenburg High School Band and Booster Club, Charlotte, North Carolina, and dedicated to Mr. Scott Clowes, director of bands, in appreciation of his 17 years of service to the East Mecklenburg High School Band Program. (8:30, 2005, Curnow Music Press, Inc.)

Midway March by John Williams, arranged by Curnow. (4:00, 1990, Jenson)

Odyssey–Symphonic Overture. Commissioned by the Massillon Ohio Band Boosters Association for the Massillon Washington High School Wind Orchestra, Clarence Crumb, conductor. (9:00, 1994, Curnow Music Press, Inc.)

Prelude on Three Welsh Hymn Tunes by Vaughan Williams, arranged by Curnow. Commissioned by the University of Illinois Bands, Dr. Harry Begian, conductor. (7:43, 1983, Jenson)

Sinfonietta for Band. Commissioned for the dedication of the new high school facility in Howell, Michigan, and dedicated to the Howell High School Band, Douglas Roose, director. (8:00, 1981, Composer's Editions, Jenson)

Slavonic Dances–Symphonic Suite by Dvořák, arranged by Curnow. Commissioned by the University of Illinois Bands, Dr. Harry Begian, conductor. (8:17, 1982, Jenson)

To Bind the Nation's Wounds. Commissioned by the University of Central Oklahoma Wind Ensemble, Dr. Ron Howell, conductor, and dedicated to the victims and survivors of the bombing of the Murrah Federal Building in Oklahoma City on April 19, 1995. (9:00, 1996, Curnow Music Press, Inc.)

Toward the Sunrising. Commissioned by the Davidson Fine Arts Bands, Augusta, Georgia, Michael A. Katterjohn, conductor, for the dedication of the new fine arts facilities. (5:00, Curnow Music Press, Inc.)

Transfiguration–Sacred. Commissioned for the dedication of the Church of the Transfiguration, Orleans, Massachusetts, June 17, 2000. (12:30, 2001, Curnow Music Press, Inc.)

Welsh Variants–Variations on "Suo-gan." Commissioned by the Concord Band, Concord, Massachusetts, William Toland, conductor. (8:06, 1988, Jenson)

Where Never Lark or Eagle Flew. Commissioned by the Graduates Association of Tenri High School Band in honor of the 50th anniversary of this association and dedicated to the Tenri High School Band, Japan. (10:17, 1992, Jenson)

Grade 6

A Moment in Time–Symphonic Poem in Three Movements. Commissioned by Yamanashi Gakuin University (Japan) Wind Ensemble, Hitoshi Shiratori, conductor. (12:40, 2004, Curnow Music Press, Inc.)

Lochinvar–Symphonic Poem. Winner of the prestigious *Coup de Vents* band composition competition Le Havre, France, 1994. Commissioned by the United States Army Band "Pershing's Own", Colonel L. Bryan Shelburne, Jr., leader and commander, in honor of Colonel Eugene W. Allen, retired. (15:00, 1994, Curnow Music Press, Inc.)

Mutanza–Symphonic Variations. Winner of the 1980 ABA-Ostwald Award. (16:27, 1981, Jenson)

Praetorius Variations–Variations on "O Come, O Come, Emmanuel." Commissioned by the Lake Braddock Secondary School Symphonic Band, Burke, Virginia, Roy Holder, conductor. (12:30, 1996, Curnow Music Press, Inc.)

Symphonic Variants for Euphonium and Symphoinic Band, Orchestra or Piano. Winner of the 1984 ABA-Ostwald Award. Commissioned by and dedicated to my teacher and friend, Dr. Harry Begian, and the University of Illinois Bands. Phillip Franke, soloist, 1982. Second place winner in the first Sudler Band Composition Competition. (18:00, 1998, Curnow Music Press, Inc.)

Variants on an Ancient Air. Commissioned by the Gamma Phi Chapter of Kappa Kappa Psi and the Beta Zeta Chapter of Tau Beta Sigma at Stephen F. Austin State University and dedicated to Mr. and Mrs. Mel Montgomery. (11:43, 1987, Jenson)

37

johan
de Meij

I consider myself more a composing musician than a
composer. And when I conduct, I consider myself more a
conducting composer than a conductor.

A. Biography

Johan de Meij was born in
Voorburg, The Netherlands, in
1953. He studied trombone
and conducting at the Royal
Conservatory of Music at The
Hague. De Meij earned international fame as a composer and arranger.
His catalogue consists of original compositions, symphonic
transcriptions, and arrangements of film scores and musicals.

The Symphony no. 1 "The Lord of the Rings," based
on Tolkien's best-selling novels of the same name, was his first
substantial composition for wind orchestra and received the
prestigious Sudler Composition Award in 1989. In 2001 the
orchestral version was premiered by the Rotterdam
Philharmonic Orchestra and recorded by the
London Symphony Orchestra that same year. His other larger
compositions, such as Symphony no. 2 "The Big Apple," *T-bone*
Concerto, and *Casanova* for violoncello and wind orchestra are
also on the repertoire lists of orchestras and bands all over the

world. *Casanova* was awarded First Prize at the International Composition Competition of Corciano (Italy) in 1999, and a year later de Meij won the Oman International Composition Prize with *The Red Tower*.

In addition to composing, de Meij is a trombonist with the Orchestra *De Volharding* (The Perseverance) and a regular substitute with the Radio Chamber Orchestra. He is much in demand as a guest conductor and has conducted concerts and has led seminars in almost all European countries, Japan, Singapore, Brazil, and the United States.

I started my musical career at age 15 in the local wind orchestra. Holland has a blooming music culture with community bands in which people can play from age 8 to 88. My entrance into the world of wind instruments was more or less by accident. A friend of my sister's had an extra trumpet, and he volunteered to help me get started with the first few lessons. I was playing with the local band within six months.

From that point forward, everything went very fast. At one point we did not have enough trombone players and had too many trumpet players, so the conductor asked me if I would like to play trombone. That's how I ended up with this instrument! Quite early in life I went to the library to listen to recordings of the symphonic repertoire and to study scores. That is, I think, what planted the seed of my knowledge of orchestration. I never took lessons in arranging or composing. I am self-taught, and I learned a lot on the job. I consider myself more a composing musician than a composer. And when I conduct, I consider myself more a conducting composer than a conductor.

When I was 15 and in high school, I had not yet considered a career in music. I played a lot of soccer, but I gave that up because I often had to play in the wind band on weekends. I always hungered to create things. I already began writing and arranging pieces as soon as I could play the trumpet.

In 1972 I landed in the Teacher's Training College to become an elementary school teacher. During this same period, I played in various orchestras and acquired a reasonable level of playing within a fair bit of time. The idea that I would be a professional musician was still unthinkable at the time, so I took classes in education, even though I never had concrete plans to teach in primary schools. The thought of a life as a musician dawned on me during my military service. By auditioning for the Band of the Cavalry in Amersfoort, I again ended up in music. First, I played bass tuba, then baritone and trombone. That made me quite a versatile musician. During this time I arranged my first pieces. There was soon an opening for euphonium with the Amsterdam Police Band, and I had a successful audition and started only three days out of the service.

I became a professional musician one day at a time, even though I did not yet have a degree from the conservatory. Because I had a lot of spare time while playing with the police band, I took wind and brass band conducting and trombone courses at the conservatory from 1978-1984. Plus, I took jobs with all the Dutch orchestras and played under important conductors and composers like Valerie Gergiev, Edo de Waart, Hans Vonk, Peter Eotvos, Luciano Berio, Gunther Schuller, and Heinrich Schiff. This symphonic music later became a deter-mining factor for the aesthetic quality of my own work, even though most of my pieces are for wind band.

In 1983, I graduated with a degree in conducting and in 1984 with a degree in trombone. I wanted to learn conducting for practical reasons; I still conduct my own work regularly as a guest conductor with orchestras all over the world.

I enjoy the diversity of composing, playing, and conducting. The cross-pollination works for me. In the Orchestra *De Volharding* I play very different music, but I learn a lot from that. It triggers me. Even when I play the most avant-garde music, I want to get to work and start creating as soon as I come home. I most often write something "shamelessly tonal" just to counterbalance all of the difficult works we play in the orchestra.

B. The Creative Process

When I was 31 years old, I took conducting classes with Arie van Beek, and I had just finished the arrangement *Moment for Morricone*, a very popular arrangement even today. Just as I sometimes wonder now if I will ever shed my image as a wind band composer, I then wondered if I would ever get rid of the *Morricone*-image. With the Symphony no. 1 "The Lord of the Rings" it disappeared in one fell swoop. Right away, I was the composer of "The Lord of the Rings" and off to a flying start.

It took me four years to finish my first symphony for wind orchestra. I started reading the *Lord of the Rings* books, made notes, and rather quickly had an idea of how to build the piece. The symphony really only depicts chapters from the first book. Movements 1, 3, and 5 describe the figures, Gandalf, Gollum, and the Hobbits, and are not programmatic. In contrast, movements 2 and 4 are programmatic, and they follow the line of the story chronologically. I do not follow the sequence of the book, but I did try to connect all five movements.

I started with the fourth movement (Journey in the Dark), not because it is the golden section, but because that fragment caught me immediately when I read the story. I already had the walk-like movement in my head. I created the leitmotiv of Gandalf about halfway through the movement. At a certain moment, Gandalf falls from the bridge of Khazad Dum, so I already needed that motif, even though the character had not been introduced. I later used it in other parts to create unity. I composed everything in a rather fragmented manner.

By the way, I did not have a blueprint for the form. "The Lord of the Rings" is not a symphony in the classical sense; it is more like five symphonic poems. The form developed rather intuitively. Originally I thought that Gandalf would be the third movement, because the number three plays an important role for that character. It is divine (the trinity), in E minor, and the theme is equivalent to 3 x 3. I played with that number in a Bach-like manner on purpose, so it would be logical to make Gandalf the middle part. But when I finished, it had to be the opening, the entrance. The Gandalf theme is the most important theme of the symphony; of course, it made sense that I would have to expose it in the first part and not the third.

So Gollum became the third movement, the most bizarre of the five. Then comes Lothlórien, with a beautiful soft start and a build up of tension that seamlessly connects to Gollum. Because of that, I often perform the change from the second to the third movement in an attacca style in my own concerts. After the low flutes in Lothlórien, I immediately go to Gollum, as if he suddenly jumps onto the podium. After Gollum, I take a longer break. Then comes the fourth movement, the dramatic high point of the symphony. In the fifth movement, a lot of the themes return. That is when the sun shines through for the first time, although the piece ends in a melancholy mood, just like the book.

The music for Symphony no. 2 "The Big Apple" came about because of a commission from the US Air Force Band for a six-minute piece. I wanted to write a fast, energetic work with a lot of spirit, something like Bernstein's *Candide* or Adams' *Short Ride in a Fast Machine*, a work inspired by New York, a Big Apple Overture. But when I started working on it, I got curious about minimalist music concepts: How long can you let the process roll? I started working with that material, and in the end it became a 36-minute symphony. Even though this was not the original intent, the band was happy with it.

Much of my music is programmatic, but now I try to reach a greater degree of abstraction. I have done this a few times, and it has worked. I like to evoke images, but I want to make my pieces more exciting and search for other avenues. I want my Symphony no. 3 to use a different language and method than my first two do. Initially, I thought I would base my Symphony no. 3 on Atlantis, but I dropped the idea because the theme was sounding too Disney-like. Now the working title is "Planet Earth," but I have to emphasize that that theme is completely metaphorical and is meant to express my fascination with our planet. I want to use electronic sounds, no babbling brooks, but abstract sounds. It is meant to be an addition to *The Planets* by Holst. Earth is the only planet he did not depict. The end, when the thinly voiced women's choir fades away and the doors are closed, is where I want to open the gates again. The city sounds of "Big Apple" were already a foreshadowing of the electronic sounds that I want to use in "Planet Earth." I use the extra-musical frame not so much as a programmatic line, but more as a direction. When I create motifs and fragments, I know immediately if they fit in the framework. If not, I save them for a different work.

Most of the time when I compose, I sit down at the piano for weeks at the time and ideas trickle down, slowly but surely. For the new symphony, I start with two chords that are interwoven, two groups of three notes. I like to play with a few notes at a time; the third movement of "Lord of the Rings" is composed from four notes, and the second part of "The Big Apple" is also composed from four notes, as are *La Quintessenza* and *The Red Tower*. Those few tones also form chords. *Casanova* is based on three chords, which are almost literally from the opening measures of *Tosca*, except in minor.

I like to restrict my material and then see what I can do with it. Those motives or cells (I always seriously search for them) are created gradually. At a certain point, I start seeing structures and variations in those few notes. I look for certain seeds from which it can grow.

From within my intuition, I develop certain motifs. Sometimes I plant a seed, and nothing grows, while another motif suddenly turns out to be an enormous source of ideas. I have to be careful that I do not use this sparse material for too long in a piece. I always listen to a fragment a few times and, again based on my intuition, I determine the number of repeats.

After I have some notes down, I put them in the synthesizer so that I can listen back. When I composed "Lord of the Rings" I still had a synthesizer limited to six voices, but it was useful because I could put in the most important parts and play the other parts along on the piano. Now I have a 32-voice synthesizer, so I can get an idea of how all the voices in the ensemble will sound. It still is only a crutch because the sounds become transparent rather quickly. But I have learned to listen through that.

I wish I could use more advanced playback programs, but I am a bit clumsy with that and much prefer using the old-fashioned pencil-and-paper method. It is a ritual that is important to me. I want to let everything pass through my fingers; I think a computer screen is too impersonal. Besides it is not as easy to fall into the habit of copying and pasting, which I see done a lot by younger composers. I understand you can save the time of writing the same notes again, but it should not be a copy when you hear it in your head. Time should continue to flow.

Sometimes I try to write with a more "modern" sound using dissonant clusters, but to me the sequence always sounds so logical that it does not come across as atonal. You have to do what you do best as a composer. I think it is funny; if you write tonal music, it is called shameless. But if you write the most atonal rubbish, the word "shameless" is never used. I think a composer should use the language in which he communicates best. It is especially hard to write good tonal music because if you are not skilled, it will be immediately clear to all. I sometimes try to make the most dissonant clusters, but in the total context of my music and because of my instrumentation it always produces pleasant sounds.

The beauty of wind bands is that when you compose something, you know for sure that it will be played dozens of times. I publish and promote my works myself through my company, Amstel Music, and have developed a worldwide distribution network over the years. All the music goes; nothing stays in the closet. For outside composers who are asked to write a piece for wind instruments, publication is not a given because it may not be attractive enough. Music for wind band should sound fabulous and be a challenge for everyone if it is to find its way. It is terribly difficult to write for wind bands—maybe even more difficult than writing for symphony orchestras.

C. The Approach to Orchestration

I started arranging early in my career for the police band. *Abba Cadabra* (based on songs by Abba) was immediately printed by Uitgeverij Molenaar. The police band was sort of experimental ground. My orchestrations are anchored in the knowledge I acquired by studying scores, and I really never had to work hard to orchestrate well. I am very intuitive and playful, both with form and instrumentation, and I regularly come up with special things that I use in my arrangements, especially in my lighter pieces.

I arranged film music, for example, themes from *James Bond* and Latin-American hits like "Copacabana" and "Can't Take My Eyes Off of You." I only did that in the first three years, but those arrangements are still very popular. I enjoy making good medleys from musicals like *Phantom of the Opera, Cats, Miss Saigon,* and *Chess*. Nudged by others, I eventually started composing when I was 31. My first piece was my Symphony no. 1, "The Lord of the Rings." Maybe that is why the piece turned out so good; I was not hindered by critics and just completely went my own way and allowed myself to be free and intuitive.

I like to write things at the edge of playability, but it has to remain practical and should not be nonsense. Besides, the score should look good; that is lesson one for every composer. I play every individual part; if it feels good, if it is interesting enough, it will work.

I pay attention to instrument groupings. I put the horn section in 1-3, 2-4 placement. I carefully look at the trombones to see if the balance is good in the triads. I also do that with oboe and English horn, sometimes placing the English horn between the first and second oboe. I treat the clarinets as a choir. I always give the alto and bass clarinets their own voice and add a lot of division to the clarinets, which makes for a warm sound. I always receive a lot of praise about the horn parts, which always have a lot to do in my music. The trombone parts are, of course, correct! I play all brass instruments, so those all sound good. Through my experience I have especially learned what you should *not* do with instrumentation.

The baritones, bassoons, and lower saxophones I treat as a sort of cello group. Think about the main theme of "Lord of the Rings." It is simply a cello line. I always think of the symphony orchestra sound so my work or arrangement does not sound like a typical wind band piece. One characteristic of a wind orchestra is that you always hear the same sounds. I do not want that. I give the players plenty of rests, use doublings sparingly, and think much in terms of color combinations.

I had Henk de Vlieger orchestrate "Lord of the Rings" for practical reasons. First of all, it had to be done in a notation program, and I cannot do that. I did not want to handwrite everything again from the start. Second, I wanted to leave the orchestration to someone who had a fresh perspective. Before Henk started, I had my own ideas about orchestration, which were made clear in my score. On the other hand I gave him some freedom with the restriction that I could recall his choices at any time. I remained the final editor, and we did well together. His new division of the percussion, for instance, was very good, resulting in one less percussionist. A few things I insisted doing my way. I could have done the job myself, but at that moment it was more practical to hand it over.

D. Views from the Composer to the Conductor Pertaining to Score Study and Preparation

I always write program notes in my scores. They tell the story of where the music goes, and include directions for the conductor. In *Casanova* there are about 20 direction pointers. But at a certain moment a composer should let go of his work.

E. The Relationship Between the Composer and the Commissioning Party

In general I have good experiences with the people who commission my music. Overall, they like the music. One commissioner wanted a work with a high degree of difficulty because he said the students would not enjoy it if it were too easy. That became *Magic Garden*, which is quite a difficult piece. However, when I was finished, he complained that it was unplayable. A year later I gave him a CD recording of the piece, which proved that it was playable after all!

Most of the time I do not let commissioners nail me down with demands like how long a piece can be, that there has to be a solo for the second oboe, or that it has to have a certain subject matter. I don't work well that way. I usually try to get *carte blanche* as far as the form or contents go, but I do discuss certain aspects. In the case of *Casanova*, for instance, I suggested to the commissioner that I compose a piece for cello and wind orchestra.

F. Views on the Teaching of Composition and How to Mentor the Young Composer

Composition is a difficult profession as it is. I do not have a ready-made recipe for making a composition, and I do not have the time to give lessons. I get lots of requests from people who want to learn arranging, but I reject all of them. I would not know where to send them, either. I never took lessons in arranging. Besides, all of my secrets can be found in my scores. Study those; that's what I used to do. For a lot of people it is a revelation when I explain certain practices, while for me it was clear as a bell in the first place. As far as that is concerned, I am not a good teacher, because I am not good at predicting what will be difficult for others. Maybe I have things to say about composing, but not in a structured manner. I prefer a more informal approach.

Once in a while I help people, but I don't even want to think about having students come to my house a few times a week. That would keep me away from my own music too often.

G. Individuals Who Have Been Especially Influential in My Development and Career

The first person who though I had talent was Anne Bijlsma, the father of the cellist Anner Bijlsma. Anne played in the Residentie Orchestra, and he was a very good trombone teacher. I started with him before I was in the conservatory, and I took lessons with him when I had just started to play trombone. He always said, "Become a professional. You've got what it takes." He was a contradictory man, but he saw something. I always showed Anne what I was doing. I would come to him with a bag full of scores and records from the library, and he was charmed by my disarming enthusiasm.

Piet van Dijk, father of the bass trombone player Ben van Dijk, has been another inspiring person. He succeeded Anne Bijlsma in the Residentie Orchestra. Apart from being a fantastic trombone player, Piet was also like a second father to me. I often came to his house, and his trombone playing motivated me greatly. It was he who prepared me for the audition on the tenor tuba in Amsterdam. I have known Ben since I was 16. He also took lessons from Bijlsma and played in a different wind band in my hometown, Voorburg. I admire him for his intellect, his attitude towards colleagues, and his wonderful playing. I plan to compose a solo piece for him and to dedicate that music to his father posthumously.

I have certainly been influenced by the writing of Vaughan Williams, and some Puccini, because I played *Turandot* with De Nederlandse Opera. I can point you straight to the fragments from "Lord of the Rings" that come from *Turandot*. For instance, the funeral march at the end of the fourth movement is strongly related to *Turandot*, the fragment depicting Liu's death. By accident there is some Bartók in it, a fragment from the *Concerto for Orchestra*. I processed it subconsciously. I heard the *Concerto for Orchestra* again after it was finished, and I thought, "So that's where it came from!"

Many people hear some Wagner in my Symphony no. 1, but I know very little Wagner. The first part is very pompous, and there is a section with trombones that resembles *Tannhäuser*. But I did not do that consciously. There are some conscious citations. The start of the fast section in the first movement is from Stravinsky's *Firebird*, even in the same key. I thought I wanted that kind of clap in that moment, and I looked into Stravinsky's score and used his. It is tongue-in-cheek, and I do that a lot. "The Big Apple" is full of quotations like that.

At times I thought I would take composing lessons, but I could never decide with whom. Louis Andriessen and Roderik de Man would have been my choices, although they compose in a very different style from mine. I place a lot of value in discussions with colleagues like Jacob ter Veldhuis, Jan Van der Roost, Jan and Jacob de Haan, and Dirk Brossé. I have no secrets with them and enjoy telling them where I get my material. With those people, mutual respect is very important; they approve of what I do and vice versa. Also, Louis Andriessen is important to me. I regularly play his music in the Orchestra *De Volharding*, and he respects my work.

H. Ten Works I Believe All Band Conductors at All Levels Should Study

This is certainly my personal Top 10, based not so much on technical conducting aspects, but purely on those works in which I find great music.

1. *Le Sacre du Printemps* by Igor Stravinsky
2. Symphony no. 3 by Aaron Copland
3. *The Planets* by Gustav Holst
4. *Nixon in China* by John Adams
5. *Paradiso*–Oratorium by Jacob ter Veldhuis
6. *Romeo and Julia* by Sergei Prokofiev
7. *Tosca* by Giacomo Puccini
8. Symphony no. 2 by Jean Sibelius
9. Symphony no. 4 by Carl Nielsen
10. *The Expedition* –Opera by Klas Tortensson

I. Ten Composers Whose Music Overall Speaks to Me in Especially Meaningful Ways

Giacomo Puccini is number one, because with his verismo operas he comes so close to reality, and I think his orchestration is beautiful. The warmth, the drama, that "gasp" with Puccini is beautiful. **Leonard Bernstein** is on the list because he knew how to bridge jazz and classical music seamlessly like no one else. **John Adams** is included because of the energy in his tones and because of the fact that he developed so well after his period of minimalism. I use those repetitive elements myself.

Peter Tchaikovsky makes the list because of his beautiful melodies, **Igor Stravinsky** because of his rhythmicity, his strength, and his clarity, and **Aaron Copland** because of his transparent colors and no-nonsense writing. **Béla Bartók** is included because of his rhythmicity and his affinity for folk music. That is why I also feel attracted to the music of **Ralph Vaughan Williams**. **Dmitri Shostakovich** has such banality and **Sergei Prokofiev** such capriciousness. I also think the works of **John Williams**, the film composer, are very important. **Alfred Reed**, with his manner of orchestrating, has led me to the right path. Reed knows, like no one else, how to make instruments shine in their registers, and he is very subtle in his instrumentation.

J. The Future of the Wind Band

I think that the wind orchestra has a bright future. It is slowly developing the basic repertoire that the symphony orchestra has had for 300 years. Here and there you see good developments, non-military professional bands that are supported. But it is a slow process. The wind band has an image of uniformed, fur-hatted, beer-drinking street musicians. That is the impression most people have, and for the most part the bands themselves are responsible. We should have more composers like Adams, Reich, and Andriessen write for wind band, although that alone is no guarantee for success. What I want to say is that on the one hand I hope wind bands emerge from their isolation, and on the other hand that composers look at these bands in a less snobbish way. There is a lot of mutual ground; many symphonic musicians conduct a wind band at night. The emancipation has started, but there is a long road ahead.

Wind orchestras are in dire need of good repertoire because it hardly exists. The symphonic literature includes the likes of Mahler, Bruckner, Mozart, and Beethoven, just to name a few. But wind bands have only existed for about 100 years. There are a few great names like Holst, Milhaud, and Hindemith who wrote original works for wind band, but a substantial repertoire, a culture, is missing.

This discrepancy is partly because the roster of a wind orchestra is quite variable per country and per orchestra. A symphony orchestra is standard group. You always have exactly what you write for as far as a composer is concerned. With a wind band you just have to wait and see. And that is the fun and charming part. I solve that problem in my own pieces by writing the number of players required for each instrument (2 only, 1 only, tutti). This is a good practice because sometimes there are 100 people in a wind band, and many parts are doubled. Moreover, the roster is undergoing a slow evolution. Instruments like harp and piano, for example, are now being included in Holland, but 20 years ago they were practically unthinkable. I think that my music has had a positive influence on the expansion and preservation of compositions for the wind band.

K. Other Facets of My Everyday Life

I have a lot of good friends whose company I enjoy. I love to cook and eat well, am active with sports like walking and bicycling, and go to films, theater, and variety shows. I have little time to read, unfortunately. I also enjoy modern sculpture, architecture, and museums. I love big cities, the Earth, and all that is special: beautiful skies, nature, and everything around me.

L. Comprehensive List of Works for Band
Grade 2

Jupiter Hymn from *The Planets* by Gustav Holst, arrangement. (2:20, 1989, Amstel Music)

To My Country from Symphony no. 3 by Bernard Zweers, arrangement. (3:20, 1995, Amstel Music)

Grade 2.5

Funeral Music from the melodrama *Bergliot* by Edvard Grieg, arrangement. (6:50, 1994, Amstel Music)

The Glory of Love by Köthe and Heck, arrangement. (3:30, 1996, Rundel)

Der Tod und das Mädchen by Franz Schubert, arrangement. (3:30, 2005, Amstel Music)

Grade 3

Abba Cadabra by Ulvaeus and Andersson, arrangement. Features "Dancing Queen" and "Money, Money, Money." (5:00, 1978, Molenaar)

Bee Gees Revival by brothers Gibb, arrangement. (6:30, 1978, Molenaar)

Copacabana by Barry Manilow, arrangement. (3:00, 1979, Molenaar)

Can't Take My Eyes Off You by Crewe and Gaudio, arrangement. (3:47, 1982, Molenaar)

Chanson d'Amour by Wayne Shanklin, arrangement. (3:10, 1982, Molenaar)

The Pink Panther Theme by Henry Mancini, arrangement. (2:25, 1982, Molenaar)

Shoutin' Liza Trombone with trombone solo or trio by Henry Fillmore, arrangement. (3:00, 1982, Carl Fischer)

Teddy Trombone for trombone and band by Henry Fillmore, arrangement. (3:00, 1982, Carl Fischer)

March to Mars by Julius Steffaro, arrangement. (3:30, 1984, Molenaar)

This Nearly Was Mine for tenor or baritone vocal solo and band from *South Pacific* by Rogers and Hammerstein, arrangement. (2:41, 1984, Molenaar)

Berceuse from *Mazeppa* by Peter Tchaikovsky, arrangement. (3:07, 1985, Molenaar)

Songs from the Musical *Cats* by Andrew Lloyd Webber, arrangement. Includes "Memory" and "Old Gumbie Cat." (8:00, 1985, Molenaar)

Chanson de Matin, Opus 15, no. 2 by Edward Elgar, arrangement. (3:43, 1987, Molenaar)

Aquarium (opus 5). I. Allegretto grazioso (Neon Tetra, Electric Eel, and Angelfish), II. Andante/Adagio (Sea Horse and Zebrafish), III. Finale: Allegro giocoso (Guppy & Co.). (8:30, 1991, Amstel Music)

The Exodus Song by Ernest Gold, arrangement. (4:16, 1991, Molenaar)

Jig from *St. Paul's Suite* by Gustav Holst, arrangement. (3:40, 1991, Amstel Music)

Out of Africa–Main theme by John Barry, arrangement. (4:06, 1991, Molenaar)

Ratatouille Satirique by Erik Satie I. Prélude from Jack in the Box, II. Rêverie, III. Marche: Le Piccadilly, 1904. (7:00, 1994, Amstel Music)

Madurodam (Miniature Suite). I. Reveille, II. Toy Soldiers, III. Binnenhof/Buitenhof, IV. Small Windmills, V. Intermezzo/Nocturne, VI. The Westerkerk Church, VII. The Muiderslot Castle, VIII. "Grande" Finale. Madurodam was commissioned by the NIB (Dutch Wind Music Institute) with financial support of the Composition Trust. (9:30, 1997, Amstel Music)

Triumphal March from *Mlada* by Moussorgsky, arrangement. (4:00, 2003, Amstel Music)

Grade 3.5

Patchwork for Brass Sextet. (7:00, 1979, Molenaar)

Moment for Morricone by Ennio Morricone, arrangement. (8:25, 1980, Molenaar)

Midnight Cowboy with trumpet and alto saxophone solos by John Barry, arrangement. (3:30, 1981, Molenaar)

In the Mystic Land of Egypt for tenor or baritone solo, SATB and band by Ketelbey, arrangement. (6:25, 1985, Molenaar)

Polish Christmas Music-Part 1. Commissioned by The American School of the Hague for the 20th Annual International Honor Band and Choir Festival, 1995. (11:10, 1995, Amstel Music)

Grade 4

Beatles' Collection by Lennon/McCartney, arrangement. (7:00, 1981, Molenaar)

Cake Walk Phantasy by Peter Milray, arrangement. (4:21, 1983, Molenaar)

Highlights from *Annie* by Charles Strouse, arrangement. (7:14, 1983, Molenaar)

James Bond 007 by Barry, Norman, and Conti, arrangement. (7:00, 1983, Molenaar)

Honky Tonk Ragtime by Willy Faust, arrangement. (3:06, 1984, Molenaar)

Some Enchanted Evening for baritone vocal solo, TTBB, and band from *South Pacific* by Rogers and Hammerstein, arrangement. (5:44, 1984, Molenaar)

Il Trièllo for trumpet solo and band by Ennio Morricone, arrangement. (4:34, 1986, Molenaar)

American Suite–Opus 98b by Antonin Dvořàk, arrangement. (9:00, 1988, Molenaar)

The Phantom of the Opera by Andrew Lloyd Webber, arrangement. (15:19, 1988, Molenaar)

Pentagram for fanfare band. I. Introduction, II. Capriccio, III. Song Without Words, IV. Alla Marcia, V. Finale. (11:30, 1989, Amstel Music)

Aladdin Suite by Carl Nielsen. I. Oriental Festival March, II. Aladdin's Dream/Dance of the Morning Mist, III. African Negro Dance. (10:30, 1992, Amstel Music)

Highlights from the Musical *Chess* by Ulvaeus and Anderson, arrangement. (15:53, 1992, Molenaar)

Two Songs from *Porgy and Bess* by Gershwin, arrangement. (6:30, 1993, Molenaar)

Miss Saigon–A Symphonic Portrait by Schönberger and Boublil, arrangement. (18:57, 1994, Molenaar)

Continental Overture. Commissioned by the California Band Directors Association and premiered February 23, 1997, at the 40th annual CBDA Conference in Bakersfield, with the composer conducting. (6:50, 1997, Amstel Music)

Elisabeth–The Musical by Kunze and Levay, arrangement. (8:25, 2000, Amstel Music)

Concerto for Bass Tuba & Wind Orchestra by Alexander Aritiunian, arrangement. (15:00, 2001, Editions BIM)

Tintin-Prisoners of the Sun by Dirk Bossé, arrangement. (13:30, 2002, Amstel Music)

Grade 4.5

Loch Ness, A Scottish Fantasy. Commissioned by the Uster Musiktage – Switzerland. (12:00, 1988, Amstel Music)

Trois Rag Caprices by Darius Milhaud, arrangement. (7:00, 1994, Amstel Music.)

Jazz Suite no. 2–Six movements by Shostakovich, arrangement. (20:00, 1995, Amstel Music)

The Wind in the Willows. I. The River, II. Ratty and Mole, III. Mr. Toad, IV. The Return of Ulysses. Commissioned by the Metropolitan Wind Symphony, Boston, Massachusetts. (17:00, 2002, Amstel Music)

Klezmer Classics. (7:50, 2004, Amstel Music)

Andante & Alla Marcia from Symphony no. 4 by Dvořàk, arrangement. (5:00, 2005, Amstel Music)

Grade 5

Les Papillons–Ballet suite by Coby Lankester, arrangement. (10:00, 1985, Molenaar)

Star Wars Saga by John Williams, arrangement. (13:01, 1987, Molenaar)

Symphony no. 1 "The Lord of the Rings." I. Gandalf (The Wizard), II. Lothlórien (The Elvenwood), III. Gollum (Sméagol), IV. Journey in the Dark, V. Hobbits. The symphony was written between March 1984 and December 1987 and had its premiere in Brussels on March 15, 1988, by the "Groot Harmonie-orkest van de Gidsen" under Norbert Nozy. In 1989 Symphony no. 1 was awarded a first prize in the Sudler International Wind Band Composition Competition in Chicago, and a year later the work received an award from the Dutch Composers Fund. (42:00, 1987, Amstel Music)

Pavane pour une Infante défunte by Ravel, arrangement. (6:03, 1990, Molenaar)

La Quintessenza. Commissioned by the Carroll County (Maryland) Public Schools and premiered by the Carroll County All State Band, conducted by Harlan Parker, in Westminster February 28, 1998. (11:30, 1998, Amstel Music)

Voice of Space, Venetian Collection Part I. Commissioned by L'Orchestre d'Harmonie de Strasbourg, France. (8:20, 2000, Amstel Music)

The Red Tower, Venetian Collection Part II. Commissioned by La Banda Civica di Soncino, Italy. (8:20, 2000, Amstel Music)

Magic Garden, Venetian Collection Part III. Commissioned by the Hofstra University Symphonic Band, Hempstead, New York. (8:00, 2000, Amstel Music)

Empire of Light. Venetian Collection Part IV. Commissioned by the ACCBDA (Atlantic Coast Colleges Band Directors Association). (9:25, 2000, Amstel Music)

Grade 5.5

Extreme Makeover–Metamorphoses on a theme by Tchaikovsky for brass band. Commissioned by the European Brass Band Association as testpiece for the European Championships, April 29–30, 2005, in Groningen, The Netherlands. (16:55, 2005, Amstel Music.)

Romeo and Juliet–Ballet suite by Prokofiev, arrangement. (17:00, 1991, Molenaar)

Symphony no. 2 "The Big Apple." Commissioned by The United States Air Force Band in Washington, D.C., by Lieutenant Colonel Alan L. Bonner, commander and conductor. The official premiere was given March 1994 during the American Bandmasters Association Convention. (36:00, 1993, Amstel Music)

T-Bone Concerto. Commissioned by The Kentucky Music Educators Association. The world premiere of the complete work was performed by Jacques Mauger and the Band of the Royal Dutch Marines, conducted by Maurice Hamers, at the Concertgebouw Amsterdam March 1, 1996. (24:03, 1996, Amstel Music)

Casanova for cello and symphonic band. Commissioned by the Dutch
   Music Foundation at the request of the band's conductor, Heinz
   Friesen. Soloist Roeland Duijne gave the world premiere
   performance April 2, 2000, at the Vredenburg Concert Hall in
   Utrecht. (26:30, 2000, Amstel Music)

chapter 3

julie
Giroux

I think it boils down to this: Some composers write good stories. Some composers are good storytellers. Great composers are both.

A. Biography

Because the point of this book is to bring composers and conductors closer together (although I will be the first to admit a great number of composers belong far, far away from other human beings). I thought perhaps the details of my musical formative years would help give conductors some insight to my music and me. I could easily use this section to state the cold, hard facts about my career up to this point but that information is easily retrievable on the Internet and is more like a postcard of my life, a souvenir at best. I would rather tell you about the trip, to share with you not necessarily what makes *a* composer, but what made *this* composer. I want you to know my *real life* biography.

I have three memories of music that go back as far as I can remember. In fact, I have no memories of any kind that precede these other than a couple of physical accidents.

1. My little miniature wood and plastic toy grand piano (chromatic with a range of an octave and a half).

2. My grandfather playing the piano.

3. My mother's 45- and 33-rpm records.

My little piano went everywhere I went. I like to think of it now as the portable cordless synthesizer of the 1960s. As a young girl, I sat in front of the TV and played along with all my favorite shows. "Captain Kangaroo" was the first to teach me the octave leap and V–I progression, and with "Gilligan's Island" I learned a charming sea shanty. "Green Acres" was like a college Theory 101 voice-scoring assignment with its I–I–V–I–IV–V–I progression and an opening lick that spells out a major chord. Nifty! On and on this went. Television was my teacher, and she had an endless repertoire to share with me. After a short while, I took piano lessons, we purchased a used, but *real*, piano, and my grandfather showed me what the instrument was capable of. My mother had to lie to the piano teacher about my age because I was five, and no one younger than six could take lessons. It's nice to have a mother who will go the extra mile in the name of education.

Grandpa, known to the rest of the world as Albert Giroux, Senior, was a jack-of-all-trades and master of none. An avid softball player, he sought employment with whichever company had the best softball team at the time doing whatever work they had available. He left many lucrative positions, much to the dismay of his family and friends. Let's just say he was creative. In his spare time, he played piano in bars and restaurants and would occasionally play for me and my brother at our house. He played "by ear" and never learned to read music. For what seemed like hours on end, he made up stories and accompanied them with music on the piano while my brother Peter and I laughed, danced, acted, and sang along. Though he never specifically showed me anything, like what a chord or a scale was, he didn't have to. I watched everything he did, and when he left, I would try to imitate it. From early on, I associated words/music/actions/emotions as one in the same, inseparable. This is something I still do today. "Programmatic music?" you ask. "Is there any other kind?" will always be my reply. In my book, there are only two types of music: intentional and unintentional programmatic music.

My mother, Jeannie Ruth Giroux, (Freeland was her maiden name) loves music. When I was younger, she had an arsenal of records. Of course, my father, Albert "Pete" Giroux, did, too, but his were mostly top-40 pop and country, which are only interesting until a maximum of five chords per song no longer floats your boat. Mom had recordings of works by all the masters: Bach, Beethoven, Mozart, Chopin, Puccini, Verdi, you name it. They all taught me weekly. The music of composers long dead lived and breathed in our house, filling the air with sounds that, to me, bordered on godliness. They filled my soul with their passion and creativity.

Though I was too young to understand love, depression, death, jubilation, or even life back then, it was all in their music. And by some miracle, after listening to it long enough, it became a part of me. It is one thing to listen to a work and another to sit and physically recreate it. On my little piano I could play along with other instruments, whether the violins or the brass, or just bounce around with the melody, countermelody or bass line. The music absorbed me, and I absorbed the music. The composers, well, sometimes it felt just like they were there with me. I like to think I made some of them smile, and I am certain I made all of them wince. I know now that these were priceless lessons in not only composition, but in orchestration, arranging, ear training, and counterpoint as well.

Some of my favorite records were those featuring Liberace. Say what you will, but his recordings, especially the ones with solo piano, were fun for me to listen to. His arrangements were definitely challenging, often filled with modulations, key changes, and technical feats I had to work many hours to recreate. His "Beer Barrel Polka" and "Alley Cat" arrangements were a couple of my favorites, and I still play them every once in a while just for fun. Chopin's "Minute Waltz" and Beethoven's "Moonlight" Sonata were also a challenge but I learned those and many others painstakingly, note for note and musically verbatim, all by ear. I could see what I was hearing on the piano keys and, later, I could see it in musical notation.

It wasn't until college that I realized the true error of my ways when a kind but concerned piano instructor informed me that although I was playing the works technically and musically correct, I was playing them all in the wrong keys (usually a whole step up), and he wondered why I did so. The only answer I had was that my record player was fast, so fast that in my youth I learned everything up a whole step or worse. Thus, *my* "Minute Waltz" is in B-flat major and roughly 53 seconds in length, and although I can play the "Moonlight" Sonata in E minor, I choose to play it in Beethoven's original C-sharp minor because there, it is perfect.

All along this journey, I composed my own music as well as countless variations and arrangements of all the music I had "absorbed." Just as with anything else, the more you do it, the better you get. I had a lot of help along the way from teachers and other musicians, but I will address or pay tribute to them later in this chapter. By the way, learning music by ear, playing along with recordings until I have the whole thing figured out and memorized (no cheating and no printed music) is something I still practice today. Only now, I use a tunable CD player and a grand piano. The composers, well, they are still here teaching me, smiling and wincing.

B. The Creative Process

I like to compare the act of composing to building a fire. Although creativity is certainly involved, it is, in my opinion, just one of many elements that goes towards the composition of a work. There is the hearth (the place and the equipment), the wood (the bulk and sum of all your knowledge, past work experiences, training, techniques, and your whole bag of tricks), the kindling, or "fat" as we call it in the South (premeditated form, structure, tonality, style, and outline), and the spark (a little inspiration and another bag of tricks).

The Hearth

The workplace should be free from distractions and provide an atmosphere that is calming to the composer. If the piece is programmatic, I surround myself with as much reference material as I can, which may include pictures, essays, poetry on or hinting at the subject, books, printouts from the Web, everything that has anything to do with what I am writing about. That is one of my tricks and one that can fuel a spark when and if I need one. Among other things, I have dictionaries, a huge thesaurus, a Latin dictionary, several poetry books, references with famous quotes, and two books of musical terms within reach if I need them. I call my little room my castle or my dungeon depending on the day I am having. I even painted the walls with a faux stacked stone-block technique, which seems to amuse everybody who visits. Of course, I'm sitting in my room as I write this, and I'm not sure which one it is, castle or dungeon.

For equipment, I use a computer with an outboard sound module full of lovely band and orchestral sounds, headphones, and NO MIDI keyboard, just the typing keyboard that came with the computer. (I will come back to that because it is important.) I like the headphones because they help filter out the world and keep me focused. In the past, I owned a whole arsenal of musical equipment, sound modules, keyboards, and drum machines. You name it, I owned it. At one point I had 23 music-making objects that had to be plugged in. The problem with that is you become more concerned with the *way* the playback sounds than with the actual composition and spend hours tweaking this and that. Who cares? The whole point is to get the best possible piece of music you can make on the page.

I do *not* use a MIDI keyboard, although I did in the past. I became comfortable with getting the music on the page very quickly—too comfortable. My fingers and my brain found notes, but over the years my fingers have developed a certain way they like to play and pick out similar intervals, sounds, directions, and chords. No matter what I did, they had some influence on my music. I didn't want that to happen anymore, so I got rid of the keyboard. I would like to think I am free now, free to dream in my head, free to compose without restrictions. At some point, no composer needs a piano unless he or she can't play by ear. There isn't any combination of notes you're going to bang out that you haven't already hit before, so why do it? Why limit your music to that box? If the keyboard restrains my imagination in any way, I want it gone. The computer can play my composition back to me. If I don't like it, I erase it.

For programmatic music, imagine this. Let's say I am writing a piece about the Golden Gate Bridge. I can snatch up my laptop, go there, write the work in its entirety while sitting on the bridge, and e-mail the work to my publisher the second I am finished. Of course, I could do all of this with a piece of paper, but that is too slow and confining, and although I would like to think my inner ear is perfect, the computer can instantly shoot a handy-dandy test run back to me. If Mozart were alive today, I have no doubt he would type 100+ w.p.m., compose on a laptop (probably without a sound card), and e-mail all his scores to his patrons and publishers as a music program file with a bill attached, cash preferred, please.

In the past, when I composed on paper, the only way I could get the feel or flow of the work was to start at the beginning and play it back in my head or hash it out on the piano. Either choice takes concentration, energy, and a stop-watch. The computer saves you that hassle. It will play the piece back at any speed, in any key, as many times as I want with no wasted energy. This leaves me free to listen as objectively as I can. Cut and paste, and bam! It's done. No more writing the same notes over and over when different instruments play the same notes.

As a learning tool, the computer is invaluable. When I have the whole work done in my head, the computer is the best "dictation" machine out there. All things considered, the computer is the only way to go. Sure, I could have somebody yank out a broken or infected tooth or amputate a limb with nothing but a bottle of scotch to deaden the pain, but why would I? The world changes, and techniques and tools improve. Composition is no different, and when software publishers come out with something even better, I will be one of the first in line to try it.

The Wood

This includes all of the staples a composer must have: orchestration and scoring techniques, knowledge, concentration, and discipline. These are skills I continually try to improve by listening to music that intrigues me and studying scores if I can't figure a piece out just by listening. I have taken private lessons from other composers in the past but, truthfully, unless I want to know something personal, I think it is a waste of time. Almost everything I want to know or need to learn is on a page in a score somewhere just waiting for me. The trial-and-error method is still one of the best teachers, and certainly the more you compose, the better you get. I also try to improve my concentration and continuously strive to hone my current techniques and composing discipline.

The Kindling

This is the part of composing I absolutely love, the place where all the big decisions are made: how, what, where, when, how long, what style, and every other pertinent fact. First, I make all those decisions. Then I think about it, turning all the specifics over and over in my mind until I can do everything but hear the work. Once I have that, then I think some more, over and over and over pretty much all the time. Occasionally I may hear the music completely, for other pieces maybe only a few melodies, and sometimes there are no notes at all. I just *feel* it. It is there, waiting to explode. I call this my "simmering" stage. Finally, when I feel like my mind cannot possibly hold one more thought, I sit down at the computer and compose. My sessions generally last a minimum of 6-9 hours, and I *try* to stop after 14. I take little breaks along the way, but if I could physically compose for 40 hours straight, I would. I don't like interruptions, and I *hate* to stop.

The Spark

Inspiration, motivation, improvisation, and the Big Bang Theory are my sparks. A paycheck can create or greatly contribute to inspiration and motivation, but I will save that for later in this chapter. Instead, I will focus on the four ways I "find" notes.

One method of composing I use is what I refer to as the Immaterial Method in which I hear music in my head and write it down. The only difference between this and playing music by ear is the source, which is the music inside my head, not a recording. This is one style of composing and the way I prefer to work. I think of an emotion, event, or gesture, translate it into music in my head, and put it on the page. I have discovered that a lot of composers write in this fashion. Sometimes the Immaterial Method passes through a filter, usually a piano or a computer, to confirm what I just heard in my head before it goes on the page or is marked a "keeper." After awhile, the filter is unnecessary because it only adds more time to the process, and it can also become a crutch if you're not careful.

The other method I refer to as the Material Method. I sit at the piano, keyboard, or another instrument that has playback ability and hunt and peck for notes. Many composers use this method, and I have found that those who primarily use this technique cannot play by ear. They find a combination of notes they like on an instrument, creatively process them with their ears and minds, and then put them on the page. This is almost a reverse process of the immaterial method. It is a much slower method for me and one I rarely use anymore, but it works.

It's good when people who compose by the Immaterial Method can also compose by the Material Method. If you can't play music by ear, it is impossible to compose using the Immaterial Method. If you can't pick out a tune you hear on the radio, you sure can't pluck one out of your head. Many composers think of themselves or pose as Immaterial composers, but they are really Material.

Then there's improvisation or music on the fly. Sometimes when I compose I just improvise. The only noticeable difference between the Immaterial Method and improvisation is the amount of time I think about it. I don't think at all when I improvise. It's like breathing . . . I just do it.

Finally, there is the Big Bang method. I have never had control over this, and it happens whenever the mood strikes. Sometimes just a few notes arrive unannounced, and sometimes the piece comes in a deluge that I can hardly keep up with. A few times I have written an entire work from beginning to end riding on what feels like a magical stream, but that is a rare occurrence. The most obvious difference between the Big Bang method and improvisation is control. Out of all the methods, the Big Bang Theory is my favorite one, but I don't really use it. It uses me, and I cherish every second of it.

C. The Approach to Orchestration

Over the years, I have studied countless scores and read numerous books and articles about orchestrating. I even took a college orchestration class or two. I have written down entire pieces from recordings, which was painful, but well worth the time and effort. To this day I remember some of those "taken down" scores better than a few of my own. I have taken excellent private lessons from orchestrators and use many orchestration techniques borrowed from other composers, alive and deceased. One of my orchestration learning techniques is also my method of score preparation, which I will address in that section.

By now, these methods are all a part of me, and impossible to remove. Composers wanting to learn orchestration cannot go wrong if they take the same steps I did. I have no particular recommendation other than that the best starting place is a college-level orchestration book. Again, because somebody might actually want to know *my* techniques in addition to all the rest, I will tell you a few of the ones I am fond of.

Low-range bass lines in the concert band have always posed a problem for me. In the symphonic orchestra you have the glorious contrabass, which, to my mind, is far superior to the tuba. It has a lower practical range, is more dexterous, can play pizzicato and tremolos, and can hold the same note for an hour if needed without the player passing out (although there will be complaints . . .). Some concert bands carry a contrabass, and although I am glad they have it, I would rather see three to five of them and be done with it. But please not two. Two contrabasses continuously struggle to find the pitch center. Yes, I love the tuba. Keep the tuba. Just give it some company and give our ears something more to listen to. In lieu of that, here is what I like to do.

I use the timpani as another bass instrument nearly equal to the tuba. When rolling it can hold out a note for long periods of time and has an extreme dynamic range. It can free the tubas and low winds up for a rest and is especially nice when it is the only instrument in the range. I use the timpani for a fake pizzicato by combining a timpani note left to decay on its own with a staccato note in the mid to low reeds. Octaves are nice, too, in both the reeds and the timpani. I also use the timpani melodically quite often as the punctuation in a sentence, or even the "You don't say," or the "Yeah, I know what you're talking about" elements of a musical conversation. Quite often my music is misinterpreted when it comes to these timpani parts. Often they are not loud enough to be part of the conversation and just end up being background noise, causing a gap in the conversation. When balanced correctly, this technique is truly one of my favorites and adds not just a nice spice to the music, but gives the listener a break from the typical tuba-on-the-bottom sound.

Most of us are all too familiar with the "band sound." You go to a concert, stare at a program with 12 different composers' works listed and when the concert is over you feel like you have listened to one *long* band piece with 12 scored clapping sections. Orchestration has a lot to do with that. One of the reasons I love writing for concert bands so much is because many instrument combinations are possible, even if some of these choices can prove to be deadly. Add in all the percussion, and you have a real Noah's Ark on your hands. I try to use this diversity to its fullest. Not every piece of music calls for variety. Some works actually sound best if left in that monotone/mono-color setting. Those types of works are generally melody based, and the interest or beauty is in what the melody says and not *how* it says it. When I am not held to that or other types of restrictions, variety is essential to me. I even take this one step further by trying to make each work I compose different from the last with orchestration being an element that has the most obvious differences.

By now you have probably noticed that I consider music to be a type of communication. I strive to tell a good story. If you read a great story out loud in a monotonous string of words, it is painful at best. Read the same story out loud in a Shakespearean style, a style full of slang and profanities, or pay James Earl Jones to read it to you, and you have three completely different works of art. Orchestration affects music in the same way. It can make or break a piece of music, no doubt about it. It is a vital element in almost all types of music. When a melody is played as a solo, it is very personal. When it is played by 40 people in unison, it becomes something akin to a cold, hard fact. If the solo instrument is a flute instead of a contrabassoon, the meaning and flavor change. Everything you add to that melody and how you voice those additions continue to alter your musical sentence or paragraph.

Orchestration is a long string of decisions. You have to decide who, what, where, and when musical events happen, beat to beat, from beginning to end. Being aware of where you are in your story, exactly what you are trying to say, and how you are going to say it is essential at all times when you compose. It's not easy, and you constantly wonder if you have made the right decisions. I'm a firm believer that it's this string of choices involving a piece that makes me like or dislike the final work. When there are too many questionable "ifs" or "maybes" in a piece, there is always a modicum of doubt in the back of my mind that doesn't allow me to like it or be completely comfortable with it.

I am still learning how to compose and how to orchestrate. I'm obsessed with both because I know I can never learn everything. I just want to see how much I can discover and how many new, or at least new to me, techniques I can find. All in all, I think it boils down to this: Some composers write good stories. Some composers are good storytellers. Great composers are both.

D. Views from the Composer to the Conductor Pertaining to Score Study and Preparation

I am *not* a conductor. I am a composer who conducts on occasion. In addition to concert band, I have conducted my own film music and film music of other composers, some of which I had never heard or even viewed the score of until I got on the podium. Speed was always of the essence, which is probably *not* something most band directors are faced with. Slicing off more than $100,000 of studio time on a picture is always thrilling. I must admit I would have been much more elated if they had just given the sum to me as a nice "thank you" bonus, but you know how that goes. I almost never have a recording to work with, so my score preparation techniques don't revolve around that. If you have a recording, by all means use it, but it will only give you a better idea of the "flow" and timing of a work and not much else. I believe the following techniques I use would work for anyone in any situation, the more time the merrier.

To know and interpret a score, you have to understand every element of the music. I hate anything that resembles work, especially when it comes to learning a new score. I encourage everybody interested in score preparation, composition, and orchestration to do this at least once and

76

be able to tell me with a straight face that it was not only enlightening and educational but pretty darn fun. Get about a half dozen highlighters or crayons each in a different color. (I prefer crayons.) You may need more or less depending on the score and your degree of color definition. Save pink for the "frou-frou" elements like a triangle note here, or a "chirp, chirp" in the flutes there. Make a photocopy of one of your favorite scores. (I can hear all the copyright people screaming already. Pipe down! This score will be literally unusable for its intended purpose when we are done with it.) Don't pick a lengthy piece to start with, or this may turn into some serious work really quickly. Now start coloring!

Color the whole line, not just the starts and stops of passages. Isolate and group the unison parts first because those are the easiest to find. Use a different color for the melody, countermelody, padding, rhythmic elements, bass-type of line, and so forth. You will have to make some decisions along the way as to what each line actually contributes to the music and group them by colors accordingly. This is a very important learning factor. You may even have to invent a name for your groupings like "the fire" or the "rhythmic energy" instruments or lines. You will have some instruments that are the same color but that play very different roles to achieve a single goal together. Make those the same color. When you are done, you will have a gorgeous, unreadable color-coded score, sprinkled with pink, that shows you at a glance what the composer intended at all times, how the piece is orchestrated, and what makes the music. Colors will jump all over the page, change places with each other, and create a wonderful musical "roadmap." Go ahead and start feeling sorry for the tuba and it's color variety now.

Dynamics aren't important in this at all. This exercise is just for the sake of identifying every element of the piece's musical skeleton. The finished product is visually interesting and quite a conversation piece. You will be able to *see* and, more important, to *know* what some of the elements are that make it one of your favorite scores, not just hear why. This ability to identify elements in a piece of music is the *key* to learning and knowing a score. You now know what everybody does at all times and how or what they contribute to the music and can adjust and balance them accordingly. Every note is on the page for a reason. Many conductors tend to pass over elements as unimportant, without understanding their purposes. Notice how many colors the clarinets, saxophones, and French horns display if you're coloring a more difficult band score. Use this same technique when learning a score, but **without** the markers or crayons. It works for me, and I hope it will work for you also.

Now that we have identified the mechanics of a piece, let's address the "music." I have an interesting story to share about this subject. The very first television project I was hired to orchestrate was a monster. I had been given the job of scoring the "source" music for a mini-series set in the Civil War period ("North and South"). For those who may not know, "source" music is all the music you see actually happening on the screen like a pianist playing in a bar scene, or a string quartet sawing away at a swanky birthday party. In both instances, you see the musicians as well as hear them on the screen. Underscoring is the music you don't see but magically hear throughout a movie or television show. This is music that has no source.

Anyway, did I mention that the project was a monster? Three and a half hours of monsters to be exact, including everything from brass bands and quintets to a 40-piece bag-pipe, fife, and drum ensemble, a literal 1860s top-40 hit parade. There were around 100 cues if I remember correctly. One day I turned in a stack of cues for the following day's recording session, and the composer I was working for happened to be present. He lazily slid the top one off the stack, perused it, turned to me, and asked, "Where is all the music on this one?" Horrified that I may have turned one in incomplete, I quickly scanned the score and thought, whew . . . yes, I finished it. I asked him what he meant. He again insisted, "The music! This one doesn't have any that I can see." Now I'm thinking, this is getting personal. After further explanation I realized he was talking about the dynamics and other expressions like accents, bow markings, and slurs. In my rushed state, I had forgotten to put any of that down!

He hit the nail on the head, though, and that is something I will never ever forget. Whether you whisper "fire?" or if you scream "FIRE!" makes a world of difference. Loud, soft, short, long, fast, and slow: All these markings have meaning and greatly contribute to the mood or emotion of a note or group of notes. Staccato-style pianissimo combined with a presto tempo sounds like controlled panic or excitement. The exact same passage played legato and mezzo forte at an andante tempo might sound comforting or whimsical. Everything in the score is there for a reason. It takes time to add all those dots, lines, and markings, and to have them ignored or butchered is painful for any composer.

To interpret any piece of music well, we must ask ourselves of every passage and section: "What is its purpose or contribution?" "What is it's meaning?" and "What emotion does or could this represent?" and go forward from there. Is any piece's interpretation written in stone? Not for me it isn't. It is possible that something on the page could be performed in a different way but still convey the same emotion, message, or implication. What a composer has marked on a page is a good place to start. If the message is understood the way it is originally marked but could be played in a different way and reach the same result, I'm game, and chances are so is the composer in question. Understanding, interpretations, and personal touches vary from piece to piece and conductor to conductor, and that makes for a lot of interesting music. It also makes for a lot of musical "obituary" pages.

Tempo, tempo, TEMPO! Again, we are back to the "What is its purpose or contribution?" "What is its meaning?" and "What emotion does or could this represent?" Tempo has the ability to completely control this no matter what anybody else does with the notes, the style, or the dynamics. Play a pretty ballad too slowly, and it becomes a funeral dirge. Play a funeral dirge quickly, and it becomes a parody.

I like to compare musical tempos to one or a combination of human emotional states. This method works for me, and it is how I decide a tempo in the first place. Of course, all the other elements play a factor, but if the tempo is wrong, everything comes across wrong. Ask the questions and find the right tempo. Most music "lives" in a certain place, and it is up to a good musician to find that place, which should be close to the tempo marking already on the page, or else the composer is at fault.

Slow- and medium-tempo pieces must breathe. This doesn't usually apply to fast works, so I am going to skip over those entirely. A slow- or medium-tempo piece or section must have drive, it must breathe, and to breathe the beat has to bend or move. To slow down as you reach a musical climax feels natural and is like savoring a moment. It probably reflects human nature to want to stop time when something in our lives becomes too perfect for words. To slightly rush just before you start to slow down is a goodie too. It's like when you excitedly rip the wrapper off of a favorite treat and then slowly savor the first bite. To slightly slow down in sections or even on a few notes that sound particularly depressing or sad, just a little, not a lot, also helps to drive the emotion or pain of the moment home. It is like saying "this *really* hurts."

Don't be afraid to experiment. If you know in your soul that it works, then do it. If the composer didn't mark it, who cares? Some people refer to some of these techniques, usually the smaller, more drastic nuances as "milking" the music. Sometimes entire works sound best with *lots of milking,* such as an extremely emotional ballad. I refer to these as "Jersey cows" because milking is a must, not an option. I don't compose a lot of Jersey cows, but when I do, I *really* have fun with them.

All music is on a journey, and tempo is a big part of that journey. Tempo is also a huge factor in the "storytelling" we were talking about earlier. When I finish a work and e-mail it to my publisher, I am elated and horrified at the same time. I hope it is a good piece, and I feel satisfied that I have done myself and the music justice. But I am horrified because my new "baby" is going to land into many different conductor's musical "arms," and some of them are going to drop it. I don't even ponder on how many conductors will "drop" my piece because that scares me even more. If conductors are just going to plow from one end of a piece to the other and not make any musical gestures, then what is the point? Perhaps a nice job driving an 18-wheeler on a straight interstate route would be a better career for them. Music has to breathe, and if it isn't breathing, then it's dead.

E. The Relationship Between the Composer and the Commissioning Party

When somebody commissions a work from me, I like for them to have as little or as much control as they want, within reason. Once I receive a commission, I already know they like my music, and most of them are looking for a work of the same "me" style. If I have accepted the contract, then I have accepted the responsibility to give them exactly what they want. If they want a 40-minute band work featuring a local yodeler, then that's what they will get. I also inform the commissioner whether I think their idea is publishable or not. Regardless of what they want, I always ask for the following information:

1. Grade level.
2. Duration.
3. Number of players on each instrument.
4. Whether the work is in one or multiple movements.
5. Which instrumental sections or solo players could or should be featured and (more important) which ones I should stay away from. If there are extraordinary soloists, I want to know about them.
6. The purpose of the commission, whether it be for a special event or person, and if the work should reflect that.
7. The date of the premiere, and when they would like to receive the work.
8. Whether there are any musicians in the group who play an instrument (other than the typical instrumentation) that they would like to feature.

9. If they own the composing program I use, would they like to watch the work being written via periodic e-mails?
10. How they would like the "commissioned by" statement to read.

My fees reflect the difficulty level, time frame, and, most of all, the length of the commission. I am a fast composer. That is just how I work. The thinking process I go through before I actually sit down and put notes on the page is always the longer of the two processes. Once I sit down, though, I am off to the races. You also have to keep in mind that I am only a composer. I don't have another job. I don't have any other demands on my time. It is my life, my love, and my hobby. We take care of each other. I do like to know about a commission as soon as possible, but I have accepted commissions with less than a two-week "due" date. I will admit I am not fond of those types of deadlines, but sometimes that's just the way things happen, and we all have to make the best of it. My television series experience helps with that because composing five minutes of finished music a day is a requirement. Not just one day, every day.

Past commissioners like to reminisce and laugh over the barrage of e-mails they receive from me while I am composing. People who ask a composer about their works are in for an earful, and this should only be undertaken by the strong of heart. I am no exception. If a director has commissioned me, I assume he or she is up to the challenge. If not, that little "delete" button is right there on the e-mail page, and I encourage its use if the director has reached the limits of "creative outpouring" pain. I like to offer these private thoughts of mine as a part of the process, too. I have never composed a piece of music without at least one small dog in my lap. They are good listeners, but every once in a while, it is nice to have someone who can comprehend my creative thoughts.

The commissioning process, outside of raising funds, should not be a painful experience. Quite the contrary, it is a chance to play a leading role in the addition of works to the concert band repertoire. When I look at my own commissioned works, it always brings a smile to my face. Each one represents a group effort and a variety of "special" moments. For certain, none of them would exist if it hadn't been commissioned. The stories told by each are unique with emotional ties invested in many people besides me. They have an "of the people, by the people, and for the people" soul. I highly recommend those with the financial ability to commission as many works as they can with composers they feel are worthy of the task. I truly believe commissioning is a timeless contribution to the art of music that has the ability to shape the future of concert band literature.

F. Views on the Teaching of Composition and How to Mentor the Young Composer

I don't teach at a university or school, so I have the privilege of only tutoring composers. My students are not "never be's" or "gimme degree's." They are composers who are composing for a living or at least trying to. My philosophy is always the same. Give them what they need and stay out of the way. Their needs may be the use of a computer or program, tips on orchestration or tonality, or just the simple recordings and scores to study to expand their knowledge. Real composers are on fire. All a teacher needs to do is give them a good variety of informative fuel. They will do the rest. I believe the path of a true artist is only wide enough for the individual. It is a solo journey. Everything else is just scenery that enhances or momentarily sets the tone of the trip.

G. Individuals Who Have Been Especially Influential in My Development and Career

The influential people in my life all have one thing in common: I love them. Funny how it works that way.

My mother and my father, A. "Pete" Giroux, gave me what I needed as best they could. My father was a shy, quiet man, but I could make him laugh, and I loved to do it. I wanted to make him proud of me, and I strived for it. I was 28 when he passed away, and my life was changed forever. Shortly after he died, I received my first nomination for an Emmy Award. That experience was both elevating and devastating. All the little things I should have asked, should have done, and should have said but for one reason or another didn't, haunt me. The love I have for him—and the regrets—are a constant presence and influence in my music.

My mother saw to it that everybody in the house had what they needed, one way or another. Period. She was also a "Band Mom" who slung chili fries, hot dogs, and cokes in the band concession stands with the best of them for nine years. She carted me, my brother, and usually our friends to every rehearsal, solo and ensemble contest, all-region, all-district, and all-state band performance, band camp, music store, and every-where else we needed to go. She was there for us, always went the extra mile, and still has the energy of ten people. She is a true joy and inspiration in my life.

Charles Minifield was my junior high band director, and he greatly influenced me as a musician and as a composer. He made up stories for everything we played and related the music to us in that manner. That was right up my alley. He is an African American Vietnam veteran who took a bullet in the back and suffers constant pain from it. He almost never took off his sunglasses during class, and he plays a mean jazz trumpet. Today, he is a district attorney practicing in Louisiana. His stories are, shall we say, unique? It was in the early 1970s when I told him I wanted to write music for the band. He replied, "Great idea! Do your thing, girl, and just ask me whatever you want to know." I wrote my first full band work when I was in the eighth grade. He is a major reason that I was able to do it.

My teachers at Louisiana State University pushed me along my way. I was recruited by one band director, spent my first year with a different band director, and finally landed with another, Frank B. Wickes. I have always been a handful, and what Frank got stuck with was exactly that. His personality and teaching techniques were good for me, although they were very different from what I had experienced before. I think of him when I write every piece. I ask myself, "Would he like it?" or "Would he play it?" It's like a creative barometer I use in my head. I have picked his brain numerous times and still continue to do so. Frank has affected my life and music on many levels and always will.

My college French horn instructor was Richard F. Norem. He was like my father away from home. Yes, he taught me about music, the horn, and other musical things, but he tended his flock with a moral and conscientious crook and never let us stray. He was a great teacher of music and life and a good friend. He and his wife, Sally, are part of my extended family.

My true mentor can only be William "Bill" Conti. He gave me my Hollywood "break" and taught me the dos and don'ts of film scoring. He and his wife, Shelby Conti, welcomed me with open arms into their lives both professionally and emotionally and even put me up in their home when I first moved out to Los Angeles. Shelby was a pillar of strength in addition to being a good friend I could talk to. Bill is what I consider to be a master of the art. I will always be grateful for the wealth of knowledge he passed on to me freely with love and passion. Bill and Shelby will be with me always and are consistently a part of my music.

Lt. Col. Alan C. Sierichs, currently conductor of the USAF Band of Flight at Wright Patterson Air Force Base, has become not only a very close friend but has shown me what I think to be the perfect relationship between a composer and a commissioner. We have had a great time over the years brainstorming pieces we would like to be composed for band, and I actually managed to write one or two. When I look at my list of published works, his influence stands out like the North Star.

My publisher, editor, and good friend Bruce Gilkes has become invaluable to me personally and professionally. The e-mails we toss back and forth, phone calls, and endless banter on many levels have kept me composing for bands when, chances are, I probably would have stopped and taken up foraging roots and berries for a living. He is also responsible for keeping my composition titles and program notes "G" rated and comprehendible. I'm not really grateful about such matters, but I'm sure the rest of the world is. Bruce is a part of my inner creative circle and always will be, whether he wants to be or not.

Now, I come to my Rock of Gibraltar, the person who has been there every step of the way, if not always physically, spiritually. He is the one who totally by coincidence can start singing the exact same tune, at the exact same time, on exactly the same pitch as me, who I always know is calling, whom I always "bounce things" off of. The person who has been the most influential not only in my music, but in my life, is my brother and kindred spirit, Peter Wayne Giroux. No poet has the words for the bond we have and the best part is, we don't need them.

H. Ten Works I Believe All Band Conductors at All Levels Should Study

I have tortured myself over this list, but in the end I decided that people should study their list of all-time difficult favorites. By that I mean pieces that are difficult technically, musically, and in every other way. These personal favorites make the learning process not only as painless as possible but hold your interest not just technically, but emotionally. That being said, I think all conductors should also study **and** conduct an opera. If there is a musical "testing ground" for conductors, in my mind that is the place.

I. Ten Composers Whose Music Overall Speaks to Me in Especially Meaningful Ways

My list of favorite composers is in progress and always will be. It changes with my age, my moods, and my color preference of the month. Many of my favorite composers aren't on this list because I'm supposed to list only ten and not 100. The following 11 (sorry, couldn't leave anybody out) composers are my "staples" who, for various reasons, are either currently loaded in my CD player or not far from it.

1. **Guiseppe Verdi** (1813-1901)
2. **Gioachino Rossini** (1792-1868)
3. **Wolfgang Amadeus Mozart** (1756-1791)
4. **Richard Wagner** (1813-1883)
5. **Giacomo Puccini** (1858-1924)
6. **Peter Ilyich Tchaikovsky** (1840-1893)
7. **Maurice Ravel** (1875-1937)
8. **Igor Stravinsky** (1882-1971)
9. **Samuel Barber** (1910-1981)
10. **Richard Strauss** (1864-1949)
11. **Richard Rodgers** (1902-1979)

Puccini's "Si. Mi chiamano Mimi" from *La Bohème*, Act 1, contains one of my all time favorite musical moments, and I can directly blame Rossini Overtures for two of my four speeding tickets. Looking at this list I am even more reminded of why I listen to music. It can make me laugh when I need to, and when I need to cry, music helps me do it. Music helps me think, can make me feel good, and can make me get up and dance in strange ways. (My dogs are the only ones that can confirm that last one.) The composers I listed make me run to the piano to play along, they can stop me dead in my tracks as I am wandering around the house, and they can make me weep. My favorite composers will always be the ones who touch my soul on some level in a way that changes me forever. I could analyze my list and probably ascertain why they are my favorites, but that would remove the magic; I want to keep it.

J. The Future of the Wind Band

I started playing French horn in our junior high school band in 1972. Since that time, the number of fine composers for the genre has multiplied at least 20 fold. I believe the generation of more and more popular standards and great literature for the wind band will increase the demand for the ensemble itself. Commercially, I do not see it replacing the symphony orchestra, but I do see the possibility of wind band reaching the same stature. I am hopeful that someday, though perhaps not in my lifetime, the wind band will become an ensemble staple of serious music not only to "band people" but to music lovers everywhere.

K. Other Facets of My Everyday Life

I am going to start this off by pointing out that I, for the most part, am a hermit. I am perfectly content to go days without seeing anybody outside my little circle and *do* go days without talking on the phone. I landscape in my yard, take long walks in the woods, and spend a good amount of time on the upkeep and loving care of my many animal friends living with me. I currently have five dogs, two cats, an aviary with around 18 society finches (they don't stay still long enough for me to count), and a very large koi and goldfish pond with a waterfall and a bridge. The fish don't let me count them either, but I have managed to train a few to come to me and let me rub their bellies (just the big ones—the little ones don't seem to care for this at all). I regularly fall into the pond while cleaning it. I don't know why. It is accidental to be sure and mainly happens when the water is frigid. I think the fish lay traps for me.

I love movies, plays, musicals, and operas. I love to laugh and make people laugh. I spend a great amount of time with my best friend, V. Kay Case. She is in no shape or form a musician and has been my grounding force for years. With her I am myself minus all the notes, and she struggles to keep me "socially acceptable" to normal people. Thank you, Kay. God knows I love you. I listen to public radio and am addicted to "Prairie Home Companion." I enjoy history and The History Channel, and biographies are interesting to me also. I spend a fair amount of time reading information in books and on the Internet about my current interests. As a bi-product, I have composed music on some of these subjects. I am addicted to online gaming and am a huge fantasy fan. The making of *Lord of the Rings* into a movie just about made my millennium.

Mostly, I daydream, and as I dream I hear music. Sometimes it is worth writing down. Occasionally, I actually do write it down. Ninety percent of my music is not published but sits in a filing cabinet behind me: band, orchestra, ensemble, and piano music for the most part. And, yes, part of the reason I have not attempted to get them published is the fear of rejection. But mostly those pieces are there because they were good enough for me to keep and earned a spot in the physical world. Currently, I have half a drawer left in a huge four-drawer cabinet, and when it gets filled I will start another one. Everything is on disk, but I print out one copy of those I feel are extremely worthy and file them away. They are all immobile, and I could count them but don't want to. It would be like giving my life's work a number, and I just can't tolerate that. It sounds like I am hoarding them, but it's not that, either. It would take time to make a decision about them, and I would rather be doing something else. Anything else.

What the future holds for me is anybody's guess. My love for opera and musicals is beginning to affect my band writing, and sooner or later I will have to write at least one. I feel it will be sooner. In the meantime, I will continue to compose away the hours and spend the rest of my time with my loved ones, my animal companions, and my dreams.

L. Comprehensive List of Works for Band
Grade 2

I'll Be Home A'fore Ye. (3:20, 2003, Musica Propria)

Wagon Trail. Premiered at the 2003 Midwest Clinic. (3:00, 2003, Musica Propria)

Grade 2.5

Let Your Spirit Sing. (3:30, 2003, Musica Propria)

Grade 3

Kalanu. Commissioned and premiered at the Midwest Clinic, Chicago, Illinois by the Rice Middle School Ravens Band, Plano, Texas with Jason Tucker, Jackie Digby, and Elisabeth McConnell, directors. (6:15, 2000, Musica Propria)

March of the Sun-Dried Tomatoes. (3:00, 1993, Musica Propria)

Mystery on Mena Mountain. (5:30, 1984, Southern Music Company)

Ouachita. (4:00, 1985, Southern Music Company)

Prisoner of the Ring. (6:30, 1985, Southern Music Company)

What Goes in the Night. Performed at the 2000 Midwest Clinic and the Texas Music Educators Association 2001 Clinic/Convention. (6:10, 1999, Musica Propria)

Grade 3.5

"Nothing That Is..." Commissioned by the United States Air Force Band of Liberty, Major Alan C. Sierichs, commander/conductor. (4:00, 1999, Musica Propria)

Grade 4

Boston Liberties. 1. Boston Harbor, 2. Facts are Stubborn Things, 3. Granary Grounds, 4. A Penny a Ton. Premiered March 8, 2003, in Concord, Massachusetts, by the Concord Band, Dr. William G. McManus, music director. (2:00/2:00/2:45/3:40, 2003, Musica Propria)

Hands of Mercy. Premiered at the Kappa Kappa Psi/Tau Beta Sigma Convention, July 24, 2001, Corpus Christi, Texas, composer conducting. (7:00, 2001, Musica Propria)

Louisiana Parish Sketches. Commissioned by the New Orleans Concert Band with Dr. Richard C. Dugger, conductor. (7:30, 1999, Musica Propria)

The Necromancer. (6:00, 1984, Southern Music Company)

Grade 4.5

All Good Things. Commissioned by the Milwaukee Lutheran High School Music Boosters and the Janet Zastrow Memorial Fund for the 100 years of Lutheran Secondary Education in Greater Milwaukee. Premiered September 21, 2003, by the Milwaukee Lutheran High School Symphonic Band, Del Schmidt, conductor. (8:00, 2003, Musica Propria)

Culloden-Movements 1 & 2. 1. Heilan Lochs, Bairns & Heather, 2. "I Hae' Grat for Tho' I Kend" ("I have wept for those I knew"). Culloden in its entirety was commissioned by Kappa Kappa Psi and Tau Beta Sigma. It is dedicated to the thousands of men and women of Kappa Kappa Psi and Tau Beta Sigma who have served university bands because of their love of bands and music. (6:00/3:00, 2000, Musica Propria)

The Greatest Generation. Commissioned by Dr. Daniel P. Bolin in memory of his father Gillespie G. Bolin, premiered in 2002 by The United States Navy Band, Captain Ralph M. Gambone, conductor, Indianapolis, Indiana. (8:00, 2002, Musica Propria)

Three Fanfares. I. An Epic Fanfare, II. Heroic Fanfare, III. Fanfare for the Fallen. The first movement was premiered December 17, 2003, at the Midwest Clinic, Chicago, by the United States Army Field Band with Colonel Finley R. Hamilton, commander and conductor. (1:12/0:47/1:20, 2003, Musica Propria)

Tiger Tail March. Titled and premiered by the Louisiana State University Wind Ensemble, November 7, 2000, Frank Wickes, conductor. (3:00, 2000, Musica Propria)

Grade 5

Circus Franticus. Commissioned by the United States Air Force Band of Liberty, Major Alan C. Sierichs, commander/conductor. (8:00, 1999, Musica Propria)

Culloden-Movement 3. "We Toomed Our Stoops for the Gaudy Sodgers" ("We Emptied Our Glasses for the Handsome Soldiers") See *Culloden*-Movements 1 & 2. (9:00, 2000, Musica Propria)

Fort McHenry Suite. 1. "The Rockets Red Glare," 2. "Dimly Seen Through the Dark Mist," 3. "When Freemen Shall Stand." Commissioned by the United States Air Force Band of Liberty, Major Alan C. Sierichs, commander/conductor. (3:00/3:00/3:00, 2000, Musica Propria)

"Il Burlone." (3:00, 1999, Musica Propria)

To Walk With Wings. Commissioned and premiered by the United States Air Force Band of the Rockies, Colonel H. Bruce Gilkes, commander/conductor. (7:20, 1998, Musica Propria)

Grade 5.5

The Nature of the Beast. Composed for the Tara Winds, Atlanta, Georgia, Dr. David Gregory, conductor. Premiered December 21, 2001, by the Tara Winds at the Midwest Clinic, Chicago, with Colonel Lowell E. Graham, USAF, guest conductor. (8:31, 2001, Musica Propria)

Grade 6

"To Fly." I. To Fly, II. Un Mouton, un Canard et un Poulet, III. Impossible, IV. They Touched the Sky, V. Parachute Hankies, VI. The Name of a Plane . . ., VII. To Fly-Finale. Premiered and commissioned by the United States Air Force Band of Flight, Lieutenant Colonel Alan C. Sierichs, commander/conductor. (28:00, 2003, Musica Propria)

chapter **4**

donald
Grantham

Many of the band conductors I have worked with equal or surpass conductors in other media, as they must to handle the demands that appear in some of the current literature. Most have a hunger for challenging new works, actively seek them out and promote them with performances and recordings, and support their creation with commissions.

A. Biography

Donald Grantham, the eldest of three brothers, was born in Duncan, Oklahoma, on November 9, 1947. He has received degrees in composition from the University of Oklahoma (bachelor of music, 1970) and the University of Southern California (master of music, 1974; DMA, 1980). He was a scholarship student of Nadia Boulanger at the Conservatoire Américain in 1973 and 1974. Since 1975 he has been a member of the theory/composition faculty at the University of Texas at Austin.

Grantham is the recipient of numerous awards and prizes in composition, including the Prix Lili Boulanger, the Nissim/ASCAP Orchestral Composition Prize, First Prize in the

Concordia Chamber Symphony's Awards to American Composers, a Guggenheim Fellowship, three grants from the National Endowment for the Arts, three First Prizes in the NBA/William Revelli Competition, two First Prizes in the ABA/Ostwald Competition, and First Prize in the National Opera Association's Biennial Composition Competition.

His music was praised for its "elegance, sensitivity, lucidity of thought, clarity of expression and fine lyricism" in a Citation awarded by the American Academy and Institute of Arts and Letters. His orchestral works have been performed by the orchestras of Cleveland, Dallas, and Atlanta and by the American Composers Orchestra, among many others. His wind ensemble music receives frequent performances worldwide. Grantham's music is published by Piquant Press, Peer-Southern, E. C. Schirmer, and Mark Foster, and a number of his works have been commercially recorded on the CRI, Klavier, Gasparo, Centaur, and Summit labels. With the late Kent Kennan, he is coauthor of *The Technique of Orchestration* (Prentice Hall).

B. The Creative Process

The creative process is much easier to discuss than the creative impulse. I wrote my first piece at the age of 13, a work for trumpet and piano to be played by my best friend and me. I have no idea what prompted me to do this, but since then thinking about music and composing have been the central activities of my intellectual life. I can't remember any period of time longer than a few weeks during the past 30 years when I didn't have a piece in progress.

The actual process of composing is, for me, a challenging and anxious pursuit. In the early stages of a new piece, I'm always concerned that I won't be able to refine and polish my ideas to a point that will satisfy me. When I have ideas I'm excited about, I'm concerned I won't be able to realize their potential. Tensions of this sort generally persist throughout the entire writing process. The strength of my initial musical ideas was a source of paralyzing concern until a revelatory conversation with Nadia Boulanger freed me of it. When I first studied with her in 1973, I was having trouble with writer's block, largely because of this lack of confidence in my initial musical impulses. I won't attempt to recreate Mlle. Boulanger's idiosyncratic English, but when I explained my difficulty to her, she dismissed it with a snort. She observed that many of the great masterpieces are based on what she characterized as "discouragingly simple" material. She played the opening melody of the Schubert B-flat (Posthumous) Piano Sonata and the opening motive of Beethoven's Symphony no. 5 as examples. "Who could *not* invent this?" she asked. "It's not the material you base your composition on but how you handle this material that will determine whether your piece succeeds or fails." This was a hugely liberating observation for me, and I turned my attention to developing my technical compositional skills rather than obsessing about how inspired my beginning sketches were.

At one time I thought that she must have considered me quite a dull student to need to have this pointed out, but years of teaching composition have shown me that everyone has blind spots and very different ones. Sometimes a seemingly obvious statement at the right moment can be surprisingly enlightening and just what a student needs to hear. As to the actual mechanics of composition, I am able to arrange my teaching schedule so that my mornings are free for composing. I teach during the afternoons, and in the evenings I orchestrate. I believe that on some level, I'm composing nearly all the time. When I work on a piece, there is always some aspect of it that I'm concerned about—something that's not quite right that needs attention—and whenever I have idle moments, I'll dwell on that problem. Very often the next time I return to the piece the problem will be solved. I suppose that's partially due to some subconscious mental activity, plus the experience of many years of wrestling with problems and coming up with solutions. I always work with pencil and paper, away from the piano, for the early stages of a piece and at the piano for the final stages. I have never used the computer for notation or for playback.

Many of my works have a programmatic element or are somehow inspired by past reading that I've found compelling. Sometimes this material will gestate for years before resulting in a piece. For instance, in my most recent wind ensemble work, *Baron Cimetiére's Mambo*, a number of extra-musical factors came into play during the course of composing the work. For the past several years, I've wanted to try my hand at a fiery Latin dance work, probably because of some of the fine *salsa* and *merengue* music I've heard in the Austin area. From the beginning, the composition seemed to have a dark, sinister character. This brought to mind a novel I had read years before, *Continental Drift* by Russell Banks, which deals with the cultural collision between south Floridians and the Haitian "boat people" during the late 1970s and 1980s. Voodoo was a strong aspect of this novel, as was the colorful character of Baron Cimetiére, the keeper of cemeteries and one of the *Loas* of death. This suggested the inclusion of a highly distorted version of the *Dies Irae*—something that otherwise would not have occurred in the piece. On rereading the novel, I was reminded of the importance of the *mambo* (a female priestess) in voodoo, and naturally I found the double *entendre* of this word appealing. All of these influences coalesce and inform the character of the completed composition, and without them the piece would have been something quite different. Most of my "programmatic" pieces have similar histories.

Preexisting music has also served as a basis for a number of my compositions, whether they be from a particular musical style or genre (shape note music, spirituals, bebop, Cajun music, etc.) or specific works by other composers that have particular significance for me (Bach, Gershwin, Elizabethan madrigalists, etc.). It is my hope and intention when I undertake the composition of such works that, like Stravinsky, Copland, Bartók, Tchaikovsky and many others, I can put my own stamp on the material and show it to the listener in a fresh light. When this is accomplished, one is justified in claiming the role of "composer" of the work. It is never my intention to simply imitate or arrange.

Most of my works are based entirely on my own ideas, although everything in my musical background—my performing and conducting experience, my listening and score study, and the compositions I've written based on borrowed material—contributes to whatever is distinctive about my musical voice.

C. The Approach to Orchestration

Like many experienced composers, I don't regard orchestration as a process separate from composition. When writing for instruments, whatever the medium happens to be will determine the compositional thought process, and the ideas seem to arrive already conceived for strings, winds, or whatever.

I always work in short score (two to four staves) and always with pencil and paper. Occasionally I'll show my sketches to a student if it happens to be relevant to what that student is working on. The first comment is almost always, "But there are no instruments indicated!"—and this is true. I know what the instruments are, and it would be redundant and troublesome to write them all in. "In any case," I counter, "you should be able to tell what they are simply by the way the part is written." A clarinet part should not look like an oboe part or a trumpet part or a violin part, even though they share a good portion of their respective ranges. Examine any score by Ravel, Stravinsky, or any other first-rate orchestrator. One doesn't need to look outside the brace to know what instrument is playing. Undifferentiated writing for the instruments is one of the most amateurish and common reasons for dull orchestration.

A second, and often remarked upon reason, is over-doubling of parts. For me, the least interesting and least colorful sound an orchestra or wind ensemble makes is a tutti at a *fortissimo* level. Much of the music for bands and wind ensembles I hear would profit from thinner, more transparent textures, less unison and octave doubling, more emphasis on contrasting registers, and more "chamber-like" writing. Debussy's *Prelude to the Afternoon of a Faun* is a model of this, and it's instructive to go through that work looking at the relative proportion of tutti and "chamber" sections and see how little doubling is employed. In so many ways it's like a chamber piece. It famously relies on solo winds a good deal of the time, and the work is nearly a third over before a truly significant, extended string passage occurs. There is only one full-blown tutti section, all of about 20 measures, and this is scored in such a way that strings and winds retain their identities. The tutti is followed by a chamber-like section that presents most of the significant motives of the work, except for the opening flute solo, which immediately follows. From the standpoint of color, this is ideal orchestration.

D. Views from the Composer to the Conductor Pertaining to Score Study and Preparation

Few of the conductors I've worked with need advice from me on score preparation or on how to achieve convincing proportion, effective pacing, or passion. If the composer has done his job, there should be sufficient information in the score for the conductor to realize all of these goals. But, of course, the composer cannot foresee everything, and it is surprising what a huge difference a small oversight can make.

In particular, I remember how soggy and enervated the opening section of *Bum's Rush* felt during the initial rehearsals. I had marked it *Mysterious, foreboding.* Finally it occurred to me to suggest, "Yes, mysterious and foreboding, but also crisply articulated." This completely cleared up the problem. I added that phrase to the opening designation and have never had a problem with the section since. It's hubristic on the part of the composer to think, "Everything is shown in the score that is necessary for the effective performance of my music." This is never true, but it's a goal the composer should constantly strive for.

One of my major concerns in performances of my works is tempo. A number of my pieces contain fast, technical sections that are right on the cusp of performability. This is not accidental; I am aware of it. I always write these sections with reluctance; they are risky in performances, a drain on rehearsal time, and a demand on the performer's practice schedule. They undoubtedly cost me performances. I nevertheless include them on occasion because some pieces would not be as convincing without them. I make the following dangerous generalization in regard to the performance of these sections: I would prefer to have my music performed at tempo *a little bit messy* rather than perfectly at a significantly slower tempo. I do not mean, of course, that the performance should be at tempo if there's a high likelihood of a breakdown or if a passage is going to be unrecognizable. It's a judgment call for the conductor, but a performance "on the edge" is almost always more satisfying than a "safe" performance designed to minimize mistakes.

I am often asked how much "freedom" a conductor can take in the performance of my music, and, of course, this depends on what is meant by "freedom." Modification of dynamics for balance, personal shaping of phrases, and judicious use of rubato are fine. Omitting sections, radically altering tempos, or changing rhythms, pitches, or octave placement are not. (I am not opposed, however, to reassigning important solo passages to other instruments in instances when the designated instrument or an adequate player is not available. In most of my scores I provide cues when I believe an alternate might be called for.)

Despite my general objection to taking liberties with the score, one of my favorite performers was Glenn Gould, who was (in)famous for the liberties he took with his repertoire. I don't agree with all of his interpretations, but I always find them of interest. He was a performer who seemed to think like a composer. He got inside a piece, recreated it from the inside out, and made it his own. I never sense that his decisions were arbitrary, even when they strike me as eccentric. Bernstein's famous remark before conducting Gould's 1962 performance of the Brahms Piano Concerto in D Minor (which I'll paraphrase as: "I don't agree with this interpretation, but I think it deserves to be heard") sums up my feelings about some of his interpretations. On the other hand, Gould's performances of Bach and repertoire from the Fitzwilliam Virginal Book are among the most satisfying I've heard.

I have written one opera, *The Boor*, based on the Chekhov play. I slaved over this work and thought that I had completely conceptualized everything I wanted—from costumes, lighting, and staging to how every note should be sung and played. The singers, musicians, and technicians involved in the premiere were experienced professionals, and when the opera went into rehearsal, it quickly became apparent to me that the best thing I could possibly do for my own work was to get out of the way and let them exercise their own imaginations and recreative powers. Almost everything on opening night was different to some degree from what I had originally conceived, but almost everything was better. I profoundly respect the contributions a gifted conductor and performer can bring to a performance and am flattered when that individual thinks enough of my work to offer his own ideas about it.

E. The Relationship Between the Composer and the Commissioning Party

Theoretically, the relationship between the composer and commissioner should be perfectly smooth and amicable. The commissioner admires the work of the composer—or why would he be commissioning him or her?—and wishes to have a work that somehow reflects his or her own musical values, while perhaps celebrating some particular occasion. The composer knows or becomes familiar with the musical abilities and proclivities of the commissioner and tailors a work to suit the occasion and the performers. It seems straightforward enough, and I'm happy to say that my experiences with commissioners have been almost universally positive (and I sincerely hope they feel the same about with me!).

In the early discussions about a commission there are a few things I must know: the size of the ensemble, the duration of the piece, the character of the piece, and the desired date of delivery. Naturally, all of these will influence whether or not I'm able to accept the assignment. I need to know about the "character of the piece" because it takes me longer to write a fast, brilliant piece than a slow, reflective one, although this is probably not true of all composers. The former type of piece will also likely be more expensive to computer-engrave and to duplicate, because it obviously requires many more measures to fill ten minutes at ♩ = 120 than ♩ = 56. When these details are settled, I need to know about the strengths and weaknesses of the ensemble. I don't find it at all difficult to emphasize or de-emphasize particular instruments or sections.

I am completely open to suggestions from commissioners about the nature of the commissioned work. I may decline to take them, but I'll certainly consider them. My experience has been that commissioners are rarely more specific than the general instructions discussed in the paragraph above, and, of course, this is perfectly agreeable.

The contract or letter of agreement needn't be lengthy but should be crystal-clear about the delivery date, the fee and the payment schedule, the duration of the piece, the party responsible for the expenses of computer-engraving and duplication of score and parts, and the level of difficulty. It is important to include clauses concerning ownership of copyright (always the composer) and the prohibition of the commissioner's loaning, selling, or renting performance materials to third parties (this is the composer's prerogative). In addition, there may be stipulations about the period of time during which the commissioner has exclusive performance and/or recording rights.

F. Views on the Teaching of Composition and How to Mentor the Young Composer

I don't agree that it's impossible to teach composition. Students are frequently required to compose in theory, counterpoint, and 20th-century style courses, just as students are required to write essays, papers, and even poetry and short stories in literature and language classes. What cannot be taught is creativity. One can write a perfectly decent essay, a "mistake-free" two-part invention, or an acceptable original piece without being the least bit creative. A person who has great difficulty in coming up with imaginative musical ideas is unlikely to be a successful composer and would be better off pursuing some other endeavor. Until proven otherwise, I assume at the beginning of composition study that my students are creative. What we work on in lessons is the craft of composition, because there is nothing to be done about the presence or lack of a creative gift.

I think one of the most important aspects of teaching composition is being able to evaluate, even "diagnose," each student based on that individual's particular musical personality. What unique musical attributes does this student possess, and what can I offer that will help him or her realize his or her potential? Nadia Boulanger was a master of this. She seemed to instinctively understand the voice I was trying to develop as a composer and also could see what was preventing me from doing so. Her lessons were designed not so much to remove these obstacles as to help me see what they were and to address them in my own way. I am still amazed at how frequently she used indirection in her lessons with me, forcing me to think about an issue rather than delivering a dictum. Some of the most valuable musical insights I have received came from her and are still an important part of my musical thinking. In my teaching, I try not to impose my own creative and aesthetic biases. Like her, I try to get inside a student's musical skin and help that student to develop an individual voice and then to express that voice in the strongest possible way.

At the beginning of composition study there are usually a number of common weaknesses that need to be addressed, matters such as pitch and tonal redundancy, square phrasing, undifferentiated instrumental writing, and so forth. As the student progresses and matures, the criticisms and suggestions gradually become more subtle and sophisticated until at the end of formal study (in ideal situations anyway) the lesson is more of a give-and-take discussion between equals. I feel that I've accomplished my job as a teacher when this occurs. (Many composers, myself included, take pains to develop and maintain a similar relationship with a friend or fellow composer so that we can try out new works while serving as a sounding board and providing helpful feedback to each other.) An important aspect of the mentoring process is to probe and find out what music the student does and does not know. As a teacher, I make weekly references to scores and recordings for the student to investigate and also frequently recommend passages from the literature relevant to what the student is composing.

It is very important for the teacher to emphasize the necessity of professional career maintenance. Being a composer is, for most of us, at least three jobs: writing the music, promoting the music, and doing something to make a living. Composing the music is only the first and perhaps the easiest step in the life of a piece. Then come the letters, the phone calls, the mailing of scores and recordings, etc., to each and every conductor/performer/publisher who might be interested.

Some young composers also need to be encouraged to network with their fellow music students and to develop the knack of enticing performers to play and record their music early on. I've found that most student players are perfectly willing to perform a new work that's well written and gratifying to play. If a composer cannot interest performers in his works after repeated attempts, some serious self-examination is in order. Of course, it is critical for student composers to attend all the concerts they possibly can, to enter competitions and respond to calls for scores, and to take advantage of any summer programs or music festivals they can attend. It is the responsibility of the teacher to see that students become aware of these possibilities and the students' responsibility to pursue all such future opportunities on their own.

G. Individuals Who Have Been Especially Influential in My Development and Career

From my previous comments, it is obvious that Nadia Boulanger was one of the most important influences on my development as a composer. I remember the two summers I spent with her at the Conservatoire Américain with deep gratitude and affection.

I had three other very fine composition teachers, all at the University of Southern California, who were quite helpful in different ways. Halsey Stevens was a master of vocal music and text setting, and I have utilized many of his ideas and methods in my own vocal works. Robert Linn was a charming and witty composer with a distinctly French sensibility. He helped me through some very specific technical problems and greatly improved the overall shape and forward momentum of my work. My own composition teaching is something of an amalgam of the practices of these three teachers.

Ramiro Cortes, the third composer I studied with at Southern California, was quite another case in that he was the most "intrusive" teacher I've ever had. Ramiro was the kind of teacher that students loved or hated; they either studied with him to the end of the degree or left at (or before) the end of the first semester. He held very strong opinions, was quick to voice them, and quick to find flaws and inconsistencies in weak responses. I remember lessons in which he literally pushed me off the piano bench to erase something I had done and replace it with his own revision. The saving grace was that he was as fast to praise and encourage. There was never any equivocation, and one had no doubts about the sincerity of his remarks. In addition, he was usually correct in his assessments, and I have never had a teacher who was better at pointing out unseen possibilities in the material I produced or at suggesting alternate and intriguing directions in which a piece could develop. I thoroughly enjoyed my time with him and was very disappointed when he left Southern California at the end of my first year of graduate study to become composer-in-residence at the University of Utah.

In summation, I would say that my experience with all four teachers was one of absorbing and internalizing as much of their individual approaches to composition and musical aesthetics as possible. In the course of our lessons, I learned to ask myself the questions that they asked me and recognized for myself the weaknesses they pointed out. I learned to regard my initial musical ideas objectively and with healthy skepticism, as something to be manipulated, tweaked, fussed over, and perhaps tossed out in part or in whole. On a personal note, I went to my lessons with Halsey Stevens and Robert Linn at ease and with a comfortable sense of expectation. I went to my lessons with Nadia Boulanger and Ramiro Cortes with a knot in my stomach.

Kent Kennan was another individual who had a strong impact on my musical thinking and career. Kent was a member of the search committee that hired me to teach at the University of Texas at Austin, where I have been since 1975. We shared an office together for several years during which time we exchanged ideas about teaching orchestration and composition and had numerous discussions about contemporary music, composers, and performers. This resulted in his inviting me to coauthor the third and subsequent editions of *The Technique of Orchestration* (Prentice Hall). It was a revelation to observe the care and precision he brought to bear on the book's content and preparation, and, of course, this is the reason for its extraordinary 54-year life as the most-used orchestration text in English.

By the time I met him, Kent had chosen not to teach composition. I think it was because he did not want to risk saying something to a young composer that might inhibit his or her development. This degree of respect for every individual informed all aspects of his life. Fortunately, he was not reticent about sharing his opinions with composers he considered to be mature, and I had the benefit of his advice about much of the music I wrote during the nearly 30 years I knew him.

Many people in the music community—particularly those with Austin connections—lost a dear and valued friend when Kent Kennan died November 1, 2003. This chapter is the poorer for want of his spidery handwritten suggestions and criticisms across the draft.

The musicians who lived in my hometown when I was growing up went out of their way to help me become a successful musician. J. Kenneth Smith, my band director from the seventh grade through high school, offered comments and suggestions about my first band piece, *American Overture*, and programmed it on our spring concert during my senior year in 1966. To my surprise, he invited me to conduct the work and gave me my first conducting lesson: "This is a three pattern, this is a four pattern. Don't mix them up." Then I was in front of the group to do what I could with them.

The choir director of our church, Gere Brock, performed several of my vocal works and also programmed my numerous original compositions and arrangements of Bach and Handel choruses for brass ensemble. Gere was also the first conductor I encountered who programmed works considered "adventurous" by her singers and audiences—and felt strong enough about it to take the heat and weather the resistance. Mary Helen Wade, my high school piano teacher, was a fine musician who was up on current musical trends and introduced me to music by Walter Piston, Samuel Barber, Wallingford Riegger, George Gershwin, and Claude Debussy that I otherwise would not have encountered for several more years.

I was unbelievably fortunate in the support of my parents. When I became interested in composition they saw to it that I received the best instruction available, which meant weekly trips to two nearby colleges to study with music faculty members. I enjoyed their wholehearted backing in what they must have considered to be a quixotic undertaking.

Finally, and most importantly, my wife Suzanne has made possible whatever I've been able to accomplish as a composer. A fine musician herself, she has offered much perceptive (and pointed!) advice about my work over the years. Moreover, she has been utterly selfless in our nearly 30-year marriage. The reason I was able to write an opera, the nearly 20 wind ensemble works, and all the other music was because she was caring for our three small children, handling the household and family affairs, seeing to the publication of my music, and in general picking up my slack and making up for my deficiencies. I owe her more than I can ever repay.

H. Ten Works I Believe All Band Conductors at All Levels Should Study

Having read Volume One of *Composers on Composing for Band*, I am aware that my friends and colleagues have named very nearly every piece that would be on any musician's top ten list.

Rather than repeat many of the same pieces, I'm going to recommend my "B List" of works, all of which I believe are just as helpful and stimulating to study. Conductors might find my first three choices unusual. I offer these suggestions because I have found them to be so personally valuable and because I think that every musician would be well served by spending 10 minutes a day sight reading and considering the construction of selections from these collections—or whatever alternatives one finds appealing.

1. Chorale Harmonizations by J. S. Bach. I recall coming across an instance of parallel fifths in my old Riemenschneider edition of the chorales as a graduate student. I was surprised, naturally, and made a notation on the back inside cover. Over the years, I've filled up that cover with what theory textbooks would consider to be errors and eccentricities—including one instance of two successive parallel fifths in the same voices (see #214, "Mitten wir im Leben sind"). I am by no means priggish about these things and in fact delight in discovering such "departures" from what is taught as standard practice. It's always interesting to speculate about why Bach made these decisions, and one can usually arrive at an explanation. It's inconceivable that they're accidental. I highly recommend the Dantalian edition, which compares different settings of the same chorale tune and contains translations of the texts. (I am also extremely interested in Bach's Chorale Preludes because I employ similar compositional procedures when I'm handling preexisting music. My setting of "Wondrous Love" in *Southern Harmony*, for instance, uses techniques similar to a number of Bach's settings.)

2. Mazurkas by Frédéric Chopin. Chopin achieves astounding variety in the 51 pieces, despite the fact that they all share the same constructive characteristics. I admire how he is able to use an utterly conventional accompaniment figure so relentlessly, yet keeps it viable by slipping in and out of it in unexpected ways. There's a similar tension between the conventional and the unconventional in the harmonic language and the phrasing that I find very compelling.

3. Preludes and Fugues op. 87 by Dmitri Shostakovich. These pieces, especially the Preludes, have proven very useful in teaching composition. The Preludes are terse and precise demonstrations of how one can fashion an entire piece from a minimal amount of motivic material. The Fugues are the opposite. They're usually quite expansive and contrapuntally intense. I don't think they always work, and occasionally the Fugues seem too long to be supported by the material. A few seem contrapuntally overwrought. The best of them exude wry wit and humor, and the ones with eccentric subjects (e.g., D major and A major) remind me of the tongue-in-cheek subjects of some of Bach's organ Fugues (BWV 532, for instance).

4. *Cantata Academica* by Benjamin Britten. This piece is a superbly unified and richly contrapuntal work for soloists, chorus, and orchestra that I regard as one of Britten's finest achievements (and that he regarded as a trifle). The 13 movements of this work feature a wide array of contrapuntal challenges (hence the "academica") including elaborate canons, the combination of a slow section with a fast section to create a third section, much retrograde and inversion, a fugue, etc., all held together by a 12-note series presented in the central movement of the work that is

treated in a completely unconventional manner. The most impressive thing about the piece, though, is that it sounds completely natural, lyrical, and unaffected. An audience can hear the entire thing spinning out as though it were a through-composed piece.

5. *Alborada del Gracioso* and *Une barque sur l'ocean* by Maurice Ravel. This is as close as one can come to having an orchestration lesson with Ravel. The piano version (from *Miroirs*) can be compared with his own orchestral scoring of the movements. For the composer, it is an object lesson in how to transcribe delicate filigree textures. For the conductor, I think it gives some idea of what is "essential" in a score versus what is decorative.

6. Violin Concerto by Alban Berg. Formally, this is one of the most perfect works I know. The beauty and persuasiveness of its harmonic language is unsurpassed. I admire the way Berg manipulates serial procedures to his own ends to exactly fit this work's particular requirements.

7. *Agon* by Igor Stravinsky. This work offers some of Stravinsky's quirkiest, most daring orchestration—how else to describe a movement scored for solo violin, xylophone, tenor and bass trombones, and cellos? It is also one of his most entertaining pieces, a work that can cause an audience to laugh aloud with delight. The piece is a sure-footed high wire act made up of dozens of disparate, seemingly disconnected parts that add up to a satisfying, convincing, unified whole; it is a compositional *tour de force.*

8. *Scenes Revisited* by Verne Reynolds. I have just recently gotten to know this work and the composer's Piano Concerto. Both strike me as some of the strongest music

I've heard for wind ensemble. The atonal harmonic language of both works never loses momentum, and the orchestration exploits the power and the delicacy of the ensemble. Both works are well proportioned and have intriguing formal designs.

9. *John's Book of Alleged Dances* for string quartet and electronics by John Adams. This work is one of the most successful recent works I know in combining popular and classical elements. It is also very witty, polished, highly absorbing, and just plain fun to listen to. *The New York Times*, in a story on the composer, wrote about a "note of optimism" in his works that is missing in much of the music of the 20th century. This seems accurate to me, and I believe that this work represents that aspect of his output. The direction Adams is taking could go far toward developing a larger and more appreciative audience for concert/symphonic music.

10. *Eight Etudes and a Fantasy* by Elliott Carter. I've used this piece in teaching composition and orchestration. Each of the etudes is based on a single constructive device, and elements of all eight etudes are combined in the concluding fantasy. Carter has stated that this piece was originally conceived to demonstrate particular orchestration principles and so is of interest to conductors and composers.

I. Ten Composers Whose Music Overall Speaks to Me in Especially Meaningful Ways

1. The composers of the Fitzwilliam Virginal Book. I love this enormous collection of Elizabethan keyboard music. It is a true "come one, come all" hodgepodge, with masters (Byrd, Gibbons, Morley, et al) presented cheek by jowl with rank amateurs. All of them are wrestling with emerging tonality, and it's plain to see those who are handling the material with authority and aplomb, those who can't quite come to grips with it, and others who are heading off in bizarre and dead-end directions. To me it seems analogous to similar struggles at the beginning of the 20th century. An excellent two-volume reprint is available from Dover, and Glenn Gould has recorded a representative selection of the pieces. John Bull's *Saint Thomas Wake* is the basis for a highly vitruosic orchestra work of the same title by Peter Maxwell Davies.

2. **Hector Berlioz**. It's hard for me to believe that *Symphonie Fantastique* dates from just three years after the death of Beethoven. The risks Berlioz takes in his orchestration, and the sounds he envisioned are still breathtaking and intimidating today. I admire his no-holds-barred, fearless approach to music and to life in general.

3. **Claude Debussy** and **Maurice Ravel**. Despite their pronounced differences, I mention them together because I admire both for the same reasons: unparalleled orchestration, exquisite harmonic sense, and subtlety of form.

4. **Benjamin Britten**. I have known some of Britten's works for 35 years, and they remain as fresh for me today as when I first heard them. I have recently either sung or conducted *Hymn to St. Cecilia*, *Rejoice in the Lamb*, and *Ceremony of*

Carols and am always highly impressed by how well they work and how "right" they feel to the performer. All of his music possesses that sense of inevitability that exists in the works of the greatest composers. I'm constantly amazed by how he is able to derive the most spectacular results from material that is familiar and simple.

5. **Dmitri Shostakovich**. Like Britten, Shostakovich is able to use familiar, even unpromising material to create vivid and imaginative structures. A number of his larger works have a Mahlerian pathos that plays out convincingly over long durations. Symphony no. 14 in particular appeals to me.

6. **Béla Bartók**. If I had to teach orchestration from only a single source, text or score, it would be his *Concerto for Orchestra*. It's a masterpiece of clean, rich, economical orchestration. The string quartets are pieces I return to again and again and in which I always find something new and stimulating.

7. **Igor Stravinsky**. In matters of reinvention of older musical forms and in reformulation of earlier musical styles and conventions, Stravinsky is unsurpassed and has been an inspiration to me. His personal stamp on familiar forms, phrasing, and the tonal/harmonic spectrum is unique, unmistakable, and a constant source of delight.

8. **George Crumb**. One has to admire a composer who has so convincingly created his own musical universe and maintained its viability over such a long and distinguished career. I think *Dark Angels* is one of the most distinctive and inventive string quartets of the 20th century.

9. **John Adams**. I think Adams is one of the most imaginative composers working today. He has incorporated pop elements into his music more successfully than any other

composer I know of, and his emotional range is most impressive.

10. **Steve Reich**. His music is clean, edgy, urban, American, and highly original. He has the best sense of timing and proportion of all the minimalists.

J. The Future of the Wind Band

The future of the wind band appears to be healthy, solid, and bright. I think the music being written for the medium is more varied, sophisticated, and wide-ranging than ever before, and the number of fine young composers being attracted to it seems to be growing exponentially.

Many of the band conductors I have worked with equal or surpass conductors in other media, as they must to handle the demands that appear in some of the current literature. Most have a hunger for challenging new works, actively seek them out and promote them with performances and recordings, and support their creation with commissions. This is quite in contrast to the orchestral world, where performances seem to be given grudgingly, and commissions are more rare and difficult to obtain.

One of the real joys of working with the wind ensemble is interacting with the performers. Most are young, sharp, hardworking, willing to try anything, and more and more often exceptionally accomplished on their instruments. I must confess that this stimulates me to take chances, and I find my orchestration for the wind ensemble is much more adventurous than for any other medium.

K. Other Facets of My Everyday Life

In 1999 my wife, Suzanne, and I founded our own publishing venture, Piquant Press, and she has handled the publication of most of my music since then, including all the wind ensemble music except for *Fantasy Variations*. This has been an adventure for both of us, and we have thoroughly enjoyed the surprises and the challenges. It has been wonderful to have her in charge of the business; she gave up a very busy piano studio to do so, and the enterprise would be impossible without her.

Our three children, Ellen (24), Mark (21), and Ben (16), are in college or high school. All are musical but have chosen to pursue other endeavors. Ellen was a dancer and choreographer with Ballet Austin but returned to the University of Texas to pursue and achieve a degree in government and art history and is now attending graduate school at the LBJ School of Public Affairs. Mark is on the Texas Tech Lacrosse team and is majoring in political science and psychology with plans to attend law school. Ben is a boxer, weightlifter, and computer whiz who is still considering his options.

I have been the choir director of St. Luke's on the Lake Episcopal Church in Austin for 24 years. I thoroughly enjoy making music with this small (20-25 voice) choir of friends, largely because they are so dedicated to it and are so willing to tackle intimidating projects—the most ambitious of which was probably the Stravinsky *Mass*. Most of them are also involved in the Austin arts community, attending the opera, ballet, and symphony, and it's very instructive to hear how they react—positively and negatively—to what they hear. The only uncommissioned music I've written in the past 15 years has been for this choir, and it's a considerable challenge to try to create something they like, the congregation likes, the clergy likes—and I like. It has been very good for me as a composer to try and meet this challenge.

For the past two years, I've sung in a large community chorus and a small, auditioned *a cappella* choir. I didn't realize how much I missed performing until I started singing again, and I expect I'll continue to make time for this activity for as long as possible.

My consistent and constant activity outside music is reading. We subscribe to numerous magazines, everything from *Mother Jones* to *Scientific American*, and my other reading is just as wide-ranging (or unfocussed, depending on how one looks at it) and includes lots of poetry, essays, and more than my share of historical fiction.

L. Comprehensive List of Works for Band

All works are published by Piquant Press with the exception of *Fantasy Variations*, which is published by Warner Bros. Most pieces range from difficult to advanced. (www.piquantpress.com)

Baron Cimitiére's Mambo. Commissioned by the J. P. Taravella High School Band, Nikk Pilato and Neil Jenkins, conductors. (5:00, 2004)

Bum's Rush. Commissioned by the University of Texas at Austin Wind Ensemble, Jerry Junkin, conductor, and winner of the 1995 NBA/William D. Revelli Prize. Recorded by the University of North Texas Wind Ensemble, Eugene Corporon, conductor, Klavier, KCD-11099,www.klavier-records.com. (12:00, 1994)

"Cloudless day...bitter sky." Commissioned by the Angelo State University Wind Ensemble, David Scott, director. (8:00, 2002)

"Come, memory..." Commissioned by Kappa Kappa Psi National Band Fraternity and Tau Beta Sigma National Band Sorority to honor the "Lives Lost, the Heroes Found, and the Enduring Spirit of America on the September 11, 2001, attack against the World Trade Center in New York City and the Pentagon in Washington, DC." (12:30, 2002)

Concerto in One Movement–Bass trombone and wind ensemble. Recorded by Donald Knaub and Rex Woods, Crystal Records. (12:00, 1979)

Don't You See? Commissioned by a consortium of university and high school ensembles organized by the Universities of Oklahoma, Arizona, and Oregon in memory of Stephen J. Paul. Based on three African American spirituals. (6:00, 2001)

Fantasy on *"La Golondrina."* Commissioned by the Texas Tech Wind Ensemble, Cody Birdwell, conductor, in memory of O.J. Garcia. Based on a Mexican folk song. (8:45, 2003)

Fantasy on *Mr. Hyde's Song.* Commissioned by the United States Navy Band, Lieutenant Commander John R. Pastin, conductor. (7:00, 1998)

Fantasy Variations. Commissioned by a consortium consisting of the wind ensembles of the University of Texas at Austin, University of Oklahoma, Michigan State University, University of Florida-Gainesville, University of Nebraska, and the University of Illinois. Winner of the 1998 NBA/William D. Revelli Prize. Winner of the 1998 ABA/Ostwald Award. Recorded by the University of North Texas Wind Ensemble, Eugene Corporon, conductor, Klavier, KCD-11098, www.klavier-records.com. Recorded by the University of Texas Wind Ensemble, Jerry Junkin, conductor, Mark Records. (14:00, 1997)

Farewell to Gray. Commissioned by the United States Military Academy Band, LTC David Dietrick, conductor. Recorded by the United States Military Band. (6:30, 2001)

Fayetteville Bop. Commissioned by the University of Arkansas Wind Ensemble, W. Dale Warren, director. (10:00, 2002)

J'ai été au bal–"I went to the dance." Commissioned by the University of Texas at Austin Wind Ensemble, Jerry Junkin, conductor. Recorded by the University of North Texas Wind Ensemble, Eugene Corporon, conductor, Klavier, KCD-11109, www.klavier-records.com. (10:00, 1999)

J. S. Dances. Commissioned by the University of Akron Symphony Band, Robert Jorgensen, director. Based on two dances from J. S. Bach's Partita no. 1 (*Clavierubung*, part 1). (8:00, 2003)

Kentucky Harmony. Commissioned by the Austin AISD, former students of Crockett High School, and friends of Paula Crider. (10:00, 2000)

Northern Celebration for wind ensemble and SATB chorus. Text adapted from Carl Sandburg's "The Prairie." Commissioned by Northern University in honor of its 100th anniversary. (10:00, 2001)

Southern Harmony. Commissioned by the Southeastern Conference of Band Directors. Recorded by the University of North Texas Wind Ensemble, Eugene Corporon, conductor, Klavier, KCD-11099, www.klavier-records.com. Winner, 1999 NBA/William D. Revelli Prize. Winner, 1999 ABA/Ostwald Award. (14:00, 1998)

Phantasticke Sprites. Commissioned by a consortium of university and high school ensembles including Riverside Community College Wind Ensemble (Kevin A. Mayse), California State University at Fullerton Wind Ensemble (Mitch Fennell), Los Altos High School Wind Ensemble (Mark Gunderson), Mount San Antonio College Wind Ensemble (Jason Chevalier), University of Texas at Austin Wind Ensemble (Jerry F. Junkin), and Upland High School Wind Ensemble (Ernie Miranda). Based on six Elizabethan madrigals. (10:00, 2002)

Variations on an American Cavalry Song. Commissioned by the United States Army Field Band, Colonel Finley R. Hamilton, commander and conductor. (12:00, 2001)

chapter **5**

robert
Jager

As with cooking, the score needs musical flavor, spices, and color. Have you ever been served a meal where all the food is essentially the same color? Take, for instance, a plate of fish, mashed potatoes, and corn! I've heard scores that reminded me of such a meal.

A. Biography

The youngest of three children, I was born in Binghamton, New York, in 1939 to Mary Virginia and Gerrit Joe Jager. (My brother and sister were twins.) Music was always an important part of our family life. My mother and father met while playing in Salvation Army bands, and so there were two trumpets in the house from my very first days. My father was a minister in the American Baptist Church and dedicated his life to rescue mission work, so we moved around the country quite a bit, to New York, Pennsylvania, North Carolina, Michigan, and Tennessee. He continued to play the trumpet almost to the day he died, and he was the one who started me on the trumpet (actually, my mother's trumpet). We would frequently play duets at the mission and when he was a guest pastor. It was as a result of these duets that I started to become interested in composing. I would not only arrange hymns for my father and me to play in services, but I also wrote a number of hymn variations for solo trumpet and piano, as well as trumpet trios for my friends and me to play.

I wrote my first composition for band when I was a sophomore at Western Michigan Christian High School in Muskegon. We had read a story from *Walden* by Thoreau entitled "The Battle of the Ants," so I wrote a tone poem for my high school band based upon that story. The work has since disappeared, but as I remember the music sounded a lot like Tchaikovsky. In fact, I know that I lifted some material from his Symphony no. 6. Nevertheless, I remain grateful to Klaus Kuiper, my high school band director, for giving me that chance to hear my first effort. With his encouragement, I kept writing and arranging, especially for the Pep Band, for which I made arrangements of current tunes like "Rock Around The Clock," and "Hound Dog." I also had the opportunity to conduct rehearsals with the band when Mr. Kuiper was absent. I like to use these events as examples for how present-day directors can encourage their students to arrange and compose.

I spent my first year of college at Wheaton College in Illinois but transferred the next year to The University of Michigan, where I had the marvelous opportunity to work under Dr. William D. Revelli. It was Dr. Revelli's assistant, George Cavender, who took me under his wing, encouraging my writing and introducing me to people on the faculty who shaped my musical life. Among the most important of those people was Elizabeth A. H. Green. She, along with Dr. Revelli and others, made a strong impact on my life, both musically and ethically.

Unfortunately, I had to leave school at the end of my junior year at Michigan. My father had accepted a job in Tennessee, and I lost my residency. College suddenly became too expensive and I joined my parents in Knoxville. I spent two years teaching brass instruments privately and playing trumpet in the Knoxville Symphony. The year was 1962, and the Vietnam conflict was rapidly heating up. Because I knew that I would be called up soon, I decided to enlist in the U. S. Navy and try to get into the music program. Fortunately, after boot camp in San Diego, I was sent to the Navy School of Music in Washington, DC. (In 1964 the school moved to Little Creek, Virginia, and was renamed the Armed Forces School of Music.) By this time I was a basic theory instructor at the school.

Later in 1964, I won the first of my three Ostwald Awards with Symphony no. 1 for Band. My commanding officer at the time, Captain John MacDonald, asked me to be the staff arranger/composer as a result of this award, and I remained in that position until my honorable discharge in 1966. These were wonderful years for me, because I got to write a lot of music for various Navy events and heard those works almost as soon as they were written. It also gave me the opportunity to meet guest musicians and work with them—artists such as Arthur Fiedler, Fred Hemke, Mark Hindsley, John P. Paynter, James Neilson, Pete Fountain, and so many more.

I returned to The University of Michigan in 1966, and, thanks in part to the G.I. Bill and a great job doing some film scoring for Michigan's Audio-Visual Department, I was able to complete both my bachelor's and master's degrees. By the time I returned to Michigan, I had 13 published works, but I continued my pursuit of degrees in music education, which I'm glad that I did for a lot of reasons. Not the least of these is that

I was required to learn the basics of every instrument, a requirement that should be made of every composer. Another wonderful opportunity came by way of Dr. Revelli, who allowed me to rehearse the Michigan Symphony Band on some occasions when he was out of town and even to conduct some of my works in concert! Not bad for a guy who considered himself "principal last chair trumpet" in the Michigan Band.

My first teaching job was a "catch-all" position at Old Dominion University in Norfolk, Virginia. I taught conducting, music appreciation, and sometimes theory. However, in my third year at Old Dominion, I became the band director, and the job was a real challenge. Up to that point, the band had consisted of 15 students augmented by musicians from the community and the military bands in the Norfolk area. I changed that emphasis and began recruiting students from other departments at the university so that by the end of the first year I had 75 players. It wasn't the best band in the world, but having only students perform in it gave the band a sense of self that was important to morale—theirs *and* mine!

In 1971 I accepted the position of Director of Composition and Theory at Tennessee Tech University in Cookeville, Tennessee. The music department at Tennessee Tech was, and continues to be, one of the leading music programs in Tennessee, and I was thrilled by the fact that I was finally in a position that dealt with my main interest. For 17 of my 30 years at Tech, I was the coordinator for the annual Composer Festival. (I later changed the name to Festival of Winds and Percussion.) During this time I hosted composers Aaron Copland, Vincent Persichetti, Karel Husa, Morton Gould, and Warren Benson as well as conductors John P. Paynter and Arnald Gabriel. In 1998 I was selected to receive the university's highest faculty award, the Caplenor Faculty Research Award, and I was the first faculty member in the arts to receive this distinction. I retired from Tennessee Tech University in May 2001 as professor emeritus.

I have been fortunate enough to receive performances from bands, orchestras, and choruses from around the world and have conducted and lectured throughout the United States, Canada, Europe, Japan, and the Republic of China. I have received commissions from some of the finest ensembles in the world, including the Tokyo Kosei Wind Orchestra, the Republic of China Band Association, many of the top university bands in the U.S., the Michigan State University Children's Choir, and all five of the Washington-based military bands. My music for orchestra has been performed by the National Symphony Orchestra of Washington, D.C., the Nashville Symphony Orchestra, the Virginia Symphony of Norfolk, the Minot (North Dakota) Symphony, the Bryan Symphony Orchestra of Tennessee, the Charlotte (North Carolina) Symphony, and the Omsk Philharmonic in Russia.

I am the only three-time winner of the American Bandmaster Association's Ostwald Award and am a two-time winner of the National School Orchestra Association's Roth Award. In addition, I have received the Kappa Kappa Psi Distinguished Service to Music Medal in the area of composition, the Friends of Harvey Gaul bicentennial competition award, and the American School Band Directors Association's Volkwein Award. My *Dialogues for Two Pianos* won the 2000 Delius Award from Jacksonville (Florida) University. In 1986 I received a MacDowell Colony Fellowship, and I was awarded the Individual Artist Fellowship in Composition from the Tennessee Arts Commission in 1996.

I am a member of the American Bandmasters Association, the American Society of Composers, Authors and Publishers (ASCAP), Phi Mu Alpha Sinfonia, Kappa Kappa Psi, Phi Kappa Phi, and an honorary member of the Women's Band Directors Association.

B. The Creative Process

If you have ever visited the Stephen Foster home in Bardstown, Kentucky, maybe you have seen the painting that shows Foster sitting at a grand piano, gazing in an ethereal manner toward the heavens. From out of a cloud, a beautiful angel reaches to him and touches his forehead. At the point of the touch is a little glimmer of light. The painting is called *Inspiration*.

I am extremely happy for Mr. Foster, but that kind of event has never happened to me, or to anyone else that I know in the creative business. In fact, after composing music for more than 45 years I still don't know how it all happens! That doesn't mean that I don't receive musical ideas out of the blue, so to speak, but I don't have any magical formula that I can use to summon them up. Of course, the concept of the composition will often suggest a theme, a set of harmonies, or a rhythm. But, more times than not, it is a process of searching for ideas, weeding them out, and then manipulating them to the task at hand. As I have frequently told my students—*listen*! Listen to the music and the sounds around you. For Messiaen it was the songs of birds, for Honegger it was a train, and for me it has run the gamut from the sound of fireworks to a squeaky door to an isolated chord played during a rehearsal. I believe that composers are more sensitive than the "normal" person to the sounds around them, and they are able to more readily draw upon that sensitivity to create their music.

I mentioned above that the "concept" of the composition will often lead the composer in the direction he or she needs to go. Once I've determined what the character and style of the work will be—joyous, triumphant, melancholy, playful, sad, dramatic—I usually begin to map out the structure of the piece. I call it "graphing." The graph is a guide, a kind of tonal roadmap, of what I want to have happen and approximately how long it will take for it to unfold. I'm never bound by the graph, but it does keep me from wandering aimlessly toward the double bar.

The next step is to begin to write the music. I have tried over the years not to write the same piece of music twice. This part of composing is always an adventure—often frustrating, sometimes exhilarating. As I grow older I am more drawn to thematic ideas based upon short motives, usually four or five notes. Sometimes, however, (as in the case of my *Preamble*), the impetus is a rhythmic figure. It could just as easily be a chord progression, as in *Mystic Chords of Memory*, which is a free adaptation of the 12-bar blues. To make this step work, I have to be completely isolated. When my wife, Sally, and I built our retirement home, we designed it in such a way that our studios (she is a painter) are at opposite ends of the house. She likes to listen to music when she paints, and I have to have absolute silence. I even made the electrician who wired our house change the light unit in my studio because it kept humming a B-natural!

When I compose, I work at the piano, one of those old fashioned pianos with strings. I also use pencil and paper. My first attempts are on cheap, toss-away paper on which I can feel free to vent my "creative spleen." (I've never really understood that phrase.) Once I'm satisfied with what I've put down, I then go to either a three-, four-, or five-stave score, or if the work is very involved I go directly to the full score. This is always done in pencil. The final step for me is to complete the full score in pencil, correcting it to make sure that my sketches and my score agree. I use computers for e-mail only, so I give my score to a very talented young man, who is a former student of mine and currently a band director in Tennessee, and he does the computer work for the "clean" score and parts.

When I taught at Tennessee Tech University, I found that the afternoons were the best time for me to set aside to compose. I was never able to write at school because I made it a point to always keep my door open to students (except when I was teaching). Now that I am retired, I still find that afternoons are the best time for me to write. I usually work on my landscaping during the morning and then go to my studio after lunch. Like most composers, I need a solid period of time during the day, usually 3 or 4 hours, to compose. However, there are always those times when the creative-block monster rears its ugly head, and the work comes to a complete stop. I have several solutions for that, which include going back into the yard to work or relax, listening to other composers' music, taking a nap, or considering if plumbing might not just be a better occupation! In a discussion session several years ago I told the gathered students that I sometimes even take a shower (whether I need it or not) to relax and see if the musical ideas will flourish again. And often it works! Upon hearing that, one of the students went out and had a sheet of manuscript paper laminated and attached a grease pencil to it with string so that I could hang it in the shower just in case inspiration should strike. I still have the gift, but I've never used it in the shower!

However the creative process works, I am constantly amazed by it and grateful that God has allowed me to be a small part of that process. I have attempted to put into words a process that is essentially indescribable, and it is a process that needs constant nurturing. This can take the form of studying scores, listening in an analytical way to music, sitting quietly and meditating on the work at hand, or just writing down short sketches that "pop" into my head. My wife tells people that she is always finding little scraps of paper around the house, in the car, or in the garage on which I have drawn five lines with five or six notes scribbled in. Like any instrumentalist or vocalist, composers must be constantly engaged in their art to keep it alive. A few days totally away from it, and it's back to basics all over again. For a long time now, composing has been some-thing I am compelled to do because of some inner motivation, and at this point in my life it is something that I do for me.

Having said that, I want to close this topic with a thought I heard expressed by one of my dearest mentors, Elizabeth A.H. Green. "We must all remember that there are three participants in bringing music alive—the composer, the performer, and the audience. If any one of those three is not participating in the act of making music, then there can be no music. One must not forget the others."

C. The Approach to Orchestration

While I was studying at The University of Michigan, I heard a fellow student remark, "If I can write it, they can play it." This is only one reason why I am grateful to have had to study and perform on all of the instruments. Before you even begin to talk about timbre and texture, you have to know what is technically possible on the instruments, or you are doomed. There are an overwhelming number of texts on orchestration, and they are excellent for such things as tessitura and some basic technical aspects of various instruments. However, the best teacher for this is to go to the instrument and learn to play it, even rudimentally. The second best teacher, after that step, is to study scores and *listen*! For many years my favorite composers to listen to for orchestration have been Hector Berlioz, Albert Roussel, Igor Stravinsky, Béla Bartók, Aaron Copland, and, of course, Percy Grainger. Many other composers continue to attract my ear, but these composers form my foundation when it comes to orchestration.

I don't think that I have ever composed a work in which the orchestration was not an immediate consideration. I don't see how you can compose a melodic line, stack a chord, or even choose keys without knowing who is going to play what. That doesn't mean I won't change my mind during the orchestration process, but by the time I am facing an 11 x 17 sheet of paper, fully 95% of the score is already determined. I think it is important to add at this point (although doing so seems to contradict the rest of this statement) that percussion should not be an afterthought. Howard Hanson once referred to percussion as "the salt and pepper of the orchestra." That seems too much of a subordinate designation to me. Percussion provides an integral color and texture in the contemporary band and orchestra and must be treated as an important element.

Orchestration is very much like landscaping and cooking, which is why, perhaps, I love to do both. As with landscaping, the score needs color and texture for variety as well as a sense of vitality. As with cooking, the score needs musical flavor, spices, and color. Have you ever been served a meal where all the food is essentially the same color? Take, for instance, a plate of fish, mashed potatoes, and corn! I've heard scores that reminded me of such a meal. It's what I call the "dull, gray sound of band" with everybody playing all the time. It's one of the reasons that I have always been drawn to open textures in the music, frequent solos, duets, etc. Of course, this puts a greater demand on the musical abilities of the ensemble (not to mention the conductor), but it is frequently in these open moments that the heart of the music comes through.

Important considerations in all of this are the technical abilities and the characteristics of each instrument. Obviously, a tuba can't do what a clarinet can do (and vice versa), either from a technical point of view or as a color choice. It is fun sometimes to ask instruments to assume a role not normally assigned to them, but caution must be exercised when doing this. Again, we return to the importance of knowing what an instrument can and cannot do. Benjamin Britten avoided the traditional cliché in his *War Requiem* when he had flutes, oboes, and clarinets play the trumpet calls in the "Bugles Rang" portion of this monumental work.

Sometimes stretching the timbral characteristics works well, but, again, this can be dangerous territory. Take, for instance, the solo bassoon at the beginning of *The Rite of Spring*. I've even heard bassoonists remark that this passage would be better served if given to the English horn. I disagree, of course. The English horn would never have been able to give that line the mystical quality that the bassoon gives it. Or take, for instance, Wagner's use of the high bass clarinet in many of his passages. I would have to think twice, or even three times, before writing a bass clarinet part above the third line B-flat in the treble clef, but because of the way Wagner uses it there is something melancholy, even mournful, about the phrase.

When writing for band, I am careful to use "color instruments" to best show off their timbre. I consider the "color instruments" to be the piccolo, English horn, E-flat clarinet, bass and contra alto clarinets, soprano saxophone, and string bass. By the way, I still love the alto clarinet (the viola of the band), even if most bands have discarded them. The most frequent criticism I hear of the alto clarinet is that they are always out of tune (the E-flat clarinet gets the same rap) and you can't hear them anyway. I don't subscribe to this statement because I believe that if the students were taught properly they would be in tune and contribute to the clarinet choir color. (Consider the Theme portion of Dello Joio's *Variants On A Medieval Tune*.) I, however, detest the B-flat contrabass clarinet. It is massive plumbing that is always in the wrong tessitura. If you keep it in the right range, it will, most of the time, be an octave lower than anyone else.

Orchestration is certainly determined, in many cases, by the grade level of the band. The chances you might take with solos, color combinations, etc., are not as wise in a grade-2 or -3 composition as they are in a grade-5 or -6 work. But that doesn't mean that everyone should play all the time, even if it is "safe." How is the individual to grow if he or she doesn't have a chance to be heard as a soloist or in combination with another player? Thank goodness for cross-cueing!

This brings me to another point: Be careful how you rewrite a solo passage, but don't be afraid to do it if you don't have the forces. In older scores the oboe was frequently cross-cued as a muted trumpet. This is a personal opinion (and, as the comic said, "it should be yours"), but a wiser substitution would be to use an "open" trumpet. If the conductor is trying to simulate the sound of an oboe with a muted trumpet, then he or she has more problems than the lack of an oboe! I will talk more about this subject in the next section.

Finally, orchestration is almost as much a part of the composer's identity as is the music itself, and it wouldn't be too far-fetched to think of it as much an integration of the composer's creativity as is the head to the body of a person. I believe that if that integration is not there, then the work is weakened. With listening, you can develop the ability to hear the separation of the compositional process from the orchestration. However, when a work is totally integrated, you have music of lasting value that be will rewarding time and time again.

In conclusion, I am reminded of a question-answer session given by Vincent Persichetti. This comment was made (by someone else): "I love your *Psalm For Band*, but it sounds like an orchestral work." To which Persichetti replied, "It was . . . the strings just never came in!"

D. Views from the Composer to the Conductor Pertaining to Score Study and Preparation

If the composer has done his or her job well, then everything the conductor needs to know will be presented on the score. In the contemporary score, because of its intricacies, this attention to detail is critical, and for a conductor to truly know the score and to interpret the composer's intentions, it is equally critical that these intricacies be discovered and understood.

I have actually heard these comments on score study: "I learn a new piece of music by listening to the publisher's CDs on the way to work each day." And "I learn the music with the band. That way we can discover new things together." I hope that it is not necessary to respond to these approaches to score study.

Every conductor comes to a new score in his or her own way, and I wouldn't pretend to think that my way is the only way. I, of course, approach any score from the perspective of a composer—specifically this composer. For me it is important to first discover where the composition is going and what its form and structure are. Not only do these two aspects give me a sense of the music, but also what it is trying to accomplish. In approaching the score this way I also discover the principal ideas (motives, themes, rhythms, etc.) and their relationship to the structure, which makes the composition succeed or fail.

I personally feel that is it vitally important to understand the harmonic language of the composer before going into a rehearsal. A chord or a melodic line may seem incorrect to you, but it may be exactly what the composer had in mind. I call this phenomenon the "right wrong note," and it is evident in much of the music of Shostakovich, Copland, Persichetti, and many more contemporary composers, even Jager. But, the "right wrong note or chord" also occurs in older music, for instance that marvelous F-major seventh in the development section of the first movement of Beethoven's Third Symphony. That must have shocked the daylights out of the audience when it premiered. Add to that the fact that it resolves next to a B-major ninth chord a tritone away, and critics surely must have said, "There! That proves it! He's going deaf!"

Some people call these moments "dissonance." When I was teaching I never let my students use the word "dissonance." It was always called "tension." The word for consonant should be "relaxation." Those two terms convey what is going on in the music so much more effectively than do dissonance and consonance. Keep in mind that even a dominant-seventh chord has tension; that's why it wants to move forward. This brings to mind a quote from the great Austrian conductor Herbert von Karajan who said, "If there are discords we must always play them as beautifully as we know how. A discord is not an excuse for ugly music-making, for playing out of tune."

In fact, many composers today utilize the overtone series as part of their harmonic language. If the music is performed out of tune or misunderstood, then the overtone series is destroyed, and the composer's intentions are not fulfilled.

Learning the score by solely listening to a tape or CD is not learning the score; it is learning what someone else did with that score. And his or her interpretation may not even be accurate. When I am asked, "How do you want it to go?" I always answer by saying, "You tell me." I want to hear the musical talent and personality of the conductor come through in my music. I don't want the conductor to parrot back what I might do. Although I hope that my scores give complete information, I don't want the conductor to be so strictly bound by that information that he or she cannot breathe something into the music. This is one of the problems I have with concert competitions in which the judges hold up the score as if it were written in stone—because this encourages stone-like performances. This doesn't mean that I want the conductor to take such liberties that the work is no longer my creation, but there is a wonderful happy medium that should be encouraged.

Another thing that I would like to encourage is creative, or at least sensible, programming. Good programming takes genuine talent, and it can make or break a concert. This applies not only to the choices of music to be performed but also the length of the concert. Leave your audiences wanting more. Have them on their feet at the end of the concert appreciating what the concert has been about, not on their feet trying to see who can get to their cars first.

Pace the concert program. Consider the weight of each composition, its place in music history (Classical, Romantic, Contemporary), the textures and moods (solos, tuttis, slow, fast, angry, sad, joyous, etc.). I like to start with my most serious works and ease up as I approach the last number. And I always include a march! The march is the band's great legacy to music, but many conductors these days refuse to perform even one. Revelli used to say that every problem that occurs in any symphony, concerto, or tone poem occurs in a great march. Solve those problems in the march, and you have it solved when you come to that larger work.

Finally, I would like to encourage every director to remember that the primary reason for having a band program in schools and universities is **education**. Although many band programs have relinquished that charge to the athletic department, educating the students (and audiences) is as important today as it ever has been. This means not only teaching a student how to play the music, but also what the music is about and who the composer is. To fail to fully educate the ensemble about the music is to fail to complete the task at hand.

I have been involved in numerous weekend festivals or a guest at this or that high school or college, and I often ask basic questions about the music. For instance, I have asked groups that played my *Third Suite* what a rondo is. Many times, no one has a clue. Can the ensemble play it? Yes! Isn't that enough?

Not for this composer. Learning the score applies not only to the director, but to the ensemble. Being prepared for a performance means mastering the music, not learning just enough to get by.

E. The Relationship Between the Composer and the Commissioning Party

A commissioning project is a marvelous way for the ensemble to get to know a composer and for the composer to write specifically for the talents of that ensemble. If careful steps are taken throughout the procedure, from signing the contract or agreement through the premiere, then a new commission can be like a marriage made in heaven. Obviously, if the parties involved in the commissioning do not communicate sufficiently, then it's rather like a marriage made somewhere else.

I have to admit that when I first started in this business I took every commission I could get. That was wrong of me! While I'd like to think that most of those works turned out to be part of the repertoire and are works that I am proud of, there were a couple of pieces that needed considerable revisions. As I learned what my capacity for composing high-quality works was, I also learned to say "no." I believe this is fair not only to me, but more important, to the commissioner. Further, I became more selective in the commissions I took. I have to be truly interested in the project to accept it. Considerations such as whether the project meets my compositional desires, or if it is a project that will challenge me and allow me to grow as a composer come into play. Composing just for the fee no longer interests me, so the commissioner would be better off finding someone interested in the project.

I prefer to have a great deal of latitude in the type of works I am asked to compose. Too many restrictions on the work will only produce a stilted composition, no matter who the composer is. For example, Richard Wagner was commissioned in 1876 to compose an overture for orchestra celebrating the centennial of the United States; it is a terrible work and seldom performed. When asked what the best thing about the commission was, Wagner replied, "The money!" The commissioner often has a specific event in mind, a celebration of some sort or a memorial; the director rarely just wants something new for the ensemble (even though the latter is the most fun).

Whatever is decided upon, there are some basic steps that should be taken. An agreement should be worked out between the composer and the commissioning body. This can be a formal contract or just a letter of agreement with the following points clearly addressed.

1. Who is commissioning the work? (This seems obvious, but it isn't always.)
2. For whom is the work being commissioned?
3. What type of work is to be written (celebration, memorial, etc.)?
4. What is the difficulty level?
5. What is the approximate length? (If the composer goes over the time allotted, there should be no extra charge.)
6. What fee will be paid to the composer?
7. When are the materials due?
8. What is the date of the concert?
9. Will I be conducting the premiere, and is this done at an extra charge or considered part of the commission?

10. The right of the premiere performance and the dedicatory and commissioning statements on the published version belong to the commissioner.
11. All other rights, including the copyright, belong to the composer.

Once all of this has been agreed to, I ask for a very recent recording of the group for which I'll be composing. I don't rely upon the conductor of the ensemble to write me a letter or send an e-mail stating that they have performed works of a certain difficulty. With all due respect, not listening to a recording can backfire on the composer. Hearing a recording makes clear what the group can and cannot do. I *do* want to know from the conductor, however, if there are any particular strengths or weaknesses that he or she feels I need to be aware of. This often helps me to "tailor make" the composition for the ensemble. During the composing of one commission, I received an urgent phone call from a conductor who asked, "I've just had an oboe transfer in from Texas! Is it too late to have something special for her?" As it was, I had already assigned that solo to the alto saxophone, but I did want to help him out, so I did a "Shostakovich modulation" (as I call it). That's when you hit the bass drum and go anywhere!

One of the most important benefits for the composer of a commission, or any premiere for that matter, is the recording of the performance. A good recording is often worth more than the commissioning fee because publishers normally require a recording before they will consider your work, and it is also valuable for Monday morning quarterbacking to see if the composition should remain as is or if revisions are necessary. If you don't get an acceptable recording at the premiere, then you may have to wait until the next concert season for one. Several times, I didn't get a recording of my new piece because the concert was not recorded or the recording engineer failed to get the work on tape or CD. Problems like this are perhaps one of the most frustrating parts of this business.

Once the rehearsals on the new work have begun and the conductor feels comfortable with the students' ability to play through the piece, I require a rehearsal tape. It doesn't have to be up to performance standards, but I want to make sure that I'm on the right track compositionally. It's easier to revise before the premiere than after it. Also, I don't like surprises of any kind, so I don't want to hear the piece for the first time at the premiere, although that has happened several times when I've been in the audience and not on the podium.

I mentioned earlier that if I were asked to travel to the performance site and conduct the premiere that the cost would be over and above the commissioning fee. Because conducting is a different task, there is an additional fee. The exception to this would be if the commissioner and I were to agree upon a fee that would include both the commission and the conducting. In this case the expanded fee usually includes meetings with the ensemble and their supporters (class lectures, etc.) to discuss the work and/or the music in general. And this last point is very important: Commissioning a composer to write a work is an excellent opportunity to bring attention and publicity to the ensemble, school, and community. These benefits should all be considered when approaching a composer about such a project.

F. Views on the Teaching of Composition and How to Mentor the Young Composer

I don't believe that you can "teach" composition, rather, you "talk" it. It is my opinion that a person either has a gift for composing, or they don't—much like people have a gift for singing, painting, or mathematics. If the person doesn't have the gift in the first place, then all the amount of teaching in the world will never make that person a composer. It reminds me of a sign our choral director had on his office wall: *Never try to teach a pig to sing. It's a waste of time, and it annoys the pig!*

If a person has the gift to be able to compose, then he or she should be encouraged from the moment the talent reveals itself. I was fortunate enough to have had a high school band director who encouraged me and gave me the opportunity to hear my efforts early on. By the time I got to college, I already had experience writing for and hearing my works for band, chorus, and small ensembles. Some colleges make the composition majors wait until their junior years to begin private composition studies. Although it's never too late to start, waiting until the third year of college is such a waste of time and talent. When I taught at Tennessee Tech University, I began my composition students in private lessons in the first year. This gave them more time with me, and it also gave them more time to hear and discuss what their colleagues were doing.

One of the best teaching devices for any composer is the performance! A teacher can talk forever to a student about his/her composition and its strengths and weaknesses, but until that student hears the work performed, it's all theory. Once the work is performed, the realities of the composition are heard, and the room for debate becomes narrower. So it is important to be in a setting where the student's works can be performed.

One of the problems with this, although it's a good problem, is that as soon as other music majors find out that one of your composition students is doing good work, they begin to assail him/her for works for their recitals. As long as I could control these opportunities, it was a "good" problem.

Instrumentalists and vocalists have etudes and preexisting compositions with which to develop their talents, but I have never found a composition textbook that is worth the purchase price. And because composing styles and the students' creative needs are so varied, a textbook would be highly restrictive. But that doesn't mean that the instruction or discussion of composing is without structure. Certainly the student needs to know how and why the materials they will be using work. Music theory is important, but it shouldn't get in the way of creative development. For instance, parallel fifths are acceptable in the composition studio. As the student becomes comfortable with the tools of his/her trade (theory, counterpoint, orchestration, harmonic styles from all periods of music), the creative base is expanded upon. The focus now becomes one of stylistic consistency (Does the piece begin like Bach and end up like Offenbach?) and experimentation. The teacher acts as a discussion leader or guide through the many possibilities.

Through all of this, and at every level, the composer must continue to *listen* to music of every period and to study scores, not only of compositions they like, but scores of pieces they either don't like or feel don't quite work. Only in this way can the student composer (and we're *all* student composers) find out how and why things work or don't work. When a student was in a bind, compositionally speaking, I would often refer them to someone else's music in which the situation was similar. The student would then come back, and we would discuss the problem to see how the solution might be achieved with the composition, in his or her style and language. I miss these discussions now that I am retired because I believe I gained as much from them as the students did. One of the wonderful things about composing is that you never stop learning!

G. Individuals Who Have Been Especially Influential in My Development and Career

Naming all of the people who have been influential in my development and career as a musician would fill a book by itself. I have been extremely fortunate to have crossed paths with some very caring and helpful individuals and have looked back upon my career in amazement that I have been blessed, not only to compose some music, but also to have had these people in my life.

First and foremost, I would have to name my parents, Gerrit and Mary Jager, who made music an integral part of our home and life. It was music that brought them together as trumpet players in different Salvation Army bands. My father was in the New York Staff Band, and my mother was in the Huntington, West Virginia, Salvation Army Staff Band. They met when the New York Band took a tour of the South. As I mentioned earlier, we had two trumpets in the house, and when my mother quit performing, I got her trumpet. My father went into the ministry, and we would play duets during the services while my mother played the piano for the congregational singing. On cross-country vacations, the whole family would sing, usually in three- or four-part harmony. It was during these times that I became very aware of harmonization, and my folks didn't seem to mind when I added suspensions, ritards, etc. I don't think this totally thrilled my siblings, however.

My brother, Joey, had a love of band music and classical music in general, including opera, and it was from him that I learned to appreciate the joys of music. He had a large collection of L.P. vinyl recordings (some of which I now have) that he treasured and that he would play constantly. Joey suffered some brain damage at birth, and, things being the way they were in the 1940s and 1950s, he didn't receive the proper attention that he would have had he been born today. He never made it past the second grade, but he was a kind of musical savant (I've never met anyone who could equal his knowledge of musical themes, composers, and compositions.) and one of the most gracious people you would ever hope to meet. He allowed me to play along with his recordings on my trumpet, reading from scores, and on many Saturdays we'd sit in the bedroom and listen to the Metropolitan Opera broadcasts, following along with scores borrowed from the local library and eating peanut butter sandwiches.

One day in 1955, we went to see a new movie entitled *Interrupted Melody* about the Australian opera singer Marjorie Lawrence. In the movie there were scenes from a number of operas, including *Carmen, Madame Butterfly* and, my favorite, *Götterdämerung.* When she hopped on the horse (which is not usually done) near the end of the opera and rode it into Siegfried's funeral pyre . . . well, I was hooked and I knew at that moment that I had to go into music. Joey passed away recently, but he left the world a much better place—kinder and more melodious—and he left me a legacy that I could never fully thank him for.

My high school band and choral director, Klaus Kuiper, encouraged my early attempts at composing and gave me the opportunity to hear those attempts with our band at Western Michigan Christian High School in Muskegon. When I attended the University of Michigan, George Cavender, the assistant director of bands, gave me that same encouragement and opportunity to hear my work with the concert band. And he brought me to the attention of Dr. William D. Revelli, the director of bands at Michigan, who in turn introduced me to composers Vincent Persichetti, Norman Dello Joio, Vaclav Nelhybel, Morton Gould, and Robert Russell Bennett. Dr. Revelli also gave me the opportunity to occasionally rehearse the symphony band when he was absent and to conduct some of my own compositions at home and on tour, including once at Carnegie Hall!

And, of course, there was Elizabeth A. H. Green, one of the dearest mentors and taskmasters I've ever known. I studied conducting with her for three years, but her influence went far beyond the classroom. She had a fabulous collection of scores, and they were all marked up in different colored pencils that showed how different conductors, such as Nicolai Malko or Bruno Walter, would interpret the music. We would discuss these interpretations by the hours, and she was never too busy to stop whatever she was doing to keep that light burning in my head. Once she told me that a certain movement in one of my larger works reminded her of "like a white daisy looks." White daisies were her favorite flowers, so after I read her description, I wrote a little string orchestra work entitled *Like a White Daisy Looks* and used her initials for the main motive: E, A, H (B-natural), G.

In the biography section I mentioned Captain John MacDonald, but he needs to be listed again in the company of these wonderful people. In the last 20 years or so I have had the privilege to be guided by Bernard Kalban, my publisher at Marks Music who is now with Carlin America and Hal Leonard. His advice, encouragement, and support have been priceless, but more than that he is a friend!

Last, but certainly not least, is my wife, Sally. She is an abstract painter who grew up in a musical family in Oklahoma. Her father was G. Ray Bonham, director of bands at Enid High School for many years, and her mother conducted the local Baptist church choir and ladies' chorus. Sally grew up in the Enid band programs as a flutist and even majored in music at Phillips University for a time, so I respect her opinions about music, especially my music. She critiques my music, and I critique her paintings! One of the joys of our home life is to sit and talk about art and music, their relationship to each other, the history of both, and current trends. She challenges me to move forward and to keep working hard to say something new and fresh. She also helps me to say "no" when I need to, and I hope I influence her in some small way.

With wonderful people like these behind me, how can I fail? How would I dare fail?

H. Ten Works I Believe All Band Conductors at All Levels Should Study

In putting this list together, I was guided by the above heading, especially the phrase "at all levels." Over the years I have noticed a tendency by conductors to perform music that is at the top technical edge of their ensembles' abilities, sometimes with disastrous or mediocre results. University bands are notoriously guilty of this, with students frequently graduating to teach at the grade-2 or -3 level after four years of performing nothing less than grade 5 music. I would love to see a top notch high school or college band program a grade-2 or -3 work to the best of their abilities.

Another guide from the heading was "all band conductors." To be honest, there is little likelihood that a conductor of bands will ever be asked to conduct an orchestra, especially one able to perform music at the level of Bartók's *Concerto for Orchestra* or Stravinsky's *The Rite of Spring*, yet I see those types of compositions on many lists. Certainly "all" good music is worth studying; that goes without saying. But from a practical point of view, and from the point of view of the above heading, I have chosen not to include any orchestral music.

I selected music from most of the band music grade levels, and I feel that every piece is good, high-quality, well-written music. The works I have chosen are also compositions that I have found serve a strong educational purpose while being artistically rewarding, and they stand up through multiple rehearsals and performances. I believe that one can always return to these pieces and reap additional benefits from them.

1. *Chant and Jubilo* by W. Francis McBeth. This is one of McBeth's earliest published works and a composition that still is as effective today as when it was written back in the early 1960s. It's a grade-3 work that many younger conductors have never known, yet it remains a foundational work in band literature.

2. *Festivo* by Vaclav Nelhybel. His music is seldom performed anymore, and therein lies a great tragedy.

Nelhybel's more difficult compositions, such as *Symphonic Movements* and *Trittico*, are brilliant displays of band power and color. This grade-3 work retains much of that power but keeps younger instrumentalists in mind. Studying the score to see how he did it is well worth the effort.

3. *Fantasy on American Sailing Songs* by Clare Grundman. This is one of my favorite works to program on weekend festivals, and I never get tired of rehearsing or performing it. I believe this is the strongest of Grundman's folk medleys. The use of color and the sense of drama and forward movement work wonderfully together. This is a grade 3-4 work that sounds harder than it really is.

4. *Psalm* by John Zdechlik. This inventive setting of "A Mighty Fortress" is a musical adventure very much in the manner of Zdechlik's *Chorale and Shaker Dance*. This grade-4 work uses color and drama well, and the wonderful thematic development begs to be shared with the ensemble. This is another piece from the literature that isn't performed enough.

5. *Psalm for Band* by Vincent Persichetti. A gem of a composition that has all but disappeared from programs, *Psalm for Band* is a solid grade-4 work by one of the 20th century's finest composers. It is truly high-quality music with not a false note anywhere in it. This is an "honest" composition that not only proves the musicianship of the ensemble, but that of the conductor. Besides that, it is fun to perform and to hear!

6. *Children's March* (Over the Hills and Far Away) by Percy Grainger. I have loved this composition ever since I first heard it on an vinyl record performed by the Goldman

152

Band. It is a grade-5 work, and you need to have low woodwind players and a pianist to do it justice, but this is Grainger at his most lighthearted (is that an oxymoron?). His use of instrumental colors is legendary, and they all come to the fore in this cascade of joy.

7. *Armenian Dances* (first set) by Alfred Reed. From the opening notes of this grade-5 work through to the rousing coda, this piece is a journey that you will want to take again and again. Reed's sense of color in this composition is at its peak, and such emotional impact is seldom felt in music for band. The conductor will need to spend some diligent, quiet time with the score, not so much because of its technical demands but because of all the little motivic joys and shadings there are to find.

8. *Sketches on a Tudor Psalm* by Fisher Tull. Using the same Thomas Tallis theme that Ralph Vaughan Williams used in his *Fantasia* for string orchestra, Tull weaves a composition that is truly his own and uniquely American in its sentiment and drive. The use of mixed meters, development of motivic fragments, frequent polytonality, and the extensive percussion requirements put this work at the top of the grade-5 level. With all that said, it must also be added that there is nothing gimmicky about this well-crafted addition to band literature.

9. *Fiesta del Pacifico* by Roger Nixon. If you have never heard or performed this work, run—don't walk—and get the score today. This is music in the tradition of Copland's *El Salon Mexico* or Manuel de Falla's *The Three Cornered Hat*, and it's just as colorful and exciting as either one of them. While this is a grade-6 "fiesta," a good grade-5 ensemble will do it justice. Everyone gets to be heard in

this remarkable work. The scoring is exquisite, the melodies and rhythms are contagious, and the spirit is boisterous. Great music and a great time for all!

10. *The Leaves Are Falling* by Warren Benson. On first glance, one might think this is a grade-4 work. But even grade 6 might be too low of a rating. This is difficult music, not so much from a technical point of view but from an emotional, sensitive point of view. To perform this music the way it should be done will take an ensemble of true musicians and a conductor who is sensitive to the composer's wishes, and the story behind the work. *The Leaves Are Falling* was composed in response to the assassination of President John F. Kennedy. It is solemn music, but ends with hope. The work is in two sections. The first section uses a gradual layering of texture to create a denseness that dissipates only to begin again. The second time the Martin Luther hymn "A Mighty Fortress" comes in, it is layered onto the first texture, so that there are layers upon layers. Benson compares the sound to looking into a plate glass window; you not only see through the window, but you also see the reflections outside the window. However you perceive it, this is one of the most powerful compositions I have ever heard or conducted, and that includes works for orchestra, chorus, etc.

I did not include the standard works for band, such as the Holst Suites, the Hindemith Symphony in B-flat, etc. because it goes without saying that these works have established their places in the literature and continue to be regularly performed. I chose the above ten works for the reasons stated earlier and because they aren't performed as frequently as they should be.

The literature for band has become very temporal, and the heritage of great music that exists for band is gradually being lost.

I. Ten Composers Whose Music Overall Speaks to Me in Especially Meaningful Ways

Several decades ago when film composer Dmitri Tiomkin received an Oscar for one of his scores, his acceptance speech began something like, "I'd like to thank Beethoven, Tchaikovsky, and Wagner for making this award possible." I completely understand what he meant by that statement. I have often said, somewhat jokingly, that I am a "derivative" composer—I steal, but only from the very best.

In the early days of composing, my influences were Tchaikovsky, Wagner, and Rimsky-Korsakov. However, in the years since then as I have grown as a composer, my influences have expanded to include mostly contemporary American composers, such as John Corigliano, John Adams, and Aaron Jay Kernis. I have also developed a new awareness in my senior years of Brahms, a composer with a rich harmonic language and a facility with rhythms that escaped me when I was younger. Still, you never quite lose the influences of those early years, which makes for quite a hybrid style. This is what gives each composer his or her own language.

Here, in historical order, are ten composers who continue to spark my imagination and to whom I am most grateful.

1. **Ludwig van Beethoven**. With the exception of *Wellington's Victory*, there is not a bad Beethoven composition. His music is not only a thrill to hear, but a constant joy and

surprise to analyze. Again and again, one can discover something fresh and exciting in his music.

2. **Gustav Mahler**. Thanks in large part to the conductor Bruno Walter we have this giant in our contemporary repertoire. Although, as Bernstein said, he straddled the Romantic and Modern periods like a "colossus," he was little known or appreciated until well into the 20th century, and his music is like the 20th century: episodic, full of surprises, and both good and terrifying. There is where the lesson is to be learned.

3. **Maurice Ravel**. Many academics place Ravel so deep in the shadow of Debussy that he barely exists, and I admire Debussy's music very much. But there is something in Ravel's music that is more personal to me. Perhaps it's his use of orchestral color, the surprising harmonic progressions, the long melodic lines, or the Haydnesque sense of humor that frequently comes seemingly from nowhere.

4. **Béla Bartók**. I hold Bartók in the same esteem that I hold Beethoven. There is so much to be learned from studying his music that just when you thought you had heard it all, something new comes at you. Just to listen to Bartók's music makes you want to become a better composer.

5. **Samuel Barber**. Classified as a neo-romanticist, Barber nevertheless pointed the way to the current period of post-atonality and post-minimalism. His use of innovative melodic lines and the craft that shows through in his use of subtle tensions and relaxations in his harmonic language make him a model for many younger composers.

6. **Dmitri Shostakovich**. Here is a composer so affected by his life that his compositions bear the noble soul, as well as the

blemishes, of the mortal man. Perhaps he did not execute his craft as well as some, but no one ever composed with more intensity. It is almost impossible to listen to his music and not align it with the politics of his time, but something at the core of this music reveals a passion stronger and more eternal than any doctrine of man.

7. **William Walton**. I have always loved Walton's music, and the older I become, the more I appreciate it. Walton was first presented to me in the form of *Belshazzar's Feast* when I was in a music literature survey class at the University of Michigan. I was thunderstruck by the work and still am to this day. I love his unabashed sense of drama, his neo-romantic melodies, and his seventh and ninth chords. His sense of development is a constant wonder, and his biting, muted brass lines are still as thrilling today as when I first heard them.

8. **Aaron Copland**. No other composer affected the way music has been written in America during the 20th century more than Aaron Copland! His mark can be heard in so much music of the last 100 years, whether in the concert hall, on television, or in the movies. The open fifths, the quartal-based melodies, the unique orchestration, and the use of jazz and folk idioms all fairly shout "America!" Yet there are two Coplands: the composer of Americana and the more strident and abstract writer. Both styles are integrally related and continue to influence composers in the 21st century.

9. **Benjamin Britten**. There is a clarity in Britten's music that I find lacking in much contemporary music. There is nothing cluttered or fussy about it. Even in its most dynamic, driving moments, there still is a sense of order. I

don't mean to imply that it is without passion, far from it. Perhaps orderliness is a British trait. On the other hand, there is not the faintest hint of the "stiff upper lip" in his scores. It is this kind of control that I strive more and more to achieve.

10. **Leonard Bernstein**. From my high school days when I first became acquainted with Bernstein's ballet *Fancy Free*, I have had to control myself not to become a Bernstein clone. His jazz-influenced scores are so infectious that it is difficult to approach them without borrowing from them. Yes, we can hear the influence in his music from other composers, especially Copland, but isn't this where I started? We are all "derivative" composers, but Leonard Bernstein did it so well. And besides that, he was a great teacher!

J. The Future of the Wind Band

The United States has the best school band programs in the world. No other country even comes close to the programs that have developed here over the last 100 years or more. In many communities throughout the land, the school band is a tremendous source of pride, and more and more community concert bands continue to form. In fact, my little hometown of Cookeville, Tennessee, formed a community concert band in 2001, and it is the major attraction of the summer concerts in the park.

Having said that, I am concerned about the future of the wind band in America. The three main reason are:

1. Funding for education in the United States continues to drop, and as it does the arts are usually the first to suffer. The arts in the public schools and colleges are considered a to be a luxury rather than an indication of quality of life, as we would prefer it to be considered.

2. There is too much emphasis on the "service" aspect of the band, rather than its educational value. Too often, bands become background music to the other school or college activities, and we have ourselves to blame for this. We must educate the public, as well as the students, about the educational value of the arts.

3. There are too many music schools in the United States and not enough qualified students to fill the classrooms and studios. In many colleges throughout the U.S., numbers are more important than quality, and the survival of a program depends upon numbers, not only those recruited, but those graduating. This results in a cycle of mediocrity that is a disservice to all programs involved.

I believe that these problems can be addressed and reversed, but it will take wisdom, courage, and a renewed commitment to education.

K. Other Facets of My Everyday Life

My family is the most important part of my life, especially now that we have six grandchildren. Unfortunately, they live all over the country, and we don't see them as often as we would like. Nevertheless, they keep us occupied and give us a reason to stay young at heart, if not physically!

One of my great joys is gardening. I gave up my vegetable garden several years ago because I got tired of feeding the raccoons and deer, but my landscaping more than makes up for the time and energy I spend outside. Gardening has always been great therapy for me, and it is so rewarding. It's also a good thing to do when the "angel of inspiration" flies off to someone else. More than once I've solved a musical problem in the garden that couldn't be solved at the piano. We have almost three acres of land, so I have plenty to keep me occupied. The climate of Tennessee is such that I can keep busy outside most of the year, and when I can't, I like to read.

I don't care much for fiction, but I do love biographies, books about history (especially the Civil War, or as we say in Tennessee, "the recent unpleasantness"), and other non-fiction. Several years ago, my wife bought me a G-scale railroad and created a monster. I have a small pond by our back patio, and now the train is a garden railroad complete with a large tunnel, waterfall, bridge, and a grist mill. There is also a little handcar on a siding that runs back and forth. It's all a trick to lure our grandchildren to our house, and I love it, too!

L. Comprehensive List of Works for Band
Grades 2-3

Bold Venture. Commissioned by the Tennessee Governor's School of the Arts and premiered by the School of the Arts Wind Ensemble, Dr. W. Francis McBeth, conductor, Murfreesboro, Tennessee, July 1988. (3:30, 1990, Kjos Music Company)

Carpathian Sketches. Composed for the East Texas State University Summer Camp Band and first performed by them with the composer conducting, Commerce, Texas, July 1979. (5:00, 1978, Marks/Hal Leonard)

Cliff Island Suite. Composed for and premiered by the Tennessee Tech University Concert Band with the composer conducting, Cookeville, Tennessee, February 1990. (7:00, 1990, Kjos Music Company)

Eagle Rock Overture. Commissioned and premiered by the Eagle Rock Junior High School, John Schooler, conductor, Idaho Falls, Idaho, December 1986. (5:00, 1986, Columbia/Warner Bros)

Japanese Prints. Commissioned by the South French Broad Junior High School Band, Patricia Garren, conductor. Premiered at the North Carolina Music Educators Association convention in Asheville, North Carolina, with the composer conducting, March 1979. (6:30, 1978, Marks/Hal Leonard)

Jubilate. Commissioned by the Japanese Bandmasters Association and first performed by the Sony Band, Toshio Akiyama conducting, Tokyo, Japan, December 1978. (5:00, 1978, Southern Music Company)

March of the Dragonmasters. For the composer's son, Matthew, and premiered by the East Texas State University Summer Camp Band with the composer conducting, Commerce, Texas, July 1984. (3:30, 1984, Marks/Hal Leonard)

Potomac Festival Overture. Commissioned by the Potomac School Band, Susan Appleby, conductor, and premiered by them with the composer conducting, McLean, Virginia, November 1990. (3:00, 1990, Kjos Music Company)

Sinfonia Hungarica. Premiered by the Tennessee Tech University Concert Band with the composer conducting, Cookeville, Tennessee, April 1998. (5:00, 1998, Mark/Hal Leonard)

Three Chinese Miniatures. Commissioned by the All-Asia Pacific Band Association and premiered by their Honor Band with the composer conducting, Taiwan, Republic of China, August 1993. (6:30, 1993, Kjos Music Company)

Under the Big Top. Commissioned and premiered by the McCracken Junior High School Band, Carl McMath, conductor. Spartanburg, South Carolina, May 1987. (4:00, 1987, Columbia/ Warner Bros)

Grade 4

Concert in the Park. Commissioned by the Quakertown Community Band, Richard Karschner, conductor, and premiered by them with the composer conducting, Quakertown, Pennsylvania, April 2002. (7:30, 2004, Kjos Music Company)

Courage to Serve–March. Premiered by the University of Michigan Symphony Band with the composer conducting, Ann Arbor, Michigan, February 1971. (3:00, 1971, Volkwein/Warner Brothers)

Hebraic Rhapsody. Commissioned by the Rock Valley Community College Wind Ensemble, Jack Simon, conductor, and premiered by them with the composer conducting, Rockford, Illinois, April 2000. (5:30, 2000, Marks/Hal Leonard)

Joan of Arc. Commissioned by the Tri-Lakes Band Director's Association of Tennessee for their 25th anniversary and premiered by their Honor Band with the composer conducting, Winchester, Tennessee, January 30, 1999. (14:15, 2001, Kjos Music Company)

The Last Full Measure of Devotion. Commissioned and premiered by the United States Army Band, Col. Bryan Shelburne, conductor, Washington, D.C., August 1995. (7:30, 1995, Ludwig Music Company)

Lord, Guard and Guide. Commissioned and premiered by the U.S. Air Force Military Airlift Command Band, Major Bruce Gilkes, conductor, Scott Air Force Base, Illinois, March 1992. (8:00, 1992, Kjos Music Company)

March "Dramatic." Composed for and premiered by the Perrysburg High School Band with the composer conducting, Perrysburg, Ohio, May 1967. (3:00, 1967, Southern Music Company)

Old Time Spirit. Commissioned by the "Friends of Wendell Evanson" for Mr. Evanson, director of bands at Henderson State University. Premiered by the Henderson State University Music Camp Band with the composer conducting, Arkadelphia, Arkansas, July 1986. (7:00, 1986, Kjos Music Company)

Pastorale and Country Dance. Commissioned by the Henderson High School Band, Paul Hooker, conductor, and premiered by them with the composer conducting, Atlanta, Georgia, March 1979. (7:00, 1979, Kjos Music Company)

Preamble. Winner of the 1976 Volkwein Award sponsored by the American School Band Directors Association. Commissioned by the Michigan Small College Band Directors Association and premiered by the Michigan Collegiate Honor Band with the composer conducting, Grand Rapids, Michigan, March 1976. (6:00, 1975, Volkwein/Warner Brothers)

Prelude: Concert Liberte. Commissioned by the Concert Liberte Band, Al Ishigami, conductor, and premiered by them with the composer conducting, Shizuoka City, Japan, November 1976. (4:00, 1976, Wingert-Jones Music)

Prelude on an Old Time Southern Hymn. Commissioned and premiered by the Louisiana Tech University Symphonic Band, Raymond Young, conductor, Ruston, Louisiana, May 1983. (6:00, 1983, Kjos Music Company)

Second Suite. Premiered by the Faculty Band at the Armed Forces School of Music with the composer conducting, Norfolk, Virginia, September 1965. (9:00, 1965, Volkwein/Warner Brothers)

Stars and Bars–March. Premiered by the Faculty Band at the U.S. Navy School of Music (now the Armed Forces School of Music) with the composer conducting. Washington, D.C., May 1963. (3:30, 1963, Volkwein/Warner Brothers)

The Tennessean March. Commissioned by the Tennessee Tech University Department of Music and premiered by their wind ensemble with the composer conducting, Cookeville, Tennessee, February 1969. (3:00, 1968, Volkwein/Warner Brothers)

Third Suite. Composed for the Granby High School Band, Leo Imperial, conductor and premiered by them with the composer conducting, Norfolk, Virginia, May 1966. (8:00, 1966, Volkwein/ Warner Brothers)

To Music. Commissioned by the Michigan State University Bands, John Whitwell, director of bands, to honor David Catron on his retirement from the university and premiered by the MSU Symphonic Band with the composer conducting, East Lansing, Michigan, March 2002. (7:30, 2003, Marks/Hal Leonard)

Tour de Force–March. Commissioned by the American Youth Festival Band for their annual tour of Europe and premiered by them with the composer conducting, June 1970. (3:00, 1970, Wingert-Jones Music)

Uncommon Valor March. Composed for Company 1, 3rd Battalion, 24th Marines (the composer's son Matthew's Marine Reserve unit) for their valor while serving in Desert Storm. Premiered by the United States Marine Band, Col. John Bourgeois, conductor, Washington, D.C., January 1991. (3:00, 1991, Ludwig Music Company)

Variants on the Air Force Hymn. Commissioned and premiered by the United State Air Force Band of Flight, Captain Kelly G. Bledsoe, conductor, Wright-Patterson Air Force Base, Ohio, February 1997. (8:00, 1996, Kjos Music Company)

Grades 5-6

Apocalypse. Commissioned by the Loyola University Wind Ensemble, Joseph Hebert, conductor, and premiered by them with the composer conducting. New Orleans, Louisiana, February 1973. (7:00, 1972, Marks/Hal Leonard)

Chorale and Toccata. Commissioned by the Pennsylvania Region IV Band Director's Association and premiered by the Region IV Honor Band, James Dunlop, conductor, Robesonia, Pennsylvania, February 1966. (6:00, 1966, Elkan Vogel/Presser)

Colonial Airs and Dances. Commissioned by the Georgia Music Educators Association and premiered by the Georgia Intercollegiate Band with the composer conducting. Columbus, Georgia, January 1987. (9:00, 1986, Kjos Music Company)

A Commemorative Suite. Commissioned and premiered by Muskegon High School Band with the composer conducting. Muskegon, Michigan, May 1987. (9:00, 1987, Ludwig Music Company)

Concerto for Band. Commissioned and premiered by the Ithaca College Wind Ensemble with the composer conducting, Ithaca, New York, April 1981. (18:00, 1981, Marks/Hal Leonard)

Concerto for Bass Tuba. Commissioned by the University of Illinois for Daniel Perantoni and premiered by Mr. Perantoni and the University of Illinois Band, Harry Begian, conductor, Champaign, Illinois, January 1980. (12:00, 1979, Marks/Hal Leonard/Presser)

Concerto for Euphonium. Premiered by the Tennessee Tech University Symphony Band, Erik Paul, soloist, and Joseph Hermann, conductor, Cookeville, Tennessee, April 1986. (15:00, 1985, Marks/Hal Leonard)

Concerto for Percussion and Band. Commissioned by Garwood Whaley and premiered by the Bishop Ireton/St. Mary's High School Wind Ensemble, Garwood Whaley, conductor, with Pat Roulet and Eric Scorce, soloists, Alexandria, Virginia, March 1985. (9:15, 1984, Meredith Music)

Concerto no. 2 for Saxophone. Commissioned by Nicholas Brightman and premiered by him with the Butler University Wind Ensemble, composer conducting, Indianapolis, Indiana, March 1978. (10:00, 1977, Warner Brothers)

Diamond Variations. This was the winner of the 1968 Ostwald Award of the American Bandmasters Association. It was commissioned and premiered by the University of Illinois Band, Dr. Mark Hindsley, conductor, Champaign, Illinois, November 1967. (10:30, 1968, Volkwein/Warner Brothers)

Epilogue: Lest We Forget. Commissioned and premiered by the United States Army Field Band, Lt. Col. Jack Grogan, conductor, at the Kentucky Music Educators Association convention, Louisville, Kentucky, February 1992. (7:30, 1991, Kjos Music Company)

Esprit de Corps. Commissioned and premiered by the United States Marine Band, Col. John Bourgeois, conductor, at the National Band Association convention, Knoxville, Tennessee, June 1984. (5:15, 1984, Marks/Hal Leonard)

First Suite for Band. This is not the "original" First Suite. Commissioned by the band parents and alumni of John Overton High School, JoAnn Hood and Richard Jolley, co-directors, and premiered by them with the composer conducting, Nashville, Tennessee, May 1996. (9:00, 1995, Kjos Music Company)

Heroic Saga. Commissioned by Kinki University Band of Osaka, Japan, and premiered by them with Frederick Fennell conducting, Osaka, Japan, November 1986. (7:00, 1986, Columbia/Warner Brothers)

In Sunshine and Shadow. This is a work for soprano and bass soloists, chorus, and wind ensemble based on the poetry of African American poet Paul Laurence Dunbar (1872-1908). It was a joint commission from Wright State University and the University of Dayton in Dayton, Ohio, and was premiered by them with the composer conducting. Dayton, Ohio, February 2003. (22:00, 2003, Marks/Hal Leonard)

Meditations on an Old Scottish Hymn Tune. Commissioned by Nebraska Wesleyan University and premiered by the Plainsman Festival Honor Band with the composer conducting, Lincoln, Nebraska, February 1993. (7:30, 1993, Kjos Music Company)

Mystic Chords of Memory. Commissioned by the United States Navy Band, CDR. Ralph Gambone, conductor, and premiered by them on the band's 75th Anniversary Concert. Washington, D.C., March 2000. (7:15, 1999, Southern Music Company)

Shivaree. Commissioned by the Springfield High School Band, Malcolm Rowell, conductor, and premiered by them with the composer conducting. Springfield, Vermont, April 1976. (7:30, 1975, Shawnee Press)

Sinfonia Noblissima. Premiered by the Granby High School Band, Leo Imperial, conductor, with the composer conducting, Norfolk, Virginia, May 1965. (6:30, 1965, Elkan Vogel/Presser)

Sinfonietta. This was the winner of the 1972 Ostwald Award of the American Bandmasters Association. It was commissioned by the Butler University Wind Ensemble, Dr. John Colbert, conductor, and premiered by them with the composer conducting, Indianapolis, Indiana, February 1970. (14:30, 1970, Volkwein/Warner Bros)

Symphony for Band no. 1. This was the winner of the 1964 Ostwald Award of the American Bandmasters Association and was premiered by the U.S. Air Force Band of the West, Major Samuel Loboda, USA, conductor, at the 1964 ABA Convention, San Antonio, Texas, March 1964. (20:00, 1964, Volkwein/Warner Brothers)

Symphony no. 2. Commissioned by Rissho Kosei-Kai of Tokyo, Japan, and premiered by the Tokyo Kosei Wind Orchestra with the composer conducting, Tokyo, Japan, November 1976. (20:00, 1976, Kjos Music Company)

Tableau. Commissioned and premiered by the United States Marine Band, Col. John Bourgeois, conductor, at the Midwest Band and Orchestra Clinic, Chicago, Illinois, December 1982. (7:30, 1982, Marks/Hal Leonard)

Testament. Commissioned by the Six Flags Organization of Atlanta, Georgia, and premiered by the United States Navy Band in Constitution Hall with the composer conducting, Washington, D.C., October 1988. (5:30, 1988, Kjos Music Company)

Triumph and Tradition. Commissioned by the University of Michigan Band Alumni Association to honor William D. Revelli upon his retirement and premiered by the University of Michigan Symphony Band with William D. Revelli conducting, Ann Arbor, Michigan, November 1985. (9:00, 1985, Southern Music Company)

Variations on a Theme by Robert Schumann. Commissioned and premiered by the North Hills High School Band, Warren Mercer, conductor, 1969 Eastern Region, MENC, Washington, D.C., April 1969. (10:30, 1968, Volkwein/Warner Brothers)

The Wall. Commissioned and premiered by the United States Air Force Band, Lt. Col. Alan Bonner, conductor, at the Texas Bandmasters Association convention, San Antonio, Texas, July 1993. (14:00, 1993, Marks/Hal Leonard)

pierre **La Plante**

As long as music and music making remain a viable part of high school and college life, bands will be a part of it. Music educators have long believed in the power of music to enhance and transform one's life, and now it seems there is an ever-increasing pile of empirical evidence that music is, indeed, a positive force in people's lives, contributes to the learning process itself, and belongs in the curriculum of every primary and secondary school. There probably isn't a successful high school band, choir, or orchestra anywhere that doesn't count as its members some of the school's best athletes, scholars and school leaders, many of whom are the best musicians in the group.

A. Biography

Pierre La Plante, a lifelong resident of Wisconsin, was born in the Milwaukee suburb of West Allis. His family lived in the towns of Cedarburg and Plymouth for a brief time before moving to Sturgeon Bay, where La Plante grew up and attended high school. He was active in band and choir and held leads in several high school operetta productions.

He attended the University of Wisconsin at Madison on a Music Clinic tuition scholarship, where he earned his bachelor of music (1967) and master of music (1972) degrees. He began teaching in fall 1967 in the Blanchardville public school system, where he directed the high school band and chorus. From 1972 to 1975, La Plante directed the high school concert band, marching band, and choir in Prescott, Wisconsin, before returning to Blanchardville (now Pecatonica Area Schools) to teach general music for grades K-6 and beginning band. He held this position from 1975 until his retirement in spring 2001.

La Plante has adjudicated for solo and ensemble contests and played bassoon in regional orchestras, including the Dubuque Symphony Orchestra and the Beloit-Janesville Symphony. He is currently a member of Madison Wind Ensemble and resides in Oregon, Wisconsin, with his wife, Laurie. Their daughters, Amy and Elizabeth, enjoy careers in the graphic arts and teaching, respectively.

I can still recall my very first "formal" music lesson. I must have been in kindergarten or first grade when my dad brought home a soprano saxophone. Dad was at various times a salesman, chef, and professional musician (a self taught saxophonist and a stride piano player). I guess I could carry a tune fairly well, and I think my dad decided on a whim to see how much of his musical ability I had inherited. After a day or two of trying to finger and honk out some simple tunes, it became apparent that I had received only a partial inheritance, and we gave up on the saxophone lessons. "Formal" musical instruction did not resume until fifth grade.

There was always music being played around the house; my parents enjoyed listening to recordings of Nat King Cole, Earl Hines, and Eddie Condon's band in addition to other pop stars of the day. I eventually had recordings of my own, but what passed for children's records in the 1940s and 1950s were often familiar classical pieces reworked with inane lyrics fitted to the melodies. I'm sure these "kiddie klassics" were well intended, but even after all these years it's hard to listen to this music in its original form without hearing the goofy lyrics.

I began piano lessons in fifth grade. By this time, my two younger sisters were born, and we lived in Sturgeon Bay, where Dad worked in clothing sales at the town's largest department store and Mom applied her skills as a beautician in one of the local salons. I had originally wanted to take clarinet lessons, but my dad intervened and convinced me to take piano lessons instead. He explained that piano lessons would give me a much greater foundation that could be applied to learning a band instrument later on when I was a bit older. I was somewhat disappointed, but he was right, as I would later find out. I enjoyed practicing, so the piano occupied much of my after school time.

I didn't actually get around to joining the band until I was a high school sophomore. The school owned a bassoon, but there was no one around to play it, so our director, who was a trumpet player, asked me to give it a try. After a few basic lessons that included the "Andy Gump" embouchure, a fingering chart, and a month in the practice room, I joined the band, playing whatever notes I could. (The piano lessons *had* paid off!)

I eventually became involved with just about every musical activity that was available: band, choir, operetta, accompanying, solo and ensemble, and music club. The music room became a second home, and I enjoyed it all so much that I thought I could stay on the scene forever if I became a music teacher! Several of us even made our TV debuts, singing and playing classical selections or show tunes on the local Cerebral Palsy Telethons, usually at three o'clock in the morning! I had always been interested in classical music, so I began buying LPs of concerti, symphonic works, and solo artists (mostly pianists) that I played almost all of the time. Besides listening to recordings, I was able to attend many symphony concerts over the years at the Peninsula Music Festival held each summer at Fish Creek, a 40-minute drive from Sturgeon Bay, and I never missed a Saturday morning broadcast of Leonard Bernstein's Young Peoples' Concerts.

In fall 1962 I enrolled at the University of Wisconsin-Madison School of Music. Earlier that summer while attending the university's music camp, I auditioned for and was lucky enough to receive a tuition scholarship offered to students attending the Milwaukee or Madison campus. The scholarship was good for all four years as long as I kept my grade point average up and lent my talents to one of the performing organizations (band, choir, etc). I recall that very few music majors graduated in four years, especially music education students, unless they took a full load that was pretty well planned out and did not take extra courses or work part time. Those students (including me) who studied extra theory, continued piano beyond what was required, took part time jobs, and practiced usually took five years plus a summer or two to graduate. I did not graduate until August 1967.

The arranging and writing bug bit me at about the time I started arranging classes with Jim Christensen, who was Ray Dvorak's assistant and director of the marching band. I had always done a little composing on and off that took the form of poems set to music for voice and piano. I also began arranging movie themes and standard pop/rock tunes for the woodwind quintets I played in and for other quartets, trios, or any groups that would consent to read through them. I was interested to hear how The Beatles and Burt Bacharach would sound in a different context.

I should mention that I am not a jazz musician, although I have always enjoyed playing ragtime and listening to jazz, especially music from the 1920s and 1930s. Several of my college roommates and friends were well versed in jazz, and one night I tagged along to a gig, bassoon in hand, and sat in on a rendition of "When Sunny Gets Blue." My soprano saxophone lessons may have lasted only a couple of days, but my jazz bassoon career ended that evening!

In 1967 I took my first job teaching band and chorus in Blanchardville, Wisconsin. I relied on (as did many band directors at the time) the compositions of Clare Grundman and James Ployhar. They worked very well with young bands without balanced instrumentation or strong players in all of the sections, and my initial composing efforts were modeled after these arranger-composers. After three years at Blanchardville, I returned to the University of Wisconsin-Madison to work on a master's degree. It was during this time that I had the opportunity to do some college teaching as a part-time instructor of piano on a one-year appointment at Milton College. Although the college has since closed its doors, their music department was well respected and had an overflow of students who wanted to take lessons or needed instruction for piano proficiency. It was a great experience, but I realized that college teaching was not going to be an option for me for various reasons. I was awarded my degree in August 1972. Laurie and I were married that same month, and two days after the wedding ceremony I left for Prescott, Wisconsin, to get started at my new teaching position while Laurie stayed behind to get things ready for the move up north.

At Prescott High School, I was again responsible for all of the high school music activities, including the marching program. The superintendent hinted during my interview that he wanted the marching band part of the program "toned down" a bit, and because I was not temperamentally suited nor really well qualified to run a marching band program, I was the ideal candidate. It was during this time I continued to arrange and had my first band piece, *A Western Portrait*, published.

As much as my wife and I enjoyed being so close to the Minneapolis-St. Paul area, the work seemed never ending. After our first daughter, Amy, was born in October 1974, I realized I wanted to have more time to be at home and work on composing. The school district in Blanchardville where I started had an opening for general classroom music and beginning band, which I applied for and was offered. I accepted, and we moved back to southern Wisconsin in 1975, where I taught until my retirement in June 2001. I continued to write and arrange when I could (mostly on weekends and during the summer when I wasn't busy working a summer job), attended workshops, taught summer band, and painted or fixed up our old two-story house that was only a couple of blocks from the high school.

After our youngest daughter, Elizabeth, was born in February 1977, I decided to keep up my playing by joining the Beloit-Janesville Symphony as second bassoonist. Playing the second part has always been a pleasure for me. As a fourth horn acquaintance of mine once said, "I get to put on my tux, walk around with my horn, and act smart without having to worry about playing solos." I am no longer with the symphony but play in the Madison Wind Ensemble, which draws its membership from area band directors, serious amateurs, and professionals who enjoy playing high-quality repertoire.

B. The Creative Process

I am sometimes uncomfortable with the word "composer" because what I do, to some extent, is what my arranging teacher, James Christensen, called "creative arranging." On the other hand, John Cacavas writes in *Music Arranging and Orchestration* (Belwin-Mills) that "to be a successful arranger one must also be a composer. The various counter-melodies, figures, introductions, and modulations in any orchestration do not just appear by chance." I suppose it just depends on how one defines a composer.

When I go about the business of putting a piece together, I think about who is probably going to be playing it, what the technical demands are going to be, and what elements I need to consider, including choice of key, fingerings, slide combinations, rhythmic complexity, and so forth. Those of us who have spent our professional careers primarily teaching and working with school bands have the advantage of knowing what kids can or can't do in a given situation and what might or might not work with a young band. My technique on bassoon or piano was never up to the level of the applied majors, so I am somewhat sympathetic toward students or amateur players who struggle to play the music they see in front of them, and I try to put myself in their place.

In writing for young bands, I believe the musical ideas, the expression, or the intent of the composer always have to trump whatever technical demands are made on the players. If they are struggling with excessive range, rhythmic complexity, or superfluous notes, it takes too much time and energy away from the music making. Obviously, putting limitations on the technical demands also puts limitations on the musical elements as well. The challenge is coming up with a piece that is interesting and musical, yet making it reasonably accessible to the players.

There are numerous pieces that may look "easy on the page" but are satisfying and often challenging musical experiences regardless of the age or grade level of the band. The example that comes to mind most often for me is Bruce Houseknecht's setting of *Salvation Is Created* by Pavel Chesnokov. I first played this at music camp and have heard, conducted, and performed the piece on numerous occasions over the years. There is so much that can be taught in terms of phrasing, control, dynamics, intonation, and tone (aside from it being an exhilarating musical experience) without having to stumble over a cascade of notes and fingerings. My most memorable and unforgettable performance experience was hearing H. Robert Reynolds conduct the piece when he was director of bands at the University of Wisconsin-Madison. I hesitate to start a list of other examples of accessible, worthwhile music because there are many worthy of mention, but I would also include Larry Daehn's *A Song For Friends*, Donald Erb's *Star Gazing*, several of Timothy Broege's pieces, and, more recently, Michael Colgrass' *Old Churches*.

My choice to use traditional materials, hymns, or "composed" music, is a deliberate one, and I did not think I had a particular style of writing that was different from what other band composers were using for their compositions. I began writing for band as nothing more than a creative hobby, or as a diversion from my teaching activities. It was as close to serious composing as I was going to get, and I had absolutely no intentions or pretensions of writing the Great American Band Symphony.

The material I use is basically Western, tonal music, so the use of traditional harmony and the usual compositional approaches and devices seems appropriate. Most of the traditional songs and tunes that survive and stay with us over the years have one thing in common—good melodies. Traditional melodies and folk songs are often challenging to use because many of these pieces are complete in themselves and do not seem ripe for development in the traditional sense. Aaron Copland said that folk music "presents a formal problem when used in a symphonic composition. Most composers have found that there is little that can be done with such material except to repeat it." (*Copland 1900-1942* by Vivian Perlis, St. Martin's Press, p. 246.)

I attempt to solve this problem by using devices such as variation, canon, augmentation, diminution, changing timbre, and modality and incorporating motives or sections of the tune being used. These are all fairly obvious musical tricks and forms of repetition to some extent, but these methods are very useful when teaching young players about the elements of music in a cohesive piece.

I think there is a common bond between vocal and instrumental music. Generally speaking, vocal music "works" when played on wind instruments, and although it is reasonable to assume that music based on songs will be somewhat programmatic, the music itself needs to promote an enjoyable and satisfying experience on its own terms, with or without any knowledge of the title or reading the program notes. Consider, too, all of the great band classics by Grainger and Holst based on traditional tunes that, in the hands of these master composers, transcend mere arranging. "Old wine in new bottles" is a familiar saying that Gordon Jacob borrowed for the title one of his pieces and best describes what I try to do.

In terms of work habits, I am a morning person and get the most accomplished by getting up ahead of the sun. I tend to sketch things out in sections on a two- or three-line score at an electronic keyboard, record the section on several tracks, and play it back before turning it into a full score using Sibelius. I have always felt the need to *see* what the sounds look like on the page in full score. I can't mull over a problem too long, or it all starts to sound the same. Allowing my subconscious to toss an idea around seems to work because sometimes when I am out for a walk, digging in the garden, or straightening up the garage, I may start thinking about it and come up with an idea or solution to a problem. When I visit a band rehearsal and kids ask how long it took me to write a piece, I tell them that I don't really know.

I try to get a live band to test the end result of my composing because I don't trust the computer or my inner ear. I was relieved to read somewhere that even Sergei Rachmaninoff would have his orchestrations tried out if he wasn't sure of what he was "hearing."

"Educational" music often gets a bad rap, and those who write for young bands need to approach it with the same seriousness and sincerity as though they were writing the next Hindemith Symphony in B-flat.

C. The Approach to Orchestration

Although I have only written a couple of pieces for orchestra, I listen to a lot of orchestral music and sometimes get ideas that "morph" into sounds for the wind band. Learning how instruments sound together is an ongoing process for me.

In arranging class we were told to create a "sound dictionary" in our heads and study scores with the recordings so we could see how these sounds were put together and what they looked like on the page. I suspect that all composer-arrangers steal from each other, and when I listen to an interesting piece, I find myself wondering how the composer "got that sound." I buy CDs, tape music off the air, and find scores to study for ideas I can use. I listen for transitions and "behind" the melody to hear the harmony, how the countermelody is written, and, more important, how satisfactorily it resolves.

Generally speaking, there is a tendency to "play it safe" when scoring pieces in the lower grades because the composer is never quite sure of the group in terms of ability, instrumentation, or what parts should be doubled or reinforced. As a result, there can be frequent overscoring that results in a sameness or a "gray" sound. Often, as a result of heavy scoring, melodies or important moving parts get lost. On the other hand, young people do not like sitting around counting rests with "nothing to do." One solution from the composer's perspective is to cue extensively, although there are conductors and composers who would disagree with this procedure. There are built-in limitations that come with writing music for players who are learning to finger, articulate, listen, and play together. Perhaps the biggest challenge in terms of orchestration is keeping the sound fresh by coming up with ways to avoid or minimize the dreaded "gray sound syndrome."

The following general "approaches" are the nitty-gritty things I keep in mind when orchestrating for bands of grade levels 1-3. I would vary or modify these approaches depending on the specific grade level.

- Keep the ranges reasonable. Divide high flutes. Very low saxophones are difficult to play softly, but don't score "thumb tones" all of the time. The last five or six semitones on bassoon are sometimes awkward for first or second year players. Decide if the clarinet(s) will play above the break.
- Give fast and furious passages to the alto saxophoness if the clarinet break presents a problem.
- Let the snare drum play after the beat, and give the horns some harmony or a countermelody.
- Allow the low brass and woodwinds to play the tune or something interesting at least once.
- If something is not working in "functional" harmony, improving the bass line is often the key to fixing the problem.
- Don't allow anyone to repeat anything ad nauseum, even if it's the bass line of Pachelbel's celebrated Canon in D.

There is an informative article in the July 2003 *Instrumentalist* (pp. 25-29) that I highly recommend titled "The Difficult Art of Writing Creative Music for Young Bands" in which Deborah Sheldon interviews several composers about the challenges of writing for young players.

D. Views from the Composer to the Conductor Pertaining to Score Study and Preparation

When I taught, my score preparation actually began with score selection. Any director of a young performing group knows that one of the most difficult and time-consuming jobs is coming up with worthwhile music that is suitable for his or her group. I would devote time to going over scores, listening to demos, and considering whether the piece would work with the particular group of students I had to teach that year. Was the piece interesting? Did it teach something? Was it too hard? Did the inner voices and instruments repeat the same four notes from beginning to end? Were the trombone parts too wimpy, or too challenging? Can I afford to buy the piece?

The selection process could involve picking out music that is too difficult to play in public but would work in class for learning and instructional purposes. The ideal selection is enjoyable and rewarding to rehearse and perform, but also serves as a vehicle for teaching tone, style, phrasing, and musicianship. Regarding difficulty, I would tend to program music that is easier than what many students might be capable of playing. Some directors would disagree with this approach, but my thinking is that it is preferable to avoid bogging down the band with technical and demanding passages that are worrisome and might detract from or mar their performance. Sometimes "tweaking" a part can help the situation. As long as the composer's intent is not violated, I have no problem altering or rewriting a part in order to make it a bit easier to play or doubling a weaker part or one that is missing from the ensemble. I once had some flute players complain about how bored they were with their part because the notes hardly ever left the staff. (This was a pretty sharp group that was truly bored.) So I wrote some passages an octave higher. They were sufficiently challenged, and the grumbling stopped.

As far as the actual preparation of the score is concerned, I agree with James Barnes' notion in Volume One of *Composers on Composing for Band* that it shouldn't take the conductor too long to figure out what is going on in a grade-1, -2, or -3 band piece. I would look through the score to see how the piece was put together and play through it on the piano, checking for trouble spots, unity and contrast (form), use of dynamics, tricky fingerings, and countermelodies, all things one would do with the most sophisticated score. (Electronic keyboards enable anyone who struggled through a piano proficiency jury to "realize" a score at the piano.)

Sometimes it is fun to find something quirky or under the surface that may or may not help with the actual musical ideas or understanding. For example, it occurred to me that my *American Riversongs* is in three or four parts and played without breaks between the sections. The form is a kind of metaphor of the rivers themselves (Ohio, Missouri, and Mississippi), which are all connected and flow in the same direction to an inevitable climax or end, into the ocean.

After selecting a piece that met my teaching goals and criteria, I might ease the students into the piece by introducing it in lessons, particularly if there were unfamiliar notes, rhythms, or passages that were problematic in one way or another. I think it is very important for beginning players experiencing their first full band rehearsals to sound as good as possible when playing as a large group. I might begin with a section that everyone could play at an acceptable level without getting lost and falling apart. An arrangement of the "Ode to Joy" ("Odey to Joy" as one student innocently put it) from

Beethoven's Ninth Symphony was always a favorite that kids clamored to play even after they grew beyond it. They usually said they had heard it in church or on TV, and I explained that it came from a much larger work and even played an excerpt from the original. The phrase structure is AABA, so once they played the first phrase, they realized they had learned three-fourths of the theme. The one thing I have never done with students is to use the "kiddie klassic" lyric method I experienced eons ago!

E. The Relationship Between the Composer and the Commissioning Party

When asked about writing a piece for a group, I first try and to make a "connection," if possible, with the commissioning party and ask what type of music they want me to write. It might relate to some aspect of local history or tradition, a special event at school or in the community, or a piece of music that has great appeal to the students. *American Riversongs* was written for the Oberlin (Ohio) High School Band, so I used a song about the Ohio River to serve as a springboard for the beginning and evolution of the composition. *Norwegian Sketches* was written for the Mt. Horeb (Wisconsin) Eighth Grade Band to celebrate the anniversary of the band program in a community that takes pride in its Norwegian heritage. The occasion of Wisconsin's bicentennial gave rise to the use of Wisconsin folk tunes in *Prairie Songs* for the Waukesha Middle School Band's performance at the state capitol.

Two other considerations are the size of the ensemble and the strengths or weaknesses regarding the instrumentation and players. Obviously, it is not a good idea to write something that is too difficult and demanding. Making a judgment about that is sometimes difficult. It is very helpful if a recording of the group is available because it allows you to hear what they are capable of playing.

Composers generally hope that their work will have a life beyond the premiere. Most of the time this is possible, unless the piece is too specific in terms of the occasion or makes extraordinary demands from a player or group of players that need to be changed prior to publication. The composer generally retains the right to use the piece after the first performance. Anything mutually agreed upon should be listed in the contract.

I have the commissioning party draw up the contract, and the only specific item that seems worth mentioning is that I always include a clause stating that neither party can be held liable for any monetary damage or loss if the piece is not delivered or if the commission falls through, etc. I regard a commission as a "work in progress," and I am always open to suggestions, revisions, or changes as long as any compromises are reasonable and doable.

F. Views on the Teaching of Composition and How to Mentor the Young Composer

I tend to side with those who say the "creative act" of composing is somewhat intuitive and elusive in nature and can't be taught in the same way as other subjects. I have never studied composition in the formal sense nor have I had the opportunity to teach and mentor composition students, so all I can do is share some ideas that have worked for me.

A century ago, aspiring composers and conductors had to attend live concerts or play in a band or orchestra to hear and experience music. There are still concerts and recitals, but the amount of recorded music currently available in every culture, style, or genre is practically unlimited. In addition, full scores, particularly standard repertoire and works coming into public domain, are readily available at relatively low cost (i.e., the Norton editions). Full band scores are now the rule. In other words, if there is a need to learn repertoire or brush up on orchestration, the opportunities for self-directed study are endless.

If you are in charge of a band or an ensemble, one good place to start composing is for your own group. Students appreciate a piece written just for them, but if this is not possible, rely on the kindness of colleagues to make a tape of the reading. Sometimes it is hard to tell if the "problems" are with the piece or the ensemble itself. Common wisdom would suggest that you find a group that plays at a level that is a notch or two higher than the piece to better analyze your efforts. I did not write as much for my first- and second-year students as many people tend to assume, although I always wrote an arrangement tailored to their needs for their first performance, which was the Christmas concert a few months after they began lessons.

A music notation program can save much time. My handwritten manuscripts look terrible, and in the past I would have to allocate huge blocks of time to copy parts.

If you are not sure of where to start, go with what you know. One of the first recordings of classical music I bought was the César Franck Symphony in D minor. I think it was the only symphonic record they had in the store, and it cost a mere 99 cents. Essentially, what I write is quite traditional, conservative, and reflects what I listened to while growing up.

Be persistent. If something doesn't sound right, rewrite it. If a publisher rejects your submission, send another piece or try another firm. Most rejection letters have "boilerplate" writing that doesn't take long to recognize, but if real comments or suggestions are offered, pay attention. Desktop publishing and notation programs have enabled many enterprising arrangers and composers to become independent publishers, with the advantage of being able to do as they please.

G. Individuals Who Have Been Especially Influential in My Development and Career

Fran Buboltz came to Sturgeon Bay High School when I was a freshman. Her energy, enthusiasm, and musicianship breathed new life into the choral program. She gave us all a chance to shine in chorus and in our annual Gilbert and Sullivan production. Miss B campaigned for music camp scholarships in lieu of expensive overnight trips to the state solo and ensemble contest and convinced me that the University of Wisconsin-Madison was the place for me to go to college. If memory serves me right, Fran was an environmentalist long before it became fashionable and supported efforts to clean up the Wolf River.

I have been very fortunate to have had piano teachers who not only taught musicianship and repertoire but understood and taught proper technique, which is essential for playing the piano effectively. In other words, they actually taught one *how to play* the piano. My first piano teacher, Gustav Abrahamson, had what was (and probably still is) one of the largest classical music collections of anyone in Sturgeon Bay. Many of these were LP recordings made from scratchy old 78s or piano rolls with music played in the "grand style" of the 19th-century virtuosos. The contributions that Gus has made to the music scene in Door County are inestimable, and goodness knows how many miles he logged on his car hauling students and adults around to Fish Creek concerts and cultural events.

In college, I studied with ellsworth snyder (lowercase intentional) who, though traditionally schooled, has been a life-long advocate, champion, and performer of new music. His personal friendship and collaboration with John Cage spanned some 30 years. In the past few years, ellsworth has embarked on a new career as a successful minimalist painter and sculptor.

Walter Gray taught history and especially loved the music of Schubert and Brahms as well as being a Beatles fan. He took every opportunity to remind us that Schubert was really a Classical composer. We always joked about starting a Madison chapter of the "Davidsbund." (The Davidsbund, or "League of David" was Robert Schumann's fictitious organization devoted to promoting good music and high artistic standards, while at the same time denouncing mediocrity and "waging war" on the musical Philistines of the day.)

I never took formal composition classes, but I need to credit Jim Christensen's arranging classes and Hilmar Luckhardt's thorough and demanding study of Renaissance polyphony and Baroque counterpoint as contributing mightily to my composing skills, such as they are.

Larry Daehn has been a friend and colleague since the early 1970s. Larry is a gentleman and master teacher who put to rest the myth that band directors need a big school, big budget, or big job to have an outstanding band and career. He always had 90 or so kids in his group, which at times approached half the student body of New Glarus High School. Larry came across a saying that he posted in his band room: *Do the best you can with what you have, where you are, right now!* Every time his band returned from a Six Flags competition they brought back not only high accolades but the "Best in Class" trophy. Larry has a delightful sense of humor, loves telling jokes, and is an avid accordion player who's heard 'em all!

Finally, I need to acknowledge the encouragement and support of my parents, Joseph and Effie, not only during my college years but while I was growing up and pursuing various hobbies, interests, and projects. They were young adults during the Depression and relied on their skills, Dad as a cook and musician and Mom as a beautician, to help them through those times. Like others of their generation, they hoped their children would have an easier time and live a good and prosperous life. The key to that was to go on and learn to do something worthwhile and useful. I don't think there was ever any doubt that one way or another that my sisters and I would go on to college or specialized training. I'm happy to say it all worked out okay in the end.

H. Ten Works I Believe All Band Conductors at All Levels Should Study

The problem with this list is that it suffers from errors of omission. Many of the works mentioned are quite traditional and show up on almost everybody's top ten. Much has been written about them, and my comments are, for the most part, short and subjective.

1. *The Well-Tempered Clavier* and the *Brandenburg Concerti* by J. S. Bach. The purity and genuineness of his music has allowed it to survive the Swingle Singers, the synthesizer, Ferruccio Busoni, and countless other transcribers, transformations, and arrangements for every imaginable combination of instruments and voices, most of which work.

2. Any Symphony or Concerto by W. A. Mozart. He seems incapable of writing anything bad.

3. Symphony no. 9, "Choral" by Ludwig van Beethoven. I have a private theory that the older you get, the more you appreciate and understand Beethoven.

4. Quintet in E-flat op. 44 by Robert Schumann. This is a masterpiece in the chamber music repertoire and one of Schumann's finest works.

5. Symphony no. 4 by Charles Ives. Any piece by Ives is good, except that darn "Variations on America." Ives was a fascinating and very quotable individual. My favorite goes something like ". . . a day in a Kansas wheat field is worth a year's study in Rome!"

6. *Concerto for Orchestra* and *Music for Strings, Percussion, and Celesta* by Béla Bartók. It has been my impression that Bartók's greatness went largely unrecognized by many during and even after his lifetime. The *Concerto* is now generally recognized as one of the great 20th-century orchestral masterpieces; the *Music for Strings* still sounds fresh and astonishing.

7. *Lincolnshire Posy* by Percy Grainger. Speaking of masterpieces, Grainger's ear for the traditional folksong and his gifts of orchestration and imagination resulted in what many believe to be one of the greatest pieces in the wind band repertoire.

8. Ballet Music and Piano Variations by Aaron Copland. His name is synonymous with American music. How can anyone who is a serious musician not have heard his music?

9. *An American in Paris,* Concerto in F, *Porgy and Bess*, and the Gershwin Songbook by George Gershwin. I was told there was a time when conservatory students would have been given the heave-ho if they were overheard practicing jazz or pop music in the practice facilities. I'm guessing that is no longer the case, thanks in part to Gershwin's music.

10. *The Rite of Spring* by Igor Stravinsky. This is probably the single most celebrated piece of 20th-century music. It still jolts and astounds as it nears the century mark (2013). One hundred years young!

I would also suggest *Silence,* a collection of John Cage's lectures and writings.

I. Ten Composers Whose Music Overall Speaks to Me in Especially Meaningful Ways

This list is also quite traditional, and the comments made before can apply here.

1. **Robert Schumann**, **Béla Bartók**, **Dimitri Kabelevski**, and **J. S. Bach** all wrote splendid music for young (and old) musicians.

2. **Gian Carlo Menotti**. I recall seeing *Amahl and the Night Visitors* when it was broadcast each Christmas, and it was the first music to affect me emotionally.

3. **Franz Schubert**. Beethoven often compels you to listen; Schubert invites.

4. **Scott Joplin**. I remember a critic describing the recording of *The Red Back Book* when it came out years ago as "some of the happiest music ever written." I have always enjoyed playing his rags.

5. **John Philip Sousa**. He was a master tunesmith who was able to take basically simple ingredients (a diatonic scale, the open tones of the bugle in *Semper Fidelis*, or two or three chords) and create thrilling, memorable, unmatched marches.

6. **Robert Schumann**. I have always been drawn to his music, which is highly personal and hardly ever outwardly flashy or virtuostic for its own sake. (The performer is well aware of the difficulties.) His music for piano students is essential repertoire.

7. **Sergei Rachmaninoff**. He was the last of the great performer-composers. Many would say his piano artistry was greater than his composing, but I have always found his music irresistible. Melodic, lush, and sprawling, the slow movement of the Symphony no. 2 is Rachmaninoff at his best.

8. **George Gershwin** and **Aaron Copland**. Gershwin is urban and brash, and his music has a "can-do optimism." Copland is rural and sturdy; he gave us "the promise of America."

9. **Maurice Ravel** and **Claude Debussy**. They were masters of orchestral color.

10. **Jerome Kern, Richard Rogers, Lorenz Hart, Oscar Hammerstein, Irving Berlin, Harold Arlen**, the **Gershwins, The Beatles**, and many others.

J. The Future of the Wind Band

I think there is a great opportunity for adult and community bands to flourish in the coming years because of all the Baby Boomers and *their* children who played in high school or college who might be looking for a worthwhile way to spend their leisure time. For those older adults who always wished they had stuck with trumpet or violin lessons, the New Horizons Band and Orchestra program, which began in 1991, is an organization that specifically targets adult beginners and continues to grow. (There is a fine article about the New Horizons organization in the July 2003 issue of *The Instrumentalist*, p. 18.)

I am usually able to attend the Midwest Clinic every year and am always amazed at the size and scope of this event, which continues to grow in terms of exhibitors, outstanding performing groups, and directors from all over the globe. This confirms the widespread appeal of the wind band. I think some of us get so involved with activities on our own turf that it is easy to forget that bands are alive and well in other countries and have their own traditions, many of which are beginning to catch on in America (i.e., the British brass band). I also scanned the list of new band pieces included in the 2003 Midwest program, and there were more than 700 new titles. *Somebody* must be playing all this music!

As long as music and music making remain a viable part of high school and college life, bands will be a part of it. Music educators have long believed in the power of music to enhance and transform one's life, and now it seems there is an ever-increasing pile of empirical evidence that music is, indeed, a positive force in people's lives, contributes to the learning process itself, and belongs in the curriculum of every primary and secondary school. There probably isn't a successful high school band, choir, or orchestra anywhere that doesn't count as its members some of the school's best athletes, scholars and school leaders, many of whom are the best musicians in the group.

As for new music being composed for band, I would guess (and I am really guessing) that many outstanding high school and college bands would be eager and willing to commission and play music by contemporary "A" list composers if they could afford the high commissioning fees many of these composers expect to be paid. I do have the impression that the more famous or well known the composer is, the more commissions he or she is likely committed to write for years in advance by orchestras with gifts and foundation money to spend or for chamber groups and concert soloists who wish to expand their repertoire.

K. Other Facets of My Everyday Life

I have always liked to tinker around and build things. When I was younger, that included hobbies of one sort or another: model planes, stamp collecting, fishing, and small-game hunting. I was never very good at team sports, but I learned to swim at an early age, have attempted to play tennis at one time or another, and, most recently, set forth "excavating" golf courses. Once I started piano lessons in fifth grade, music became more and more the center of my activities, except for the many jobs I undertook over the years.

I have always worked summer jobs (in "bottle factories" as a friend likes to put it) either from habit or necessity ever since I began mowing lawns when I was in grade school. They have, by choice, been blue jean jobs requiring some physical labor, which not only help to keep my weight down but serve as a counterpoint to the teaching life. At one time I did a lot of do-it-yourself plumbing and home remodeling, but when we moved out of our 80-year-old home a few years ago, I decided it was time to put away the hammer and nails, except for an occasional wine rack or set of shelves. Even though I'm retired from teaching, I still work (as of this writing) part-time at a traditional book bindery that has been family owned for five generations. My wife and I also spend a day each week caring for our granddaughter. My leisure activities include walking, gardening, and attending an occasional wine tasting or computer class. I try to keep active playing bassoon, reading, and listening to music on Wisconsin Public Radio.

L. Comprehensive List of Works for Band
Grade 1

All Ye Young Sailors—Pop. (2:00, 1988, Carl Fischer)

Barn Dance Saturday Night. (1:48, 1993, Carl Fischer e-print)

On the Colorado Trail. (2:15, 2003, Daehn Publications)

Grade 1.5

Chanson and March by Chedeville, arranged by La Plante. (2:20, 1984, Heritage Music Press)

The Red River Valley. (2:54, 2001, Daehn Publications)

Grade 2

Five Good-Natured Variations on Mr. Frog Went A-Courtin' (3:18, 2004, Great Works Publishing)

A March on the King's Highway. (2:30, 1988, Daehn Publications)

Monterey March. (2:30, 1988, Daehn Publications)

Western Portrait. (3:00, 1976, Byron Douglas)

Grade 2.5

Fantasy on a Fiddle Tune. Dedicated to Carol Kalscheur for 32 wonderful years of service to the DeForest (Wisconsin) School District. (3:00, 1997, unpublished)

A Little French Suite. (6:25, 1987, Bourne Co., print on demand)

Every Time I Feel the Spirit–Concert March. (2:30, 1988, Shawnee)

Prospect–Hymn for Band. Dedicated to Larry Daehn and the New Glarus (Wisconsin) High School Band. (4:00, 1983, Bourne Co.)

Triptych for Christmas. (4:00, 1977, Pro Art)

Variations and Fugal Finale–An Old Traditional Song. Commissioned by and dedicated to the Florida Bandmasters Association. (4:00, 1999, unpublished)

Grade 2-3

Come to the Fair. (2:58, 1995, Daehn Publications)

Nordic Sketches. Commissioned by the Mt. Horeb (Wisconsin) Middle School Band, Patty Schlafer, director, on the occasion of their 65th Anniversary Concert. (5:29, 1994, Daehn Publications)

The Thunder and the Roar. Commissioned by and for the 10th anniversary of the Tri-State Middle School Honor Band Festival. The tri-states are Wisconsin, Iowa, and Minnesota. The first performance was March 6, 2004, in Decorah, Iowa, with the composer conducting. (5:00, 2004, Daehn Publications)

The Voyageurs. Commissioned by the Wisconsin Chapter of the NBA and the Heid Music, Co. Dedicated to the Wisconsin All-State Junior Band. First performance at Wisconsin Rapids, January 26, 2002. (5:32, 2002, Daehn Publications)

Grade 3

Lakeland Portrait. (4:10, 1987, Kjos)

Grade 3-4

American Riversongs. Commissioned by and dedicated to the 1988-89 Oberlin High School Band, Stephen Johnson III, director, Oberlin, Ohio. (7:00, 1991, Daehn Publications)

English Country Settings. (7:07, 1997, Daehn Publications)

In the Forest of the King. To the Thoreau Middle School Symphonic Band of Vienna, Virginia, Richard H. Sanger, conductor. (8:40, 2000, Daehn Publications)

Legends and Heroes, American Folksong Suite, no. 1. Commissioned by and dedicated to the North Carolina Central District Bandmasters Association. (8:00, 2003, Daehn Publications)

Prairie Songs. Commissioned by the Central Middle School Band in Waukesha, Wisconsin, Laura Kautz Sindberg, conductor, with the assistance of the Wisconsin Sesquicentennial Commission. Because of an engraving error, the following acknowledgements were omitted: The Wisconsin Historical Society for "The Pinery Boy"; "The Turkey Song," reprinted by permission of the American Folklore Society from the *Journal of American Folklore,* 52, January-March 1939. (4:44, 1998, Daehn Publications)

Grade 4

The High Barbaree. (5:20, 2004, Daehn Publications)

chapter 7

david **Maslanka**

When I compose, I don't use a computer. I much prefer to sit quietly with pencil and paper. I do use a piano and am a regular worker; usually mornings are best, although when things are hot I will do three sessions a day. I can't sit for longer than two hours at a stretch. The composing is always going on, and ideas and awareness of connections will come at any time or place. I always come up with good tunes in the shower. I work on one piece at a time, but a series of pieces is always developing. I have what I call my "compost heap," the hundreds of pages of sketches that haven't made it into a composition yet. Something is always cooking in there.

A. Biography

I was born in 1943 and raised in New Bedford, Massachusetts, a former whaling and fishing town. I love the ocean but am uneasy being on or in it. My father worked for Revere Copper and Brass and was a hobby gardener and beekeeper. My mother was a housewife who raised me and my two older brothers; she had musical talent, but no training. The music gene came to me; I was the one who listened to her modest collection of classical records.

I started clarinet study in public school at age nine and played in bands through high school. The school music programs were not particularly distinguished; my best memories are of whacking away at Sousa and King marches in junior high. During my senior year, I went as a clarinetist to All-State Band, which Al Wright conducted, and was in the Greater Boston Youth Symphony Orchestra. These experiences pushed me toward music study in college.

I tried to compose a few things in high school but without guidance or success. I began more in earnest at Oberlin, where I pursued a music education degree while studying composition with Joseph Wood. A critical developmental point for me was the Junior Year Abroad program, which took me to the Mozarteum in Salzburg, Austria. My master's degree and PhD in music theory and composition were completed at Michigan State University under H. Owen Reed and Paul Harder.

From 1970 to 1990, I taught successively at the State University of New York at Geneseo, Sarah Lawrence College, New York University, and Kingsborough Community College of the City University of New York. I had my greatest development as teacher and composer while at Kingsborough, and this prepared me to take the step into freelance work. In 1990 my family and I moved to Missoula, Montana, where I have been busy writing music ever since. During the course of the last 40 years, I have found out a few things about composing and have made a lot of good friends.

B. Creative Process

Einstein remarked that he could no longer see a distinction between matter and energy, that what we called physical matter was the condensation of energy at certain points. To look closely at matter is to see it disappear into energy. Studies in quantum physics—although I am no expert—suggest that the key to what we call psychic phenomena lies in the nature of the electron—its ability to be both matter and energy, to move instantaneously (the quantum leap) from any point to any other point. We certainly seem solid enough in our daily lives, self-contained units who take care in crossing busy streets, but our minds deal with ideas, musical flow, imagination, inspiration, vision—all of which are entirely "non material"— yet the most powerful aspects of our beings.

The connection between our conscious existence in the "material" world of time and this "energy" realm is the whole point of composing. If our physical presence and our conscious awakeness can be called "this side," I refer to the "energy" realm—the realm of imagination, inspiration, vision, Higher Power—as "the other side." I think that music is one of the direct channels to and from the other side and that the human nervous system, in fact the whole human organism, is an antenna for receiving energy from the other side. However they define it, whether it be in religious, psychological, or secular terms, I think that all musicians are drawn to this connecting point like moths to the flame.

These thoughts developed over many years. As I look back I can see that from the very first eager hearing of music, I was on a path that would eventually allow me to perceive and use the joining of the conscious mind with the deep unconscious to develop a fuller sense of the mysteries of the other side.

Awareness of direct access to the unconscious first came through self-hypnosis, and then through a home-grown meditation process. I certainly felt flashes of inspiration in my early composing, but made my first conscious attempts at applying meditation to the compositional process in the early 1980s.

For me, composing begins by going into the meditation space, first to gain a sense of the energy of the people who have commissioned the music, specifically their need in asking for a piece, then to ask what wants to happen in the music. What I receive is a series of what I would call dream images that have strong spiritual-emotional feelings. People have asked how I know I'm not just "making all this up." I certainly make no absolute claim for my meditation images, but I have come to perceive a qualitative difference between these experiences and idle fantasy over time. I would suggest that idle fantasy itself is a potential first step on the continuum to powerful vision. I would also suggest that the procedure for developing useful meditation is not particularly mysterious. It is no more difficult or mysterious than learning to play an instrument. How do you get to Carnegie Hall?

I think every composer is drawn to a few powerful focal points such as preferred medium, type or period of music, or philosophical idea. One is magnetically drawn to a particular channel for creative flow. One of the most powerful of these for me has been the Catholic Mass. I am not a churchgoer, but very early in my creative life I began to think that there was something important about the Mass. It took a full 20 years before I felt ready to actually write a musical setting, which was completed in 1996. I feel that all of my composing before this lead to the Mass and that everything since has been a reflection of the Mass, although little of this is explicit. For me one of the central issues of the Mass is that of transformation, specifically the opening of the ego to receive a connection to the grace of God. This connection has literally saved my life and allowed me to grow into a useful human being.

When I compose, I don't use a computer. I much prefer to sit quietly with pencil and paper. I do use a piano and am a regular worker; usually mornings are best, although when things are hot I will do three sessions a day. I can't sit for longer than two hours at a stretch. The composing is always going on, and ideas and awareness of connections will come at any time or place. I always come up with good tunes in the shower. I work on one piece at a time, but a series of pieces is always developing. I have what I call my "compost heap," the hundreds of pages of sketches that haven't made it into a composition yet. Something is always cooking in there.

C. The Approach to Orchestration

For me, orchestration is an integral part of the conception process. The character of the music can arise out of my hearing an instrumental sound or combination in my mind. I do a lot of drawing with pastels, and this has a direct parallel to composing. My drawings rarely start as an attempt to make a picture of something but gradually emerge as different colors suggest both form and feeling.

Orchestration always starts with external requirements—the size and makeup of an ensemble or any hard restrictions. Creative work finds its point and force through restrictions, so I am not in the least bothered by them. I am particularly thoughtful about restrictions when writing for young players, and I try to hear a particular ensemble very closely and write to its strengths.

Which comes first, the chicken or the egg? Orchestral color or musical idea? It works both ways. A given music can suggest a color, or a color can suggest music. I invariably produce a short-form sketch of a piece before I make a full score. The sketch lays out the complete line of the piece, indicates textures—some fully developed, some a suggestion of what I want to do in the full score—and contains lots of indications for orchestration. This process allows the overall sound character of a piece to have a long incubation period. There are moments in composing when the full ensemble appears in the mind. When the whole quality emerges at once, there is a sense of having had a vision. There is a need to balance attention to the smallest details with an awareness of the layout of color over a whole composition. Qualities of orchestration contribute directly to form. The whole process of conceiving and orchestrating music for large ensembles is a truly complex one.

As I said earlier, I do not use a computer for composing or orchestrating; I much prefer a quiet inner hearing and feeling of the sound qualities that want to emerge. I believe that imagination is stunted by constant reference to computer playback. What seems on the surface to be a wonderful tool—you can actually hear your composition!—turns out in the end to seriously limit the ability to conceive sound. There is always a need for busy composers to get things done in a timely fashion, and the computer is wonderful for making parts. But in composing, allowing the music its full dream space is the real issue—not speed or convenience.

Even after all these years, a large, blank page is daunting. Even if I have heard a complete sound, there is still the matter of picking it apart and deciding on primary and secondary elements, blends, and balances. Over the years, I have relied on a short mantra: "Write what you know, then write what you don't know."

There is a distinct talent for hearing musical colors, and from my earliest compositions I have always had that spark. But the ability to orchestrate, like the ability to compose, most often takes long years to come to full flower. Every orchestration is a speculation, and for the young composer it is even more so. In my early work, I took my best guess and often wrote too much on the page. There is a nervousness about leaving blank spaces. My best ongoing instruction in orchestration is to hear pieces taken apart in rehearsals. I hear just the brass, just the winds, or even smaller parts from a texture, and understand that that sound would have been perfectly good all by itself. The more I have composed, the sparer my orchestration has become. Even the big moments have gotten much more specific. I am fascinated that out of a "standard" wind ensemble there are so many potential colors. It never wears out. I don't consciously try to invent new colors, but continually wait to be surprised by what wants to happen in new pieces. My scoring has been particularly noted for its use of percussion. I will say briefly that percussion has great emotional power and that I think of it not as an add-on or decoration, but as an integral voice in the wind ensemble.

D. Views from the Composer to the Conductor Pertaining to Score Study and Preparation

Conductors are very well trained in how to begin looking at scores, so I don't have a lot to say about score preparation—just a few fundamental ideas. Begin study with a metronome, and use the metronome until you have internalized the pulse rates for the whole piece. Understanding the rate at which the composer intends the music to unfold is the groundwork for opening into full power. Try to gain a sense of a piece before listening to recordings. If recordings are used too early in the process, they can wipe out your budding imagination for the music. Study a piece well in advance of having to conduct it, and let it sit quietly in your mind until it starts to tell you how it wants to sound. Visualizations can be useful. Any moment in a piece used as a point of meditation can provide access to your own dream/imagination space. Visualizations help you contact and bring to consciousness an underlying energy that is related to the music being studied.

For me, the issues of proportion and pacing emerge from that of passion, which I understand as finding the fullest value of the essential nature of a piece. The first step in finding essential nature is the conductor's imagination for sound. People have done my *A Child's Garden of Dreams* with a full band. Why? Similarly, my Concerto for Alto Saxophone and Wind Ensemble is scored for 33 players. Can it be played by 80? No. Conductors have said, "I can't do a piece for 25 players; what would I do with the rest of my ensemble?" Indeed. There is the standing ensemble, then there is what the composer asks.

It seems to me that the most interesting part of being a conductor would be finding out the true nature of something you have never heard before. This is where the conductor taps into creative flow and joins that process of creation initiated by the composer. Passion, or true musical value, begins with sound quality. Sound quality, like visible color, exists outside of time. And it is just that that makes it a direct link to the power of the other side, the power that wants to manifest itself in a performance. First of all, choose music that allows for this possibility. Finding the true value of sound means patient ensemble work with solo colors, blends, balances, and dynamics, that is, actually taking the time to get players to internalize the value that is required. As this happens, players take ownership of the piece.

Dynamics are a special issue. I have found that even with very good bands dynamics tend to merge toward an average: *ff* becomes *f*; *pp* becomes *mf*. Both players and conductors seem reticent about finding the true value of dynamics unless the composer is actually there to give permission.

A good sense of proportion and pacing emerge out of a long steeping process. There is flexibility in any music. One outcome of composing that I have truly enjoyed over the years is seeing conductors' personalities emerge through the music. There is no easy path. It is important that conductors find a composer whose music they admire and perform a lot of that composer's music over a long period of time. This allows an assimilation to a way of thinking and a growing recognition of what the music requires. It is also important to return to significant works a number of times. One of my long-time conductor colleagues, Steve Steele, has performed *A Child's Garden of Dreams* six times. On the fifth occasion he said, "I finally smiled!"

It is very useful to develop working relationships with composers. Direct visits are the best, but phone calls, e-mails, and sending rehearsal recordings are also extremely useful. I have done lots of good coaching through rehearsal recordings.

The last and most important point I want to discuss under the heading of passion is finding the point of release. Some conductors do this naturally, and for others it is the occasional happy surprise. The idea is to allow it to become consistent. There is a relationship between technical mastery and release into powerful musical sound, but the path is not direct. Finding the release point is bound up with personality and life issues, which is why it most often takes 20 years or more for the concept to develop enough to rise to the surface. After all the training and all the years of "being in charge," there comes the idea of the release point where you are no longer *in charge* of the music, but *participating with* the music. This is very hard because it feels initially like giving up control. It is not. It is expanding control to allow the music to make its fundamental movement. It is opening up to partnership with the other side. I have to write music this way. I am technically prepared with years of study and years of experience in writing. But if I try to decide in advance what a piece is supposed to be, try to impose a form or a mood, I can be shut down until I am ready to allow what wants to happen. Have I given up control? Hardly. The ego expands to accept its partnership with a much bigger circle of contributing forces.

E. The Relationship Between the Composer and the Commissioning Party

Commissioning is a grand adventure, a great leap of faith. It is hard to imagine buying anything of comparable expense that you can't look at, test drive, touch, taste, or smell before you commit to it. Like composing, commissioning, in my opinion, is neither arbitrary nor accidental. There is a coming together of the needs (known and unknown) of the commissioning party, the needs and abilities (especially the ability to be intuitively open to what wants to happen) of the composer, and the impulses coming from the other side. Commissioning and composing become a kind of deep prayer that something good, powerful, and useful will come into the world.

I don't need to say too much about the technical aspects of commissioning. Contracts are useful, but they should be simple and free of legalese. My guide for fees and contracts is a brochure on the commissioning process put out by Meet The Composer. Commissions, like everything else in life, proceed best on good faith and earnest effort from all concerned. In the whole of my professional life, I have tried to do my best work with each commission and have never missed a deadline.

F. Views on the Teaching of Composition and How to Mentor the Young Composer

I do believe that the composer is born, and, all things being equal, will gravitate toward music and what he or she needs by way of instruction. In any case, if they are to be good composers, they cannot avoid the major aspects of music: melody, counterpoint, harmony, rhythm, form, texture, and orchestration. For me, technical development from a historical perspective is essential. Most of my life has been spent in the 20th century. During that time, an amazing number of compositional procedures evolved. Some of these presumed to push aside history, to say that "old" musical language had nothing to say to modern times. I have found that the spirit of music does not pay much attention to theorists and "isms." Melody has not died, counterpoint has not died, tonality has not died, feeling from the heart has not died (just the opposite: it is so much more of a requirement these days), and live performances have not fallen by the wayside. Computers have seemingly made it easier to be a composer. This is true only in a very circumscribed way.

Music must affect the composer forcefully, and the music he or she creates must communicate an energy forcefully to someone else. Much has been made of the idea that the composer should not try to dictate feeling to a listener, that we are all separate beings, and one person cannot possibly know the experience of another or have the same response to a piece of music. I disagree with these ideas altogether. Like that of spoken language, the evolution of musical language has been a communal venture for as long as humans have inhabited this planet. The perception of music rests on thousands of years of shared feelings, and people are built pretty much like one another. The hard wiring is the same. Ways of perceiving and learning are comparable, and perception of music will be comparable. Anyone who ignores or denies this does so at his or her own peril. The young composer has to learn the language of the past and learn it very thoroughly. This in no way denies the new but gives a grounded context for the emergence of the individual voice. What the above suggests is that music is a communal process, and the young composer must trace the complex path to a useful connection with a community.

Beyond technical development, there is the "other side" of composing, the reason why composers gravitate to composing in the first place. This cannot be taught directly. I think it is a kind of "mother's milk" that the young composer absorbs by being around a good older composer. Everyone's connection to the "other side" and his or her path toward it is different. Composing is a "whole person" occupation, and that "whole person" expands and meets its life issues at its own rate. Formal education is just the briefest beginning of this process. The best that can happen for young composers is to be deeply impressed by the work of their teachers and other developed composers and to be deeply struck by music in performance. These are important first openings to what must become a lifelong exploration of the "other side."

I taught very little composition in my 20-year academic career. My most interesting work has come since then. I meet interested student composers and young professionals in my travels, and they often contact me with questions or ask me to look at their music. It has been very gratifying to see their development. Teaching is about patience and saying the right thing at the right time. People are only able to take the steps they are ready to take.

G. Individuals Who Have Been Especially Influential in My Development and Career

My family was not overtly musical, but my mother's interest in listening to classical recordings was my opening to that world. My first clarinet teacher, Frank Bayreuther, was a kindly man who steered me to join the Greater Boston Youth Symphony Orchestra. The conductor, Marvin Rabin, was also a kind man to me and a very strong musician and teacher. Being in the Youth Symphony tipped the balance in my decision to study music in college.

At Oberlin I found my way to Joseph Wood, who was, on the surface, a somewhat forbidding and curmudgeonly man. Wood allowed me into his composition class and then took me as a private student. He helped me make the transition from an undergraduate music education major to a graduate school composition major. I studied with H. Owen Reed at Michigan

State for five years. It was under Reed that I gained my first real strength and maturity as a composer, and I acknowledge him as my primary teacher and mentor. He said surprisingly little to me in lessons but was nonetheless a fine teacher. He was an energetic man, quite settled in himself, an easy, natural musician, and an accomplished and active composer. I think being in the presence of these qualities for that length of time allowed me to grow in my own way, and to understand, at least subconsciously, that I could be a composer like this composer—the real thing. Paul Harder, Russell Friedewald, and Gomer Llewelyn Jones were my teachers in 16th- and 18th-century counterpoint, and I am eternally grateful to them.

Paul Harder gave me one of the sharpest orienting lessons of my young life, and it is a moment I recall as decisive. I studied composition with Harder for one semester while Reed was on leave, at the time of the Martin Luther King and Robert Kennedy assassinations. I expressed my dismay in a lesson by asking what the point of composing was in such a troubled world. He said simply, "If that's how you feel, then go do something else." I knew very quickly that I wasn't going to do something else and that, for better or worse, composing was my path.

In my early professional life, I had the great good fortune to have several stays at the MacDowell Colony in Peterborough, New Hampshire, which is an artists colony for composers, writers, and visual artists. I met Barney Childs there in 1974. He was another curmudgeon! It seems I get along well with cranky people; what does *that* say about me? Barney became friend and mentor, offering me my first commissions and sustaining me with his correspondence through the darkest period of my life. The letters smelled like cigars. My ongoing friendship with Jim Willey dates from 1970 when I joined the faculty at SUNY–Geneseo. He has been my composing colleague and talking companion about music for the whole of my professional life.

Frederick Fennell conducted the premiere of my first wind ensemble work (Concerto for Piano, Winds and Percussion) at Eastman. He was even-tempered and highly competent and treated me and my music with sincere regard. He recommended me to John P. Paynter, who took up the Concerto and subsequently commissioned both *A Child's Garden of Dreams* and Symphony no. 2. I owe a lot to Fennell and Paynter for seeing something in my music and producing fine, energized performances of these really difficult pieces. Through these two fine conductors, my path was set in writing for winds.

I owe a huge amount to the many conductors who have steadfastly supported my work over the years. They have become colleagues and fast friends. Their passion for music and for the big adventure into unknown territory has contributed enormously to my evolution as composer and teacher. Among these are Bill Rowell, Gary Green, Steve Steele, Ray Lichtenwalter, Gregg Hanson, Jerry Junkin, Thom Wubbenhorst, Larry Gookin, John Whitwell, Tim Salzman, and John Combs.

Critical people appear at critical moments. Among them was Dr. Anthony J. DeLuca, my psychologist in the 1970s and 1980s. We were radically different, and our personalities banged into each other frequently. But I am alive today because of our work. He opened me to internal exploration, the thought of Freud and of Jung, and sparked in me the search for a spiritual path—all of which has profoundly affected my composing life.

Arthur Cohn was another gruff personality. He oversaw the Serious Music Department at Carl Fischer for many years. His whole life was spent fostering new music and new composers. He was the one who pushed me to accept myself as a really good composer—not an easy step! His committed support was one element that allowed me to move from academic life to independent work.

My wife, Alison, has been my encourager and protector of space for most of my creative life. She has been a key element in allowing my music to reach full value over the years. She is not a trained musician, but her sense of what is good and not so good in music is very sharp indeed. She says music has to make her want to sing or dance; if it doesn't, she is quickly not interested. This plain and practical view of music has kept me a little closer to earth than I might otherwise be, and has guided a lot of my music making. She is my constant emotional, intellectual, and spiritual companion—my best friend!

H. Ten Works I Believe All Band Conductors at All Levels Should Study

There are too many pieces to choose from! I have included a sampling of older works that have influenced me strongly. They are in no particular order. My approach to music study has always been to follow whatever interests me. Something will always "light up," and I go look for recordings and scores.

1. *Quintet for Clarinet and Strings* by Johannes Brahms. This is one of the last works of Brahms, written after he had officially stopped composing. Brahms had an unfailing ear

for melody, and his melodies are seldom "square." He will use a regular meter as a grid pattern for very subtle and supple rhythmic flow. He was a learned master of counterpoint and Baroque and Classical forms and was particularly adept at variations. His music was considered out of date by the "progressives" of his day. But good music is good music regardless of when it was written. Bach was another "retro" composer who did pretty well! I chose the *Quintet* because it represents the summation of Brahms' technical, emotional, and spiritual capacities—deep feeling elucidated by clear thinking.

2. *Requiem* by Giuseppe Verdi. He had the ability to write amazing dramatic scenes out of the simplest of materials. His tunes are often deceptively naïve sounding, yet he had an instinct for gut power, which he could let loose to its maximum hair-raising effect. The *Requiem* is a fully developed example of his gifts.

3. The *Goldberg Variations* by J. S. Bach show his unparalleled capacity for integrating an intellectual idea—in this case a series of canons at progressively larger intervals—with engaging musical flow. There is an effortless submergence of contrapuntal technique and structural principles into compelling musical statements.

4. 371 Chorales by Bach. Those of you who know my music know my connection to the chorales. They are miniature musical gems and comprise a method book for the study of melody. Singing them is the best way of getting inside them.

5. *L'Apres Midi d'un Faun* by Claude Debussy is, in my opinion, one of the finest small pieces ever written. His genius in this piece was to spin out a series of feelings and

moods of nature through the subtle evolution of a single motive. This process was not development in the Classical sense but a seemingly unfettered flow of feeling and spirit. The spareness of his orchestration is a lesson for all composers—everything sounds.

6. *Symphony of Psalms* by Igor Stravinsky. Everyone lists Stravinsky's *Le Sacre du Printemps* as a piece to study, and I don't see how a conducting student can escape being exposed to it. So I instead recommend the *Symphony of Psalms*. After the early ballets, Stravinsky moved deeply into a kind of formal objectivism, which he based on Classical models. The result in a piece like *Symphony of Psalms* is elegant music. Its passion arises out a sparseness and clarity of musical speech. I watched Stravinsky conduct this work at Oberlin in 1965, and the image of him on the podium is still etched in my mind.

7. *Deserts* by Edgard Varese. The Oberlin Wind Ensemble under Kenneth Moore performed this piece in the early 1960s. This was an astonishing experience for me as a young student. It not only opened my ears to that unique sound world but got me thinking about percussion. Like other "one of a kind" composers, Varese's music is riveting and compelling. The character of his sounds is bracing and refreshing to my ears.

8. Symphony no. 13 "Babi Yar" by Dmitri Shostakovich. If I have a musical hero, it is Shostakovich. His composing was an act of sheer bravery, for many years a potentially deadly cat-and-mouse game between him and Josef Stalin. He wrote 15 wonderful symphonies. Symphony no. 13 is a powerful memorial for Jews killed in Russia during World War II. This was one more political bombshell for

Shostakovich, and I am drawn to this work because of its sustained drama. Shostakovich had the ability to open a big musical space with a single gesture.

9. *Survivor from Warsaw* by Arnold Schoenberg is a brief but wrenchingly powerful dramatic work. One of his later pieces, it has all the qualities of sparseness and directness that come from knowing who you are and what you need to say. It doesn't concede anything to niceness.

10. *War Requiem* by Benjamin Britten. He was one of the easiest of natural musicians. I'm sure he worked hard at his composing, but everything has an effortless flow. He was given to clear and engaging melodies and a harmonic language rooted in English folk style. He was nonetheless a thoroughly modern and dramatically powerful composer. With words from the *Missa pro Defunctis* and the poems of Wilfred Owen, the *War Requiem* is both a memorial and a huge anti-war statement; it is a compellingly dramatic work on an epic scale.

I. Ten Composers Whose Music Overall Speaks to Me in Especially Meaningful Ways

All music is about the receiving from the "other side." This characterizes every kind of music—folk music through art music—for all time. Music is the ritual voice of a people, and is that thing that both joins them to a sacred power and is a living manifestation of that power. The progress of Western culture has been marked by the evolution of consciousness and a sense of self. This is not a straight-line or inevitable process. The names of our stylistic periods—Renaissance, Baroque, Classical, Romantic, and the less-defining designations for our own time: Modern, Post-Modern, Post-Historical (Someone in the future will have to rename us!) are all indications of qualities of consciousness and movements toward self-awareness. I can only make a suggestion here without developing the thesis fully, but each composer named below has spoken to me on that level of awareness of the connection to the deeper power. Each expanded an aspect of consciousness in their culture.

1. **J. S. Bach**. The enormity of his achievement is staggering. He was not given to "self expression" as we think of it but much more to an objective, logical construction. The effect is not easy to explain. It is not personal, not ego-passionate, yet hugely beneficial and moving. His musical message was about the music, not about himself. I think each era since Bach's has been forced to deal more and more directly with the issue of ego—first to experience its effects and then consciously to transcend it. We have come to a point in our age where this is a requirement in order that we not destroy ourselves.

2. **Joseph Haydn**. He and Mozart are the major figures of the Classical era. Without diminishing Mozart (Who could do that?), Haydn has always drawn me in more. His lengthy career was characterized by a commitment to process and to the on-time production of music to fulfill a specific need. His music is quirky and interesting; he constantly worked at odd angles to the boundaries of accepted forms.

3. **Ludwig van Beethoven**. He was the eruptive interjection of ego-self in Western culture. He was the first composer whose personality was, and remains, a major issue. I can relate to his struggle to transcend personal problems and to make a powerful statement.

4. **Franz Schubert** has always spoken to me because of his effortless flow of beautiful melodies. He was not given to development as such (and neither am I), which puts him in line with the late Romantics, especially Debussy.

5. I see in **Claude Debussy** a clear breakthrough in consciousness. He took from what existed (he started as a big fan of Wagner) but was able to follow a flow that went wherever it wanted. His music shows a connection to the deep unconscious in the Jungian sense. It appears to me that he was able to enter the deep dream space.

   My ancestry is central European, and I am drawn to the dark powers of Mussorgsky, Schoenberg, and Shostakovich.

6. **Modest Mussorgsky** had a direct, "unpretty" connection to raw musical power. He was able to tap in and let it loose. This was in the context of a very messy and unsuccessful life. A Mussorgsky fact: He started 16 opera projects in his brief career but completed only one.

7. **Arnold Schoenberg** has always been a favorite of mine. His writing has been termed "expressionistic," that is, moving toward the dark and troubled side of the human psyche. His writing is deeply rooted in Classical concepts, out of which he forged an elegant, powerful, and quite new personal voice. Pieces that I would recommend, along with *Survivor from Warsaw,* are *Five Pieces for Orchestra* and the opera *Moses and Aaron.* While, in my opinion, Debussy is Jungian, I would say that Schoenberg is Freudian—among the first "psychological" composers.

8. **Dmitri Shostakovich** is the direct expression model for my own symphonies and concertos. His work was deeply connected to the life and pain of the world around him. His large works most often had a social, political, or personal

subtext. He had an instinct for scope, dramatic pacing, and sheer sustained power. He was also extremely patient with slow and quiet music. His final String Quartet (no. 15) has five movements, all marked *Adagio*!

9. **Igor Stravinsky** has been a seminal influence for every composer since his time. He was a technical virtuoso. Whereas Shostakovich was deeply personal, it seems to me that Stravinsky backed away from personal expression. The middle and late works tend toward the enigmatic. They are finely crafted, wonderful pieces of music but removed from the mess of worldly strife. This is a quality that I admire in his work because it transcends the personal and reaches for a place beyond individual psychology.

10. **Charles Ives** reached deep into the American unconscious. We tend to look at "old-time" America through Norman Rockwell eyes, whereas Ives touched a deeply conflicted and chaotic core of late 19th- and early 20th-century American life. I greatly admire his ability to bring all of this to the surface in such works as the *Concord Sonata, Three Places in New England,* and especially Symphony no. 4. I love the raging jumble of sound in the Symphony. Rhythm moves in large glacial blocks, making the evolution of shapes and the formal process as a whole into entirely new things. I also admire his courage in writing something that he knew had little chance of being performed or accepted.

J. The Future of the Wind Band

In the 1960s, when I was a graduate student working with H. Owen Reed, he advised us with all gravity that a "serious" composer was allowed to write one work for band. If he wrote more, he would be written off as *not* serious. Well, that thinking has certainly changed, but not altogether. There has been mutual development between composers and wind bands. Bands and wind ensembles have consistently gotten better, and good composers have responded more and more with new and fine works. I know that my music has inspired wind bands and their conductors to perform really well, and that has inspired me in turn. It has allowed me to hear deeply into these instrument combinations and to write with increasing clarity and consciousness. I know that this is also true of many other composers. I believe this central musical excitement between composers and ensembles, an excitement that is shared directly with audiences, is one major key to the future of wind bands. There is still a cultural attitude that the orchestra is "high art" and that the band is a poor relation. Many band people chafe at this seeming lack of respectability, but I don't think it is particularly important. *All* concert music, from the highest professional levels to the lowest school levels, is more or less invisible in our society. We live in a visual age dominated by movies, TV, and computers. Music is seen almost exclusively as entertainment, and almost all entertainment is passively received with the push of a button.

On the other hand, there is a thirst, a soulful need, for a direct, active connection to a deeper experience, and wind bands—public school, university, community—existing as they do at the invisible grass roots level, provide this opportunity. As long as this living contact with imaginative force is available through wind bands, they will thrive. At the core of this place of contact is the willingness to have an imaginative adventure, and this challenges the best, deepest, highest, brightest, most soulful, and most thoughtful qualities in all concerned.

It is not important that the "best" composers be induced to write for winds, or that concerts be in "important" halls and reviewed by major critics. All of this will happen on its own as the inherent vitality of the wind band experience moves forward. In this regard, it is important that most wind bands are non-professional. It is wonderful to have professional bands, but school groups are freer to explore new works and can devote the hours needed to produce truly settled and insightful performances of mostly unfamiliar pieces. The future of wind bands and the music being written for them rests on this patient and largely unheralded body of work.

K. Other Facets of My Everyday Life

My composing has always been balanced and fed by other things. I feel a need to know something about the world, and that has led to persistent reading in history, anthropology, paleontology, psychology, religion, mysticism, and politics, among other things. I am not drawn to fiction but will read the occasional novel, and am a long-term subscriber to *Natural History* magazine. I have an abiding interest in the Civil War, especially in the life of Lincoln, and in watching the unfolding in our own time of the issues coming out of that war. I don't read very much at all about music, nor do I listen to a lot of music. If I am composing, which is most of the time, I don't want to hear anything else. I am involved with meditation and dream work. I do most of my meditation work while taking long walks.

My primary hobby is drawing with pastel colors. I have the drawing things set up in my composing room and will often move from one to the other. I have found over the long term that surprising and interesting themes have emerged from my unconscious through the drawing. It is parallel to composing in this regard.

Alison and I have raised three children, Stephen, Matthew, and Kathryn, and I help Alison care for her horses. I am not a rider, but I enjoy feeding the horses, hauling hay, and doing general upkeep. It is a very interesting feeling to be accepted by these large creatures. I am also the family cook and love going to grocery stores. All that food! So many choices!

L. Comprehensive List of Works for Band

I have never attached grade levels to my pieces. *Rollo Takes a Walk* and *Prelude on a Gregorian Tune* are published by Neil Kjos; all others are with Carl Fischer.

A Child's Garden of Dreams. Commissioned by John and Marietta Paynter. Premiered February 1982 by the Northwestern University Wind Ensemble, John P. Paynter, conductor. (35:00, 1981)

Concerto for Alto Saxophone and Wind Ensemble. Consortium commission headed by Jerry Junkin of the University of Texas at Austin and Gregg Hanson of the University of Arizona. Premiered March 2000 at the North American Saxophone Alliance National Convention, University of Arizona Wind Ensemble, Gregg Hanson, conductor, Joseph Lulloff, saxophone. (45:00, 1999)

Concerto for Marimba and Band. Commissioned by the U.S. Air Force Band. Premiered March 1990 at the Percussive Arts Society International Convention, Philadelphia, Pennsylvania, U.S. Air

Force Band, Steven Grimo, conductor, Randall Eyles, marimba. (17:00, 1990)

Concerto for Piano, Winds and Percussion. Premiered March 1979, Eastman Wind Ensemble, Frederick Fennell, conductor, William Dobbins, piano. (20:00, 1974-76)

Concerto for Piano, Winds and Percussion no. 2. Commissioned by Steven Hesla. Premiered February 2003 by the Hellgate High School Wind Ensemble, Missoula, Montana, John H. Combs, conductor, Steven Hesla, piano. (27:00, 2002)

Golden Light—A Celebration Piece. Commissioned by South Shore Conservatory, Cohassett, Massachusetts. Premiered by the South Shore Conservatory Senior Wind Ensemble, Malcolm W. Rowell, Jr., conductor. (8:00, 1990)

Heart Songs. Commissioned by Joe Gunn for the Harwood Junior High School Symphonic Band, Bedford, Texas. Premiered April 1998 by the Harwood Junior High School Symphonic Band, Christopher Ferrell, conductor. (15:00, 1998)

Hell's Gate—for Three Saxophones and Wind Ensemble. Commissioned by Hellgate High School Symphonic Band, Missoula, Montana. Premiered March 1997 by the Hellgate High School Symphonic Band, John H. Combs, conductor. (17:00, 1996)

In Memoriam. Commissioned by the University of Texas at Arlington Wind Ensemble. Premiered March 1990 at the Texas Music Educators Association Conference, San Antonio, Texas, University of Texas at Arlington Wind Ensemble, Ray C. Lichtenwalter, conductor. (14:00, 1989)

Laudamus Te. Commissioned by the Mount St. Charles Academy Symphonic Band, Woonsocket, Rhode Island. Premiered April 1995 by the Mount St. Charles Academy Symphonic Band, Marc Blanchette, conductor. (13:00, 1995)

Mass for SATB chorus, boys chorus, soprano and baritone soli, organ, and wind ensemble. Consortium Commission headed by Gregg Hanson of the University of Arizona. Premiered April 1996 at the St. Thomas the Apostle Church, Tucson, Arizona, University of Arizona Wind Ensemble, Gregg Hanson, conductor. (110:00, 1995)

Montana Music: Chorale Variations. Commissioned by the Bishop Ireton High School Wind Ensemble, Alexandria, Virginia. Premiered May 1993 by the Bishop Ireton High School Wind Ensemble, Garwood Whaley, conductor. (14:00, 1993)

Morning Star. Commissioned by the Grand Ledge (Michigan) High School Wind Ensemble. Premiered by the Grand Ledge High School Wind Ensemble, Michael Kaufman, conductor. (8:00, 1997)

Prelude on a Gregorian Tune. For young bands. (3:00, 1980)

Rollo Takes a Walk. For young bands. (4:00, 1980)

Sea Dreams—Concerto for Two Horns and Wind Orchestra. Consortium Commission headed by Thomas Bacon. Premiered April 1998 by the Arizona State University Wind Ensemble, Richard Strange, conductor, Thomas Bacon and James Graber, horns. (30:00, 1997)

Song Book for Flute and Wind Ensemble. Consortium commission headed by Hal Ott and Larry Gookin of Central Washington University. Premiered July 2001 at the National Flute Association Convention, Dallas, Texas, Texas Wind Symphony, Ray C. Lichtenwalter, conductor, Stephanie Jutt, flute. (48:00, 2001)

Symphony no. 2. Commissioned by the Big Ten Band Directors Association. Premiered March 1987 at the CBDNA National Convention, Evanston, Illinois, Northwestern University Wind Ensemble and Symphonic Band, John P. Paynter, conductor. (35:00, 1986)

Symphony no. 3. Commissioned by the University of Connecticut Research Council. Premiered May 1992 by the University of Connecticut Wind Ensemble, Gary Green, conductor. (48:00, 1991)

Symphony no. 4. Consortium Commission headed by Jerry Junkin of the University of Texas at Austin. Premiered February 1994 at the TMEA convention, San Antonio, Texas, University of Texas at Austin Wind Ensemble, Jerry Junkin, conductor. (27:00, 1993)

Symphony no. 5. Consortium commission headed by Stephen K. Steele of Illinois State University. Premiered March 2001 at the CBDNA National Convention, University of North Texas at Denton, Illinois State University Wind Ensemble, Stephen K. Steele, conductor. (40:00, 2000)

Symphony no. 7. Consortium headed by Stephen K. Steele of Illinois
State University. Premiere: March 2005 at Illinois State University,
Normal, Illinois, Illinois State University Wind Ensemble, Stephen
K. Steele, conductor. (30:00, 2004)

Tears. Commissioned by the Wisconsin CBDNA. Premiered at the
March 1994 WMEA Convention, Madison, Wisconsin, Allan
McMurray, conductor. (14:00, 1993)

Testament. Consortium commission headed by Joseph Grzybowski and
the L.D. Bell High School Band of Hurst, Texas. Premiered March
2002 at the TMEA Convention, San Antonio, Texas, Texas
Christian University Wind Ensemble, Bobby R. Francis, conductor.
(11:00, 2001)

Traveler. Commissioned by the University of Texas at Arlington Band
Alumni Association. Premiered April 2004 at Meyerson Hall,
Dallas, Texas, University of Texas at Arlington Wind Ensemble,
Ray C. Lichtenwalter, conductor. (14:00, 2003)

A Tuning Piece: Songs of Fall and Winter. Commissioned by Kappa
Kappa Psi. Premiered in 1995 at the Kappa Kappa Psi National
Convention, Orlando, Florida, James Croft, conductor. (17:00,
1995)

UFO Dreams—Concerto for Euphonium and Wind Ensemble.
Commissioned by the Hellgate High School Symphonic Wind
Ensemble, Missoula, Montana. Premiered March 1999 by the
Hellgate High School Wind Ensemble, John H. Combs, conductor,
Matt Maslanka, euphonium. (17:00, 1998)

Variants on a Hymn Tune. Commissioned by the Missoula All-City
Winds. Premiered February 1995 at the MENC Northwestern
Convention, Spokane, Washington, Missoula All-City Winds, John
Schuberg, conductor, Matt Maslanka, euphonium. (5:00, 1994)

chapter **8**

philip Sparke

What we need fewer of are the self-styled experts who think their opinions about programming and repertoire are better than anybody else's and clutter the band periodicals with pomposity and self promotion. Can't they see that this is a matter of taste and not an absolute? I cannot stand country music but would not dream of postulating that my taste (even though my experience and education could perhaps be considered more sophisticated) is better *than that of a country music fan. There are many more [Kenny] Rogers fans than concert band fans, after all.*

A. Biography

Born in London in 1951, I have spent most of my life in the south of England. My earliest musical experiences came rather late, I suppose, as neither of my parents were musical. My father owned a wind-up gramophone and a small collection of 78s; the only one I can remember is Beethoven's Fifth, which took up four records and therefore had a number of breaks. (I'm still perturbed when I hear it play straight through on CD!) I learned the recorder at school at about the age of 9, and my parents bought an old upright piano a couple of years later, which I never learned to play properly but did start to pick out tunes on.

I later studied violin for a few years but changed to trumpet, which I found much more fun. I taught myself to play and as a result have never been able to play it properly. I wrote a few pieces for local amateur symphony orchestras (now fortunately lost!) and, on leaving school, applied for a place at the Royal College of Music in London, where I studied composition, piano, and trumpet. I don't think I was a huge success there but had some marvelous tutors in all three disciplines who taught me more about life in general than music in particular.

I was fortunate that my composition tutor, Philip Cannon, also conducted the newly formed RCM Wind Orchestra, the idea of which was to keep the many excess wind players who couldn't get into the college's orchestras occupied. This was my first experience with a concert band; I occasionally played with the group and also wrote a couple of works for them. Luckily the first piece I wrote, *Gaudium*, was accepted for publication by Boosey & Hawkes, although I don't think anyone ever bought a copy!

While at the College, I played for several local operatic societies for pocket money and met a drummer who also played in the local brass band. They happened to be a very good band indeed, and he took me to a couple of rehearsals. So I wrote a couple of pieces for them to try out and caught the brass band "bug," which led me to eventually working for R. Smith & Co., the brass and concert band publishers, as a copyist. I wrote several pieces, which they published, but eventually left to join their local rival, Studio Music Company, where I stayed for 17 years as music editor and CD producer until I left in 2000 to become a full-time composer and start my own publishing company, Anglo Music Press.

The number of commissions began to grow and grow (both for brass and concert bands), and Studio Music was great in spreading my name internationally, specifically by taking me to the annual Midwest Clinic in Chicago from 1987 on. Contacts I made at the Clinic lead to a number of prestigious commissions, including the Tokyo Kosei Wind Orchestra (*Celebration*) and the U.S. Air Force Band (*Dance Movements*), two pieces that have been particularly good to me.

As I said, in 2000 I decided to have a go at writing full-time, something that I always thought I would not be able to do, as I had previously been a "part-time" composer. First, I wondered about having to come up with ideas all the time, and second, if I could do that, I had doubts that the world needed so much "Sparke!" So far it seems to be working out well enough, and I am combining writing with an increasing number of guest-conducting engagements and contest adjudicating, as well as the everyday needs of organizing Anglo Music Press, which mostly seems to be deleting unwanted e-mails!

B. The Creative Process

I guess most composers are asked at some time or another, "Where do the ideas come from?" It is certainly the question I get asked most often, and the answer is: "I don't know." I sometimes try to explain things a bit more by asking the questioners about *their* job and point out there are things that *they* do every day that I don't understand or have a concept of how to achieve. But my favorite analogy is the graphic designer. I'm amazed how people can see the most appropriate color for a particular design or picture because I don't have that visual capacity at all. This is by way of pointing out that we all have different skills and talents and that composing is no different from any other; it just seems to be a complete mystery to some—even some experienced musicians. Well, it's not really a mystery. It is true that I don't know where the ideas come from, but that aside, for me it is much more a question of perspiration than inspiration.

Since 2000, when I started to publish my own music, I have been writing virtually full-time. I start at 8:00 a.m. and usually work though until 5:00 or 6:00 p.m. when my wife and son come home from work and the nursery. This is not all creative composing; I also set all my work on a computer program (score and parts) so that when I have reached a compositional hiatus, I can do some part-extraction, editing, or proofing. (I don't think I could compose all day.)

If those things get on my nerves, I'll go out for a walk, do some household chores, or run some errands. If I'm stuck with a piece, I find a walk does wonders to free the imagination. In fact, most of my favorite bits have been composed while walking—I even remember some of these when I get home!

I don't think that I've written any two pieces in the same way. Usually the music has no program, but sometimes it does. Often the stimulation is a musical one, but sometimes it can be an event or landscape. The only consistent aspect of *all* my pieces is that I start with the first note and compose straight through; the music is always a result of what has gone on before. I have rarely started in the middle of a work (never, unless it was a multi-movement piece) and cannot (not that I've tried much) work by assembling a collection of sketches or ideas and forming them into a piece. That all seems a little mathematical to me. The one time I started with a melody and tried to write music to introduce and work up to that melody, it was like trying to fit a size-11 foot into a size-7 boot! So I always start with the first note and work on from there. I hope that this has the effect of making my music sound spontaneous (at least, that's the idea!), but I definitely know that it means I can write music that has some sort of logical harmonic and textural progress.

I will always start off with how long and what grade level a piece should be and and usually have a concept of the form of the piece I intend to write (multi-movement or through-composed, for example) as well as its color and texture. By that I mean I can hear the effect of the piece, whether light and bright, heavy and serious, or a mixture, before I hear any specific notes or harmonies. In nearly every case, however, the piece takes on a life of its own and goes its own way, but what I believe have been the most satisfying pieces to compose are those in which I have set the mood I want in the first bar and then go off in the direction I have in my head. The trouble is that what the composer considers successful (in my case, if the piece ends up near to the original concept) is very often of no interest to listeners or performers; those pieces of mine that seem to be the most popular are those in which I felt I had little or no control over where the piece went, and the music seemed to write itself. I think that's not a bad thing, really—the pieces I enjoy least (as a listener) are those in which I can hear the composer's brain at work (some sets of variations, for example, or when the music has an extra-musical "concept"), and I would much rather listen to someone like Mahler whose music seems driven more by his heart than his head. What I try to do is take the listener on an emotional journey as well as a musical one.

In terms of what comes first, this again varies; sometimes I hear the whole score. (One four-minute piece actually came to me in its entirety while waiting for the green signal at a traffic light—it was weird and has unfortunately never happened again!) Sometimes the initial idea is just a melodic line or a texture, and I then have to work out which notes are needed to create that texture. Every piece needs its own approach. I don't know why this is the case, except that I'm convinced most composers in the band field today only have half a tank of talent and then work hard to get the piece done. This is not an insult, I just mean that we have no Bachs or Mozarts, who seemed to be able to do exactly as they liked with their music; most of us mortals simply have to do the best with the equipment we have. Composers rarely talk to each other about this (which is why these books are such a great idea!), but I'm sure most of us simply have to put in the hours to get a piece onto paper. Unless we are very lucky, it's a struggle—well, perhaps that's putting it too strongly; let's just say it's more a question of application than divine inspiration.

C. The Approach to Orchestration

Orchestration is as personal to most composers as the compositional process itself, I guess; indeed, for many it is *part* of the process itself—certainly for me. I always hear the sound of anything I write and rarely "orchestrate" after the creative process. I'm sure this is quite common, although I know many composers who write "black-and-white" music first in a short score and "color" it later with orchestration. Whatever works best, I guess!

I think we can divide the subject into two halves: a) learning how the various instruments work (this is never-ending) and b) how to best combine them to produce the desired sounds. The first is the fun bit. Composers are generally loners, but contact with bands and players is the most enjoyable part of the job for me, and I never miss the chance to ask (or better, discover during a rehearsal) what works instrumentally and what doesn't. My latest discovery is to ensure that the oboes always enter on a downbeat. Reading orchestration books is a help but is not a patch on working with amateur players and finding out their common strengths and weaknesses, which seem to be fairly consistent around the world!

The second part of the job is also never-ending. Finding out how the myriad of colors that are available from a concert band can be successfully combined is a fascinating study. My own approach is, as I have said, a process of achieving the color and texture that arrives with the music, whether that's just the melody or the whole thing. Sometimes it arrives simply as texture, and the most satisfying part of the craft of composition is when I can produce what I hear in my head in the score.

The problem is that all bands make different sounds. I classify them from silver and gold (my favorites) to brown and dark brown (my unfavorites!). This variation seems to be much wider with bands than with orchestras. This is part and parcel of the fact that bands can vary in size from 35 to 135 and that different countries have different traditions. It's quite common in the UK, for example, for bands to use single flutes (with multiple clarinets, of course), while other countries may use three or four or more to a part. So what I may have designed as a delicate "hand over" from piccolo to flute can often go awry. Also, the numerical relationship between wind and brass can obviously vary enormously with consequent differences in the band's color and balance.

The incredible fact is that it seems to be acceptable for some concert bands to perform with instruments missing! Why we have got ourselves into this position, I don't know. No other amateur or professional form of music making buys into this culture. Even the most modest of amateur orchestras would not dream of playing a Beethoven symphony without bassoons, but some of us seem to think it's acceptable to leave them out of a band rather than make the effort to hire instrumentalists.

Publishers and some composers (I include myself here, hands up) are so frightened of losing sales that they cross-cue (or worse, over-double) in their scores so that smaller bands will buy the piece. Directors (not unnaturally) assume it's therefore the composer's intention that some instruments may be left out, and we have a vicious cycle. The net result is that orchestration for the concert band is mostly a compromise, and this means that everyone loses—the players (who get less exposed and therefore less satisfying parts), the composer (who often has to play it safe with his orchestration), and audiences (who miss out on some of the wonderful sounds a band can create). May I use this part of my chapter to beg directors to go the extra mile and fill in those empty seats for concerts at least? You're not to blame for this situation, but you are the only ones who can break the cycle by insisting on full instrumentation, however difficult that might be. Thank you!

One of my solutions to these inherent problems (and it may be common, but I don't study other composers' works much, which is a fault of mine) is to "layer" my textures; put *very* simply, this means dividing the band into soprano, alto, tenor, and bass areas and combining instruments of like sound to keep the overall texture clear no matter how many players are involved. As often as possible, I also try to avoid doubling horns and saxes (a wretched sound, which loses the best qualities of both instruments) and similarly, trumpets and clarinets. I much prefer the combination, when appropriate, of horns and clarinets or trumpets and saxophones.

Coming from the land of the brass band, I am used to the idea of "culturing" a total band sound. This does not yet seem universal in the concert band world (not this side of the Atlantic, anyway), and I would encourage more conductors to listen to the colors the *whole* band produces, rather than individual players or sections.

D. Views from the Composer to the Conductor Pertaining to Score Study and Preparation

Preparation

Being a simple soul and overly trusting, I find it hard to know what to say here. I assume conductors know what they are doing and don't need any advice from the composer that doesn't appear in the score. It would be simple and obvious to suggest that the conductor should look at every note, articulation, dynamic, and verbal instruction in the score and try to work out why the composer put it there. If the score is ambiguous or devoid of help, that is the fault of the composer. I see it as my job to put everything the conductor needs to know into the score, and therefore if I need to pass on more information here, I am not doing my job properly.

In my teens, I conducted an amateur orchestra and had the pleasure once of leading Elgar's wonderful Cello Concerto. I was used to asking the players to play this note short, that one with a little accent, louder here, softer there, but that didn't happen with this work. Everything, but everything, the players needed to know was in their parts. Elgar's writing (He's not often mentioned among the "masters" of orchestration along with Ravel and Wagner, but to me he is the very best) was *so* clear and precise that the piece played itself, and the balance with the soloist happened without the need to alter anything. So my advice would be to prepare by studying every dot and nuance and to make sure that the players see them and observe them, too. Obvious, really, as I said!

Tempo is a particular hobbyhorse of mine. Today, when most composers use some sort of computer software, they have the chance to hear a "performance" of their piece other than the one in their head, so they can usually decide on the optimum tempo for their music (bearing in mind a computer doesn't have to breathe!). We are not always right, of course, and a chosen tempo must vary a little according to the skills of the players and the venue involved. But please *try* my written tempo first, and then dismiss it if you need to!

Proportion

I have my doubts about being able offer anything helpful here. At school I remember having to analyze the first movement of a Mozart Symphony and found he had used "Sonata form," which has a first subject, second subject, development, and recapitulation. All very tidy. But I doubted then (and still do) whether working this form out would actually make a difference in how I would conduct it or perform it. It seems to me that this is done chiefly for the convenience of educators who are looking for something structured to teach. I would refer them to a marvelous quote from one of our less-than-marvelous politicians who accused someone of "looking for the copper cable when you should be looking for the electricity."

How, for example, could I make a recapitulation *sound* like a recapitulation in a performance? Mozart had already done this with the tonal structure. And if I can't do that, what's the point of the analysis in the first place? It is, of course, helpful to recognize when a theme is repeated so you can choose to either play it the same way or differently, but I have severe doubts that an analysis of the form of a piece *on paper* can do anything that will help a conductor during a performance. If the composer has the macro things right, all of this should happen naturally. I realize this opinion flies in the face of received wisdom and may explain why I'm only an adequate conductor rather than a good one (!) but the conductor should be able to *feel* the shape of a piece instead of having to work it out in his or her initial study, which I would prefer was spent studying the micro things.

So, as you can tell, dear reader, I'm not a great fan of analyzing music. Analysis is *not* the opposite of the compositional process and therefore can't tell you how the piece was put together. I am often asked for analyses of my pieces (from people who presumably wish to save themselves some work), and I always respond by asking them if a bar of chocolate tastes better when you know what the ingredients are.

Pacing

Because music notation is so gloriously imprecise, there are elements that the composer can't put in the score, and pacing is one of them. I see music (my own pieces, anyway) as an emotional journey, and the conductor can hopefully see a piece's highs and lows. His performance should ideally reflect this journey by negotiating the mood changes smoothly (when called for) and seamlessly so that the audience's emotional "attention," if you like, is not distracted. One of the other beauties of music is that this journey can take a different route from performance to performance, and this allows the conductor to stamp his personality on the piece.

Passion

I have partly covered this in the previous paragraph. I only recently recognized the "emotional journey"—I had previously looked at composing as a harmonic or textural journey (craft rather than art), but I have now seen what I have been trying to do during the last 30 years—I suppose it's never too late! So while I am reluctant to say to conductors "be passionate about your music making" because that sounds patronizing to me, at least I can ask you to look for the passion in my pieces instead of looking for the recapitulation! I have stated that I am not a fan of analyzing music; does the fact that the opening melody of Tchaikovsky's famous Piano Concerto never reappears in the work mean it is badly constructed? I wonder how many realized this before it was pointed out to them—certainly not me! And this fact has never spoiled my enjoyment of the piece, nor has the fact that none of the lines of lyrics in "Some Enchanted Evening" rhymes with any other. I would much prefer that conductors use their ears and hearts before engaging their brains!

E. The Relationship Between the Composer and the Commissioning Party

Band composers tend not to talk to each other about delicate matters such as how they work or how they see their position in the greater scheme, but I see us falling into two camps: "pragmatists" and "artists." The latter (and I could name names!) see themselves as creative gods whose "mission" is to endow the world with their masterpieces, and if you are lucky enough to have them accept a commission from you, you must give them total artistic rein and let the muses dictate. (I even know one composer who made his name writing for brass and concert bands but doesn't mention that in his *vitae*!) By far the majority, in my experience, are the former (and I include myself here) who see themselves as "jobbing" musicians whose commissioning duty is to give the commissioner exactly what is asked for. It may be, of course, that the commissioner gives no guidance by choice, but in the majority of cases, I think there is a piece at the back of his or her mind, and I feel it's the composer's job to come up with the goods. It's part of the craft. The danger arises when the commissioner is shy of tying the composer down and either under or overestimates the ability of his band and says "write what you like" when he really means, "I need a grade-3, seven-minute opener featuring bagpipes."

So I will always push the commissioner to give me as much information as possible about the band, the occasion and circumstances of the premiere, and even the type of venue. Of course, I hope to write a piece that will receive a second performance, or even more, but I believe that "he who pays the piper calls the tune." If I want to express myself in another way, then I am always free to write for my own amusement and not ask someone else to sponsor my musical foibles. One of the beauties of this book is that we composers can state how we feel about this and hopefully avoid future misunderstandings. The most satisfying part of the job for me is to hear back from a conductor that the piece is exactly what was wanted. I suppose it means my technique is in good order.

In my case, the commissioning fee usually (in practice) buys the performance material for the premiere (to publication quality), a dedication in the published score, and the right to the first performance (and recording, if requested). I used to also allow a year's sole use of the piece, but bands don't often request this these days. Outside of the first performance or series of performances, they are unlikely to want to repeat the work, or any work, within the first year. So I usually publish the work after about 10-14 months and hence publicize the commissioner's forward-thinking music policy!

Whenever possible, I try to attend a rehearsal and the first performance, but because most of my commissions are from outside the U.K., this is not possible as often as I would like.

F. Views on the Teaching of Composition and How to Mentor the Young Composer

This is something I have tried to do and failed! For a start, I have absolutely no clue how the compositional process works in my case, such as where the music comes from and why, why some pieces are easier to write than others, and why it is easier on some days than others. This is partly because I've deliberately eschewed working it out. I try to use the brain as little as possible when I'm writing (don't say it!) and prefer to rely on what musical instincts I've been endowed with. So I avoid intellectualizing the process as much as possible. I've heard pieces in which the composer has used his intellect, and I don't like them!

It's hard for me to offer practical help to a young composer in terms of how the process works and which approach will work best for him or her. My composition studies at college were wonderful, but we talked very little about compositional technique. My tutor, Philip Cannon, always spoke of the thoughts behind his music in emotional rather than technical terms and looked at the overall effect of the pieces I presented him with rather than the details.

I have often had beginning composers (young and old) ask me to look over their work, and my approach is always the same. I don't feel qualified to judge other people's work, and I don't think my opinion counts for more than theirs. So I will usually ask what *they* think about the piece and how *they* think it could be "improved." If they can point out what they consider to be its weak points, I can offer a suggestion to help strengthen the work, but if they think the piece is fine, there is no more to say. I don't believe it's productive to point out what *I* think could be improved as it's all a matter of opinion. (An aside: We too often talk of this piece being *better* than that piece, or that composer being *better* than this one. This is assuming that our opinion is the truth of the matter. What we should say is "I prefer this piece/composer to that one.")

I feel the only way a composer can grow is to have his pieces rehearsed and performed and to be self-critical, using what he or she has learned in the next piece. At least that's what happened to me! Being self-critical is not always easy, of course, especially for younger composers. (I once saw a sign in a shop that read: *If you have any questions, please ask one of the younger members of our staff—they appear to know everything.*)

239

But growth as a composer goes hand-in-hand with growth as a person, and these problems often right themselves—as we mature, our compositions mature (in most cases). The composer who thinks that everything he writes is a masterpiece will not make a career of it!

Where I think I can help is in terms of the craft, instrumentation, and orchestration, in determining what will prove to be possible in performances and what won't. But this is also an area in which a composer can learn from his own mistakes and miscalculations as much as from a teacher.

So if I were to try to help inexperienced composers, I would do it in terms of finding out *why* they are writing for band in particular and what they aim to achieve. What is it about the piece that will interest anyone else? Does it *communicate* anything? Do they know how amateurs function? (If they don't like it, they won't play it.) My goal is to help them find themselves, and I hope that doesn't sound too pompous.

G. Individuals Who Have Been Especially Influential in My Development and Career

Please excuse my reverting to lists here, but I think this will work best. These names are in no particular order.

- Philip Cannon, my composition professor, for encouraging me to write for bands.
- Geoffrey Brand, publisher, for taking a gamble on my early works.
- Stan Kitchen, publisher and my boss for 17 happy years, for nurturing my development internationally.

- Bob Walton, my trumpet professor, who realized I would never be able to play properly and never mentioned it in three years at the Royal College of Music.
- Alan Rowlands, my piano professor, similar to above, but he *did* mention it and decided to discuss Zen Buddhism instead!

H. Ten Works I Believe All Band Conductors at All Levels Should Study

I feel uneasy with this part of the assignment because I don't believe my opinion of what constitutes "great works" has much value to anyone but me. It's *purely* my opinion, and I wouldn't dream of thrusting it upon anyone else. As I get older, I find myself facing a dichotomy. I rarely hear pieces by other composers and think "I wish I'd written that." This is not arrogance at all, just a reflection of the fact that I am aware of the path I want my compositional journey to take. I know now what I want to be writing in ten years, and it's only a question of getting there; other composers are taking other paths, which is a good thing! However, I have also come to the realization that all opinions about music are equally valid. Even though I don't understand it, there are those who like Kenny Rogers, for example, and they are entitled to their opinion as much as the *sane* world is!

All I can do is draw up a list of works that I find inspiring or which have had a particular influence over me, in terms of musical or personal development.

1. *The Rite of Spring* by Igor Stravinsky. Of course!

2. Prelude to *Hansel and Gretel* by Englebert Humperdinck. Without ever analyzing why, I have always thought this is one of the most perfectly formed works in the orchestral repertoire. Now that I stop to wonder why, I think I like the harmonic and textural "rhythms" because they are very important to me when I'm writing. It takes me on the perfect musical journey. By the way, it is incredible that he produced this little masterpiece but hardly any other works that remain in the repertoire.

3. Symphony no. 29 by W. A. Mozart. This piece has a grace that's missing these days, it seems to me. There is so much violence in today's band music.

4. Prelude to *Die Meistersinger* by Richard Wagner. This is just the best trumpet part I've ever played (!), and it also has, for me, the same qualities as the Humperdinck, the same inevitability in its harmonic journey.

5. *Romeo and Juliet* by Sergei Prokofiev, for its passion and brilliant orchestral color. This is one piece I couldn't live without on my desert island!

6. *Apollo* by Igor Stravinsky. I can't explain this one fully, but it moves me in ways other music doesn't.

7. *Fantasia on a Theme of Thomas Tallis* by Ralph Vaughan Williams. This has the perfect shape and is sublime music.

8. Symphony no. 6 by Gustav Mahler, again for the passion, beauty, and menace but chiefly for his command of the large scale.

9. Piano Concerto in A minor by Edvard Grieg. I may be a simple soul, but I find the unpretentious beauty of the second movement so moving.

10. Piano Concerto in G by Maurice Ravel. I love this piece and, again, find the second movement to be one of the most beautiful moments in music.

I. Ten Composers Whose Music Overall Speaks to Me in Especially Meaningful Ways

This will cover the same ground as the previous section to a certain extent, so I'll expand on those composers a bit and add some more. The list is in no particular order, and I won't mention Mozart, as that's a given.

1. **Igor Stravinsky**. I spent many of my teenage years listening to as much Stravinsky as possible. I consider him to be a truly great composer, more than anything for his ability to write in such a wide range of moods and styles. While Schoenberg and his followers were examining their own navels, Stravinsky was writing some of the most serious music I know (*Apollo* and the *Symphony of Psalms*, for example) and the funniest (the two little orchestral Suites).

2. **J. S. Bach**. He was surely one of the composers who had the greatest command of his art. It seems to me that his music is not man-made at all, but just *is*. What I wouldn't give to have one percent of his facility! His music has beauty and restraint without peer.

3. **Edvard Grieg**. He is generally considered, I suppose, a minor composer (get it?). I really do find that his simple honesty as a writer has a charm few other composers can match.

4. **Maurice Ravel**. It's the sensuousness of his music that captivates me, as well as the delicacy of his harmonic language and orchestration.

5. **Gabriel Fauré**. He falls in the same category as Grieg, I guess. I find his restraint and taste sublimely alluring.

6. **Johannes Brahms**. The symphonies are the perfect blend of head and heart. Compelling listening.

7. **Aaron Copland**. His music always gives the impression that he knew what he was doing. I love the "outdoor" feel and optimism of much of his music, something that has been a great influence on my music.

8. **Edward Elgar**. He is another huge influence on me, not so much in terms of style, but because his orchestration is part of the piece as whole, more than in the works of any other composer I know. His use of color is so much a part of the expression of his music, and he knew so much about instrumental writing that his scores are always open on my desk.

9. **Gustav Mahler**. I never get tired of listening to the symphonies. I find the music so spontaneous that each time I hear them seems like the first time. And I would like to take the liberty of including Bruckner here, who demonstrates so clearly how *not* to do it!

10. **Jean Sibelius**. He is remarkable for his symphonies. I think it's the individuality of his voice that appeals me. He was one of the true originals of the 20th century and the directness and clarity of his thinking are so appealing to me. His works are valuable models.

J. The Future of the Wind Band

I'm not in everyday contact with bands or players, so I don't consider myself particularly qualified to add insight to this subject. I *can* perhaps add a British perspective to this largely American book!

Even though study after study continues to prove that learning a musical instrument and playing in a large ensemble are some of the most beneficial of the educational disciplines, the opportunities for students to study music in the UK are patchy to say the least. There is no national standard, and music is the only subject that unqualified teachers (who may be good players) are allowed to teach. It's nothing short of a scandal. I personally witnessed a 12-year-old's first trombone lesson. She shared her 15-minute lesson with two other kids but wasn't allowed to touch the trombone until her parents had signed a form. One of the other pupils was asked to learn a new tune for next week, but the teacher couldn't give him a copy of the music!

Some parts of the country, it must be said, have a wonderful music policy, but parents have to pay for tuition in all areas, so many pupils share a 15- or 20-minute lesson with one or two others. (The prevailing political atmosphere here in the U.K. is that taxes should be as low as possible and we should have the choice to spend our money as we please. This is a principle I agree with, but it doesn't work! We choose Mediterranean holidays and DVD players and are appalled when we have to pay for services we think should be supplied free of charge.) In my day everything was paid for by the school through our taxes, so we are not (on the whole) prepared to pay for health services, let alone for music lessons. Goodness knows how many talented youngsters can't even take the first step these days.

I think the number of people leaving school who own and play wind instruments has to be declining. This, in turn, has to have an effect on the number of community bands in this country; I'm sure this situation is common around the world. In contrast to the United States and Japan, it is rare for a U.K. school to have its own concert band. There is usually an ensemble of some sort, but it typically consists of whatever instrumentalists are available.

At the same time, the last 30 years have seen a real maturing of the concert band repertoire so that we can be proud of what we play, no matter what style it is in. Specialty composers bring a subtlety to their work, which means there has never been a better time to play in a concert band. Bands have found voices of their own with national identities, and composers of all styles are contributing so that all types of musicians can find something satisfying in the concert band experience.

I guess one thing feeds off the other: The better the available repertoire becomes, the more likely players will be to join concert bands. The more often bands select good music, the more likely it becomes that composers will want to write for bands.

All in all, I am fairly optimistic that the band experience, which is unique and priceless, is something that will continue to attract players at all levels for many years to come. While new orchestral repertoire is ossifying (they have a great back catalogue, of course!), the quality and variety of band repertoire continues to improve and diversify.

What we need fewer of are the self-styled experts who think their opinions about programming and repertoire are better than anybody else's and clutter the band periodicals with pomposity and self promotion. Can't they see that this is a matter of taste and not an absolute? As you may have guessed from my previous comments about Kenny Rogers, I cannot stand country music but would not dream of postulating that my taste (even though my experience and education could perhaps be considered more sophisticated) is *better* than that of a country music fan. There are many more Rogers fans than concert band fans, after all.

Please, please, please—if you like something, then by all means say so, but please don't delude yourself that you can judge the absolute quality of music. There is no such thing! You are confusing opinions with facts! If we don't like pineapple, for example, we just don't eat it; if we don't like a piece of music or a composer, we seem compelled to tell someone about it! What we are doing, in fact, is trying to prove that we know more about the subject than others. How arrogant is that?

I feel better now!

K. Other Facets of My Everyday Life

I have two sons, and they are more important to me than any note of music. My younger one, Benjamin, was born in 2001 soon after I started writing full-time, so I have been at home during the first three years of his short life and have loved every minute of watching him grow up. It's the best thing in the world. Were I to try to express a philosophy (apart from "just get on with it, for Heaven's sake!") in my music, my first choice would be to salute the joy of childhood innocence, but I don't think this is possible. While I salute the possibilities music gives us to communicate the subtlest of emotions and thoughts, this is one area in which it falls short. Music that is meant to be childlike so often sounds childish.

It may sound sad, but I spend most of my time writing. However, I believe that the more you compose, the better you get. I am enjoying my writing more than ever but will stop even in full "flow" if Benny wants to play with me!

In the little time I have away from music, I love eating and drinking well and am a huge fan of cricket, which is the most fascinating sport in the world, even though very few understand it and everybody plays it better than we, the inventors, do. It takes time to watch because an international Test takes place over five days and could easily end in a draw, but it's just a wonderful game that is played more in the mind than any other sport I know.

I have also lately got into soccer and am a moderately enthusiastic Manchester United fan (because I live in London). But they don't play as skillfully as they did in my day, and individual talent seems to be measured by how quickly you can pass the ball to somebody else!

I am also intrigued by outer space and our "role" in the greater scheme of things. A devout atheist, I stay at home every Sunday, come rain or shine. I don't believe anything unless I can see proof, so I find the inexplicable mystery of the universe a subject of unending fascination.

L. Comprehensive List of Works for Band

(This list omits arrangements.)

Grade 1

Infinity and Beyond.... (3:00, 2001, Anglo Music Press)

A London Intrada. (2:00, 2001, Anglo Music Press)

Pathfiinders March. (3:00, 2002, Anglo Music Press)

Simple Sarabande. (3:00, 2003, Anglo Music Press)

Grade 1.5

Chorus and March. (4:00, 2003, Anglo Music Press)

Westminster Prelude. (3:00, 2003, Anglo Music Press)

Grade 2

Ballad for Benny. (4:00, 2001, Anglo Music Press)

Big Sky Overture. (4:00, 2002, Anglo Music Press)

Carol of the Shepherds. (3:00, 2001, Anglo Music Press)

Clarinet Calypso. (4:00, 2003, Anglo Music Press)

Jamaica Farewell. (2:00, 1992, Studio Music)

Mumbo Jumbo. (2:00, 1992, Studio Music)

Processional Overture. (3:00, 1993, Studio Music)

Tijuana Trumpets. (2:00, 1993, Studio Music)

Grade 3

The Centurion. (4:00, 2000, Anglo Music Press)

Concert Prelude. (4:00, 1979, G & M Brand)

A Huntingdon Celebration. Commissioned by the Huntingdonshire Concert Band. (5:00, 2003, Anglo Music Press)

Jubilee Prelude. Commissioned by the Fanfare Concordia de Vetroz. (5:00, 1996, Studio Music)

Merry-Go-Round. Commissioned by the French Brass Open Festival. (5:00, 2002, Anglo Music Press)

Norwegian Rondo. Commissioned by Roland Recher. (5:00, 1997, Studio Music)

River City Serenade. Commissioned by the River City Brass Band. (6:00, 1992, Studio Music)

Shalom! A Suite of Israeli Folk Songs. (9:00, 2001, Anglo Music Press)

Slipstream. Commissioned by the BBC. (4:00, 1990, Studio Music)

A Tameside Overture. Commissioned by Tameside Council. (5:00, 1989, G & M Brand)

Time Remembered. Commissioned by the Woking Wind Orchestra. (9:00, 2000, Anglo Music Press)

A Yorkshire Overture. (5:00, 1990, Studio Music)

Grade 4

Carnival. Commissioned by Meinrad Brogli. (9:00, 1997, Studio Music)

Clarinet Concerto. Commissioned by Linda Merrick. (16:00, 2003, Anglo Music Press)

Diversions—Variations on a Swiss Folk Song. Commissioned by Solothurnischer Kantonal Musikverband. (14:00, 1998, Studio Music)

Fanfare, Romance and Finale. (8:00, 1990, Studio Music)

Four Norfolk Dances. Commissioned by the South Norfolk Youth Symphonic Band. (12:00, 2001, Anglo Music Press)

Hanover Festival. Commissioned by the Hanover Wind Symphony. (8:00, 1999, Anglo Music Press)

Jubilee Overture. Commissioned by the GUS Band. (8:00, 1984, Studio Music)

Kaleidoscope—Five Variations on the Brugg Song. Commissioned by the Aargau and Waadtland Music Associations. (12:00, 2003, Anglo Music Press)

Masquerade—A Willisau Celebration. Commissioned by the Stadtmusikkapelle Willisau. (15:00, 2002, Anglo Music Press)

Morning Song. Commissioned by Bowling Green State University. (9:00, 2002, Anglo Music Press)

Mountain Song. Commissioned by the River City Brass Band. (8:00, 1997, Studio Music)

Music for a Festival. Commissioned by the Hounslow Youth Wind Orchestra. (14:00, 1987, Studio Music)

Music for Arosa. Commissioned for the Arosa Music Festival. (10:00, 1996, Studio Music)

Pantomime. Commissioned by Nicholas Childs. (8:00, 1987, Studio Music)

A Pittsburgh Overture. Commissioned by the River City Brass Band. (6:00, 1992, Studio Music)

Portrait of a City. Commissioned by L'Orchestre d'Harmonie Municipal d'Annemasse. (14:00, 2002, Anglo Music Press)

Sinfonietta no. 3—Rheinfelden Sketches. Commissioned by the Stadtmusikkapelle Rheinfelden. (15:00, 2001, Anglo Music Press)

A Swiss Festival Overture. Commissioned by the Berne Music Association. (14:00, 1988, Studio Music)

Theatre Music. Commissioned by Musikpreis Grenchen. (12:00, 1989, Studio Music)

To a New Dawn. Commissioned by the U.S. Continental Army Band. (8:00, 2000, Anglo Music Press)

Grade 5

Barn Dance and Cowboy Hymn. (4:00, 1981, G & M Brand)

Celebration. Commissioned by the Tokyo Kosei Wind Orchestra. (13:00, 1991, Studio Music)

Fantasy for Euphonium. (8:00, 1978, G & M Brand)

Fiesta! Commissioned by the U.S. Army Field Band. (6:00, 1996, Studio Music)

Gaudium. (12:00, 1976, Boosey & Hawkes)

Hymn of the Highlands. Commissioned by the Yorkshire Building Society Band. (18:00, 2002, Anglo Music Press)

Invictus (The Unconquered). Commissioned by the U.S. Army Ground Forces Band. (10:00, 2001, Anglo Music Press)

The Land of the Long White Cloud—Aotearoa. Commissioned by the New Zealand Brass Band Association. (12:00, 1980, G & M Brand)

A Lindisfarne Rhapsody. Commissioned by Kenneth Bell. (14:00, 1997, Studio Music)

Navigation Inn. Commissioned by Ian Gibson. (5:00, 2000, Anglo Music Press)

Orient Express. Commissioned by the BBC. (8:00, 1992, Studio Music)

Out of Darkness, Into the Light. Commissioned by the Hofstra University Symphonic Winds. (9:00, 2003, Anglo Music Press)

Sinfonietta no. 1. Commissioned by the Friends of the Marine Band of the Royal Netherlands Navy. (12:00, 1990, Studio Music)

Sinfonietta no. 2. Commissioned by the National Youth Wind Orchestra of Great Britain. (16:00, 1992, Studio Music)

Sunrise at Angel's Gate. Commissioned by the U.S. Army Field Band. (9:00, 2001, Anglo Music Press)

The White Rose. Commissioned by the White Rose Concert Band. (8:00, 2002, Anglo Music Press)

A Wilten Festival Overture. Commissioned by Stadtmusikkapelle Wilten, Innsbruck. (8:00, 1999, Anglo Music Press)

Grade 6

Dance Movements. Commissioned by the U.S. Air Force Band. (20:00, 1996, Studio Music)

Symphony—*Earth, Water, Sun, Wind.* Commissioned by Northern Arizona University. (32:00, 1999, Anglo Music Press)

The Year of the Dragon. Commissioned by the Cory Band. (12:00, 1985, Studio Music)

chapter **9**

eric **Whitacre**

It begins with a feeling, and that feeling seems to radiate from the space between my sternum and my throat. It aches, and I feel profoundly compelled to "sing" that thing out to the world. I don't know why I do this; I just do.

A. Biography

I was born in Reno, Nevada, January 2, 1970. I lived throughout the state until I was 25 years old, and I'm proud to say that I am a fifth-generation Nevadan.

I've loved music as long as I can remember, but I had no real formal training growing up. My parents paid for piano lessons on several occasions, but the concepts didn't really stick; I just couldn't stand practicing. I played trumpet in the junior high marching band for a few years (all by ear) and was eventually kicked out because I was "impossible." I played synthesizer in a techno-pop band in high school, and I honestly thought that I would grow up to be a rock star.

After high school I attended the University of Nevada, Las Vegas and started in the music department. (Amazingly, I was admitted as a music education major even though I couldn't

253

read music.) I was sort of tricked into joining the choir (there were a lot of cute girls in the soprano section), and on the first day of class we started rehearsing the "Kyrie" from the Mozart *Requiem.* My life was profoundly changed that day, and I became a choir geek of the highest order.

I wrote my first concert work when I was 21, an *a cappella* setting of *Go, Lovely Rose.* It was published that same year. When I was 23, I wrote *Ghost Train*, my first attempt at writing for instruments. I continued writing as much as possible while pursuing my undergraduate degree, and by the time I graduated, I had a nice portfolio of commissioned and published works.

In 1995 I began my master's degree at The Juilliard School, where I studied composition with David Diamond and John Corigliano. I also met my wife there as well as two of my greatest friends, composers Steven Bryant and Jonathan Newman.

I graduated in 1997 and moved to Los Angeles, where I now live as a full time composer and conductor. In the past few years I've been invited to conduct concerts of my music in Europe, Japan, Singapore, Australia, and all over America. If you would have told me in 1988 that I would be traveling the world, making my living composing and conducting classical concert music, I wouldn't have believed you.

B. The Creative Process

I feel as though I am always composing. It's just who I am. There is always music and rhythm running through my body. At any moment of any day I can choose to acknowledge it or not, but it is with me everywhere. It seems to be somehow connected to my emotional core, and it feels as if there is no real separation between the way I feel and the way my music sounds as I am writing. I am simultaneously learning about myself and being changed by the process.

For me, "composing" music is simply focusing and refining this ever-present music. And the process is different with every piece. Sometimes I have a melody that bubbles to the surface or a little fragment that starts singing inside of me; sometimes it comes out of piano or vocal improvisations; and sometimes it is something that I hear in a movie or on the radio that resonates deeply with me and sparks an idea. Always, though, it begins with a feeling, and that feeling seems to radiate from the space between my sternum and my throat. It aches, and I feel profoundly compelled to "sing" that thing out to the world. I don't know why I do this; I just do.

As I begin to refine the essential idea, I start to develop a general palette of sonic colors to use, and in this way the little universe of the piece starts to define itself. This helps me establish certain loose "rules" about my universe: What is its harmonic language? What kind of rhythm lives in this little world? Which kind of "magic" does it contain?

(It's strange, but as I write down the description of this process it seems clinical and well planned, but in reality it is a completely intuitive exercise; I never consciously do these things but keep working at the piece until it "feels right.")

I believe that the most efficient music, music that operates on many levels at one time, is the best music. I am constantly trying to refine my palette for each piece to just a few simple brushstrokes and gestures.

I find that I do some of my best composing while in the shower, walking, or driving. Again, I don't question it anymore; I just let the muse lead me and take longer walks.

I always write by putting pencil to paper, sometimes using a piano or sequencer to check my ideas. Finale and Sibelius are evils best left in the hands of my copyist.

Above all, there is the architecture of the piece, the way that the work will unfold over time and be emotionally perceived by the players and the audience. I agonize over structure, working and working to get it just right. I strive for the most simple and elegant structures in my pieces, but for some reason it often takes me a long time to find them. It feels a little like sculpting; the statue is already inside the stone, and it is my job to chip away the unnecessary rock until the finished work is finally revealed.

This long "refining" period for me is an extraordinarily painful process. I find myself feeling the highest highs and the lowest lows, and at times it keeps me up all night. I completely agree with something that Frank Ticheli said in Volume One of this series: "Composers must put in the time." I often hear beginning composers say that they get great ideas and can't get past the first few bars. I immediately know that they just haven't worked on it long enough.

My experience has been that in order to develop an idea and bring a new creation into the world, you must go through a certain learning curve. I don't believe that you can be taught this curve, but you must suffer through and find it on your own. And the only way this can happen is by spending hours and hours and hours searching for the answer.

For me there is really no separation between my person and my music. It's hard to explain, but when I hear certain musical sounds created it is as if someone is speaking my true name. I often use the same chords or progressions in different pieces, quoting myself, and this is not because I have run out of ideas; it's because those chords and progressions represent *me*.

C. The Approach to Orchestration

I still feel like I have no idea how to orchestrate for band. I am constantly trying to improve my orchestration skills for all kinds of ensembles but am now certain that nothing is more difficult than scoring for the modern wind band.

The first and greatest obstacle lies in the ambiguity of the instrument list. An ensemble can have 24 clarinets or one on a part. It is not uncommon for the trumpets to outnumber every other instrument group. Sometimes there is a double bass, sometimes not. This lack of standardization makes for a difficult scoring process, and I find that it generally creates a "universal" band sound with every part doubled and tripled across the ensemble. To my ear, this creates a dullish "brown" sound that causes the ear to tire quickly.

There is also a lack of a homogenous group of instruments from the top to the bottom of the range of a single family. I suppose you could argue that clarinets fit this description, but clarinets seem to me to have a pointed, more focused sound, even when they are amassed in great numbers. And, generally, you will have one E-flat clarinet, a couple of bass clarinets, and a sea of B-flat clarinets, which doesn't make for a very balanced family.

Finally, the band has an extraordinarily difficult time playing softly. Solo, duet, and trio passages can be soft, but, of course, they lose the lushness of a large ensemble. I love to write soft, lush, sensual music, and I still haven't figured out how to do this with a band. And would someone *please* explain to me what four saxophones are doing in this ensemble? Are they part of the wind family? Do they always live with the horns? Why are there always two altos and rarely a soprano? I am vexed by this problem. It vexes me.

For me, each piece is a new experiment, and I'll try something different every time. *Ghost Train* was just a giant half-educated guess. I really didn't know what I was doing, and I think I ended up making some choices by accident that inadvertently made the ensemble sound fresh. With *Equus*, I was consciously working to make the wind ensemble sound like an orchestra. With *October*, I feel that I finally stumbled upon a few orchestrational ideas that truly make the group sparkle, namely treating the trumpets like the violin section and giving all of the best lines to the horns.

D. Views from the Composer to the Conductor Pertaining to Score Study and Preparation

When I compose, I feel *so* constricted by modern notation. In a very definite way, the music that I compose for live performances is vastly shaped by the limitations of standardized Western notation.

I try to do my best with my instructions to the conductor and to the players, but so much of it seems impossible to translate on the page. How do I ask for something to be played "musically?" How can I ask for a chord to sound "hollow," or "shiny," or "foggy?" This is the way that *I* experience music, and I find that I just don't have the tools with which to express these ideas. I suppose I could put these descriptive words into the score, but it always strikes me as ineffectual, and, even worse, confusing.

So, for the conductor, I tend to give only the basics: ♩=80, legato, *molto espressivo*, *pianissimo* . . . and then hope for the best.

I know that there is a tendency to rely on reference recordings when preparing a piece, but I would strongly encourage conductors to avoid this trap. Recordings are rarely accurate interpretations of my ultimate vision for the piece, and so many variables are involved when approaching the recorded version. How big was the room? How big was the group? What was the "vibe" on the session day? These are fundamental elements that go into the making of a recording, and the odds of them matching another conductor's live circumstance have got to be low. Furthermore, most recordings these days have been hyper-edited and as such make for horrible references to anything possible in the real world.

The thing that never fails to upset me is when conductors rewrite my music. Changing the notes on the page seems to be particularly popular with band conductors, and as long as I live I will never understand this compulsion. *Every* note, every gesture, every dynamic I write is on the page for a reason. The choices made are never arbitrary, and in my view they are absolutely essential for the ultimate success of the piece during a live performance. That simple gesture at the beginning of the piece causes the entire structure to collapse if it is removed or rewritten.

Above all, I find that there is a heavy emphasis on accuracy in the wind band, and I am a strong advocate of the opposite. Of course, I want the notes and rhythms to be correct, but not if the soul of the piece is sacrificed. I will gladly take a rough but passionate performance of my music *any* day over a correct but boring one.

E. The Relationship Between the Composer and the Commissioning Party

I don't really accept commissions anymore. Even when I was taking them, I never did it for the money, and I found that the pressure of finishing a piece on schedule (something I have yet to accomplish) was absolutely torturous. There is always someone trying to micromanage the progress of the piece, and believe me when I tell you that composers are under more than enough pressure from their inner critics without having to deal with some anxious commissioner freaking out.

Also, commissions always seem to be for some grand event (the 100th anniversary of a school of music, an international festival, the commemoration of a great person) and the commissioning party is spending *a lot* of money to make it happen. The expectations are huge, so they just don't want your next piece; they want your *greatest* piece. The BCM International boys and I often joke that what a commissioning party is really looking for when they contact me is *Sleepzilla Eats Ghostober*. As a commissioned composer, I end up trying to always write my greatest piece for these commissions, as opposed to my *next* piece, and it's always a rough and brutal process. I find that every time I try to impress someone with my writing, it's a big disaster, and I think my writing is much better when I just compose the piece singing in my heart.

Commissioning new works is great for most composers, though, and essential for the creation of new literature for the ensemble. I hope that every group will ask a young composer to write a new work for them. Just agree on a general length for the piece and a deadline (don't say I didn't warn you), and then let them work their magic. It is a thing of beauty to hear a new work birthed into the world.

F. Views on the Teaching of Composition and How to Mentor the Young Composer

I am often approached by other young composers seeking lessons, and I always have the same answer: I have no idea how one is supposed to teach composition. I'm sure that part of the reason I feel this way is that I am almost completely self-taught and that I can't imagine doing it any other way. Over the years my composition teachers have given me essential food for thought (particularly John Corigliano), and on rare occasions they have shown me something in the creative process I hadn't known before. More often than not, they tried to enforce upon me rules and subjective opinions that ran completely counter to my instinct, and I ended up either creatively lost or totally unimpressed.

For the most part, I learn in two different ways: looking at what other creators have done, and trying it myself. I apply this to every aspect of my life, especially composing.

The single most important thing a beginning composer can do is to **finish a piece and have it performed by actual human beings**. I cannot stress this strongly enough. So much of academic teaching has become absurdly abstract, and there is nothing like a real group of musicians waiting for their score and parts to snap you back to reality.

Composers learn so much, so quickly when they hear their work played in real time, by real people. Structure, orchestration, and technical difficulty; all of these things become instantly clear and knowable when you hear a live performance.

As a composer writing music, it is entirely up to you to find your way. There are *no rules*. You can create complete, perfect worlds of your liking. As I said before, it is painful, lonely, and difficult. But when you find the path and your muse sings clearly and bravely there is absolutely nothing like it.

G. Individuals Who Have Been Especially Influential on My Development and Career

- **David B. Weiller**. He was the choral conductor who recruited me into his chorus at UNLV and forever changed my life. He is one of the most musical people I have ever met, and his respect for art and the artistic process is unparalleled. He is that single teacher who set me on the path on which I believe I was meant to travel, and I am eternally grateful for his compassion, his friendship, and his effect on the world.
- **Tom Leslie**. If it weren't for Tom, I wouldn't be writing music for winds. He was completely fearless, allowing me to make daily changes to *Ghost Train* for months on end, literally using his rehearsal time as a real-time orchestration and composition lab for me. He has been the greatest champion of my band music (as well as that of dozens of other composers) and has remained a dear friend throughout the years.
- **John Morris Russell**. My one and only conducting teacher.
- **Jim Burnett**. My junior high band director. Always busting my chops for not being able to read music, but a *great* man.

- **My mother and father**. My mother has given so deeply of herself to support my career as an artist that I get a lump in my throat even as I write these words. My father was hesitant at first (I think he was afraid that I wouldn't be able to support myself) but in the past few years has become my biggest fan.
- **Hila Plitmann**, my astonishing wife, who amazes me every day with her artistry and her infinite capacity for joy. I have no idea how I got so lucky on this one . . .
- **Mary Anthony Cox**. The legendary (f)ear-training teacher at Juilliard. The single best teacher I've ever had.
- **John Corigliano**. My composition teacher at Juilliard. We talked only about architecture and the creative process.
- **Dr. Jocelyn Kaye Jensen**. She allowed me to write anything I liked, the more outrageous the better. I wrote several choral works for her, including the original *Cloudburst*.
- **Dr. Bruce Mayhall**. My first true champion, and the man who talked me into finishing my degree after I dropped out of college.
- **Dr. Jo Michael Scheibe** was an early champion of my choral music and became one of my dearest friends.
- **The Boys of BCM International**. Composers Steven Bryant, Jonathan Newman, and Jim Bonney, my spiritual and musical brothers.

H. Ten Works I Believe All Band Conductors at All Levels Should Study

I wouldn't dare to assume that I know what is best for an individual conductor or composer, but I believe the following pieces are essential masterpieces of Western music. For me, these pieces represent the foundation of all that I do. Much of this list looks like a greatest hits collection of classical music, but I think these pieces are great and timeless for a reason:

1. *Peter Grimes* by Benjamin Britten. Immensely beautiful and haunting music and by far my favorite opera.

2. *Knoxville, Summer of 1915* by Samuel Barber. Gorgeous, perfect vocal writing, and the Rosetta Stone of small symphonic orchestration.

3. *The Rite of Spring* by Igor Stravinsky. In one way or another, this piece is the grandfather of almost every 20th-century work.

4. *Harmonium* by John Adams. Breathtakingly fresh and exciting, I feel like I have been borrowing (read: stealing) from this piece for years.

5. *La Mer* by Claude Debussy. Never has revolutionary music also been so *beautiful.*

6. String Quartet in F by Maurice Ravel. Just perfect. Truly perfect.

7. Almost everything by J. S. Bach. Pick any piece. Analyze its structure. Now analyze the motivic development. Now analyze the layer upon layer of foreground and background counterpoint. Then forget all of that, and just listen . . . it's extraordinary on every level.

8. *Passio* by Arvo Pärt. A profound and exquisite study in elegance and restraint and probably the single greatest musical influence on my harmonic vocabulary.

9. Piano Concerto no. 23 in A major by W. A. Mozart. Sublime.

10. Symphony no. 5 by Ralph Vaughan Williams. A gorgeous, sensual idyll, and a major inspiration for my *October.*

11. Symphony no. 5 by Sergei Prokofiev. Full and complete mastery of the large form.

12. Symphony no. 9 by Ludwig van Beethoven. I know that everyone knows this, but he wrote this when he was *completely deaf*. More astonishing than the craft (which is super-human) is that the message he chose to exalt in the face of his affliction was one of brotherhood, hope, and joy.

I. Ten Composers Whose Music Overall Speaks to Me in Especially Meaningful Ways

I don't even know where to begin with this question because I feel my musical inspiration and influences come from so many sources. I could probably fill this book with the complete list of composers whose music I listen to, but in the interest of space, I'll just list a sampling. With deep humility, then, I offer ten *genres* of music that are especially meaningful to me, and within each I list some of my favorite composers:

1. **Classical Music:** Benjamin Britten, Samuel Barber, Igor Stravinsky, John Adams, Claude Debussy, Maurice Ravel, J. S. Bach, W. A. Mozart, Béla Bartók, Ludwig van Beethoven, Ralph Vaughan Williams, Claudio Monteverdi, Sergei Prokofiev, Giovanni Palestrina, Orlando di Lasso, and G. F. Handel.

2. **Contemporary Classical Music:** Arvo Pärt, Tan Dun, John Adams, Steve Reich, Aaron Jay Kernis, Krzysztof Penderecki, Toru Takemitsu, George Crumb, Morten Lauridsen, and Björk. (This is not a mistake. I truly believe she is creating some of the most innovative, important "contemporary classical" music out there.)

3. **Rock:** Queen, U2, Pink Floyd, Linkin Park, Van Halen (Sammy Hagar, then Diamond Dave), Chicago, Metallica, Journey, and Alanis Morrissette.

4. **Pop:** Thomas Dolby, Billy Joel, Depeche Mode, Prince, Stevie Wonder, Sting, Aimee Mann, Tori Amos, Duran Duran, The Pet Shop Boys, Beck, Peter Gabriel, and Tears for Fears.

5. **Musical Theater:** Richard Rodgers, Stephen Sondheim, Leonard Bernstein, Frank Loesser, Arthur Sullivan (of Gilbert and Sullivan fame), George Gershwin, and John Kandor.

6. **Film Music:** John Williams, Philip Glass, James Newton Howard, Thomas Newman, Jerry Goldsmith, Howard Shore, Danny Elfman, and Bernard Herrmann.

7. **Electronica:** Björk, Aphex Twin, Radiohead, William Orbit, Venus Hum, Vangelis, Brian Eno, Guy Sigsworth, Boards of Canada, and Vince Clarke.

8. **Folk:** Cat Stevens, Paul Simon (with and without Art Garfunkel), Bill Withers, James Taylor, and Tracy Chapman.

9. **The Beatles:** Yes, they get their own category.

10. **Opera:** Giacomo Puccini, Benjamin Britten, W. A. Mozart, and Claudio Monteverdi.

J. The Future of the Wind Band

As far as I can tell, the wind band (at least in America) has become the most popular ensemble in educational and community circles, rivaled only by choirs. As long as school districts continue to fund the programs (and that might be a big "if") I believe that the art form itself will continue to flourish.

I do believe that for the band community to grow artistically, some things are going to have to change. Simply, we need better, more interesting literature and a dedication to the creation of new, *different* works. Much of the industry is now controlled by a handful of major publishers and as such they can dictate which pieces will be popular and receive the most exposure. I think it is essential for band conductors to find and nurture the music that lies on the fringes. Only then will the rest of the concert world start to recognize the wind band for what it can become: the most influential and relevant live performing ensemble in concert music.

K. Other Facets of My Everyday Life

I'm a pretty simple guy. I mostly spend my days writing or traveling, and when I'm not doing those things I read, walk, exercise, eat sushi, watch movies, and spend time with friends and my wife. I don't think I'm a workaholic, but I do feel a little lost when I'm away from music for too long. I *love* to conduct and will jump at the chance to do so in almost any situation. I don't exactly *love* to compose music, but I am compelled to do it anyway, so I suppose that for me it is truly a vocation.

L. Comprehensive List of Works for Band

All pieces are published by Carpe Ranam Productions and distributed by Hal Leonard.

Grade 3

Cloudburst. Premiered by the Indiana All-State Band, conducted by the composer, March 2001 at the Indiana All-State Convention. (2001)

Sleep. Premiered by the Rutgers University Wind Ensemble, Dr. William Berz, conductor, March 2003. (2002)

Grade 3-4

October. Premiered by the Fremont High School Band, Brian Anderson, conductor, May 2000, Fremont, Nebraska. (2000)

Grade 4

Noisy Wheels of Joy. Premiered by the University of Nevada–Las Vegas Wind Symphony, Tad Suzuki, conductor, March 2001 at the American Bandmasters Association National Convention.

Grade 4-5

Godzilla Eats Las Vegas! Premiered by the University of Nevada–Las Vegas Wind Symphony, Thomas G. Leslie, conductor, March 1996 at UNLV. (1995)

Grade 5-6

Ghost Train. Premiered by the University of Nevada–Las Vegas Wind Symphony, Thomas G. Leslie, conductor at the March 1994 Western Regional CBDNA Convention. Complete suite premiered April 1995 at UNLV. (1993/1994)

Grade 6

Equus. Premiered by the University of Miami Wind Symphony, Gary Green, conductor, March 2000. (1999)

chapter 10

dana **Wilson**

The commissioning of art profoundly nurtured the essence of Western culture. It is what allowed Michelangelo to pay someone else to paint his house so that he could paint the Sistine Chapel.

A. Biography

The works of Dana Wilson have been commissioned and performed by such diverse ensembles as the Chicago Chamber Musicians, Detroit Chamber Winds and Strings, Buffalo Philharmonic, Memphis Symphony, Dallas Wind Symphony, Voices of Change, Netherlands Wind Ensemble, Syracuse Symphony, and Tokyo Kosei Wind Orchestra. He has written solo works for such renowned artists as Gail Williams, Larry Combs, James Thompson, and David Weiss. Wilson has received grants from, among others, the National Endowment for the Arts, New York Foundation for the Arts, New England Foundation for the Arts, New York State Council for the Arts, Arts Midwest, and Meet The Composer. His compositions have been performed throughout the United States, Europe, and East Asia and are published by Boosey & Hawkes and Ludwig Music. They can be heard on Klavier, Albany, Summit, Centaur,

Innova, Meister Music, Elf, Open Loop, Mark, Redwood, Musical Heritage Society, and Kosei Recordings. His wind works have received several awards, including the Sudler International Composition Prize, International Trumpet Guild First Prize (twice), the Britten-on-the-Bay Festival Prize, and the American Bandmasters Association/Ostwald Prize.

Wilson is coauthor of *Contemporary Choral Arranging*, published by Prentice Hall and has written articles on diverse musical subjects. He has been a Yaddo Fellow (at Yaddo, the artists' retreat in Saratoga Springs, New York), a Wye Fellow at the Aspen Institute, a Charles A. Dana Fellow, and a Fellow at the Society for Humanities at Cornell University. For more information and lists of works, please visit www.ithaca.edu/wilson.

Coming of age in Wilton, Connecticut, as a young Baby Boomer, I became involved with music through singing in choirs and playing piano in jazz groups and guitar in rock bands. It appeared to me at the time that "art music" was dominated by serialism, and that it was the card that everyone had to carry in order to be admitted to the inner circle, particularly in academia. Serialism and its pre-compositional imperatives, however, did not excite me. Concurrently, jazz and popular styles were not respected—and sometimes not even allowed—in the academy. So because I had little interest in living my life on the road as a moderately good jazz pianist, it seemed that I should pursue a career in a profession other than music.

I studied psychology at Bowdoin College, and stayed involved with music as much as possible, including directing a vocal octet and playing in various bands. Upon graduation, I was drafted to serve late in the Vietnam quagmire but was instead sent to Heidelberg, Germany, where I played piano in the European headquarters band. As virtually everyone who had run out of options was drafted in those days, the band was populated with incredible musicians, many of whom had graduated from the major conservatories, and I sensed for the first time what the world of professional musicianship was about. After my stint, I set to work developing my fledgling skills and trying to support myself as a composer and arranger while going back to school. I received my master's degree from the University of Connecticut and then went to Eastman for my doctorate. From there I joined the faculty in the School of Music at Ithaca College where I have remained ever since, in part because I have been able to explore my many musical interests. My first work for wind ensemble, *Piece of Mind*, was commissioned by Rodney Winther, then conductor of the Ithaca College Wind Ensemble, and premiered in New York City in 1986. It took me a long time, however, to consider myself a composer. As I began my professional career, I felt as though I was behind in my training, having missed the undergraduate mentoring and networking. Developing both a style that expresses the ideas that concern me and a vocabulary and syntax that feel like my native musical language has taken a good amount of work and substantial support and interest on the part of teachers, other musicians, and family.

My musical interests continue to be eclectic and reflect the various layers that comprise my background, and I'm grateful for this. The longer I live, the more conscious I am of drawing upon a breadth of experiences to help give life meaning and, I hope, to inform my music. I'm also relieved that eclecticism in composition is currently valued. The challenge now—in life as in art—is to make a cohesive whole out of all the diverse input.

B. The Creative Process

Writing a piece can be compared to writing a novel—that is, it can begin anywhere and grow in any direction from there with the final piece being some kind of unfolding in time of those initial impulses. Sometimes I have begun with what turns out to be measure one of the piece: *Dance of the New World* evolved from the layered percussion found in the work's opening measures. A piece may also begin with an image of the climax: the seminal idea for *Kah! Out of Darkness* was intense sound swirling around the hall; to accomplish that I placed two small ensembles in the rear corners of the hall. Another might begin with a concept: *Piece of Mind* was generated from a desire to represent different aspects of the mind and the way they function; this meant exploring a myriad of styles.

Sometimes I wish to express my excitement over some art, event, or other music: *Shakata: Singing the World into Existence* was inspired by various non-Western communal rituals and their social and musical power and intensity. Finally, there is intent: in *Sang!*, I wanted to write a piece that would allow young or less experienced players to perform complex rhythms commonly heard in popular dance music and jazz. I began the piece with a highly syncopated chant from which the rest of the piece is carefully derived. It was important that this chant be easily learned, aurally if necessary, as is the case with most popular music and the cultures that inspire it.

As for the writing itself, the first stage—that of staring at blank music paper with few tangible musical ideas emerging—is the most painful. Despite the desire to get something down, the fact that once materials are committed to they must be lived with for at least the next few months is always lurking as I try to determine what drama is hidden within them. Eventually ideas begin to percolate, however, and the next stage, exploring the implications of those ideas, is the most enjoyable part of the process. Well into the piece, a mix of craft and intuition takes over, one guiding and informing the other. Gradually the main materials are illuminated and a formal design becomes palpable. Then it is a matter of constantly reshaping.

Reshaping the music may be analogous to sculpting with clay. First, you often get the basic shape to work and then focus on details until the whole seems to take on its own expressive integrity. Some days may be spent adjusting proportions, while others may be devoted to shaping a melodic line until it is just right (comparable to the sculptor agonizing over the folds in the ear, even though the rest of the head is lopsided). Still other days may be spent dousing it with water to pull much of it apart. When the piece seems pretty close to completion, a long process of smoothing and sanding begins. In this entire process, the well-known and painfully huge ratio of perspiration to inspiration is clear, but both are needed in order to keep the process vital and worthwhile.

All of this takes an enormous amount of energy. Hence, for me, mornings are preferable for composing because of the combination of the "dream-state" remnants from sleep and a jolt from caffeine. Once teaching or interruptions begin, it's very difficult to return to the world of the piece that day.

It is the pleasure of living in that world that draws me to writing. Sometimes, however, it's lonely in that world, so I go to the piano for company, feedback, note checking, and to explore ideas. Occasionally I have a desire to hear the MIDI playback of the computerized notation because it can be rewarding to hear something of the piece before the first performance. I have also sometimes learned how to better pace a piece through playback. Usually, however, the playback's lack of musicality and inability to capture the natural balance and articulation of real performers (coupled with my inability and lack of desire to tweak it so that it sounds expressive) is more depressing than helpful, and I find myself wasting time trying to improve the sound quality when the notated music is just fine.

It turns out that many of my works appear to be about conjuring or exorcising, and I'm sure that composing serves as some sort of spiritual and psychological ablution, as well as perhaps a sense of connection to a greater whole. How this works I have no idea . . .

C. The Approach to Orchestration

On one level, orchestration is simply one of the parameters a composer has at his or her disposal. If the timbre and dynamics can be varied through orchestration, other parameters such as melody, harmony, and rhythm can be limited. Ravel's *Bolero* is perhaps the most famous example of this because it features repetition of almost every parameter except orchestration. It is almost exclusively orchestration that causes the piece to grow and finally to explode. Therefore, a composer's decisions with regard to orchestration are often integral to the composition process.

On another level, music is drama, and music for a large ensemble such as a band or wind ensemble has the potential for powerful drama. It is the working out of deep-seated psycho-acoustical relationships.

To consider this second level, I picture our ancient fore-bears sitting around in a cave—particularly at night, when they only had their ears to identify whether something nearby was benign leaf rustling or a life-threatening predator. Sounds getting louder suggested that something was coming closer, raising concern; sounds diminishing suggested that something was moving away, allowing relaxation. Low brash sounds generally meant trouble; high, skittering sounds meant something that fell within the spectrum from playful to annoying. Sudden, loud events were startling, and sounds that were difficult to identify created anxiety, at least until they could be identified and either be responded to or ignored.

Those cave dwellers who did not heed these distinctions usually did not live long enough to create offspring. Our forebears, on the other hand, paid close attention to the many sounds around them and had the good sense to respond to them, subconsciously defining the link between sound and emotion/survival. I feel we enter the concert hall with this link hardwired in our psyche. Listening to a piece of music is information processing that may not determine our survival, but it still engages us emotionally in this age-old way. Orchestration, then, is for me the manipulation of the sound world to generate certain emotional states.

Orchestration also helps to play out certain social and psychological needs of the listener. For me, an unaccompanied solo passage is haunting because it expresses aloneness, an off-stage solo expressing even greater human separation, if not isolation. Various accompanimental patterns express different levels of support for the soloist; if the timbre is close to that of the melodic instrument, there is a sense of even greater support and commonality. A duet is just that, a coupling whose nature is defined by the confluence or contrast of the lines. Each instrument speaks to me differently in terms of "strength of purpose," with register playing a large role in the instrument's ability to assert itself. Obviously such imagery can go to unnecessary extremes, and I don't always think consciously of these relationships when I orchestrate, but it helps me to understand the ritual intent of much music and the social nature of the concert hall, and, therefore, the compositional/orchestrational process.

Another key issue in orchestration is breathing, not just of the players, but of the music itself. The very term "inspiration" stresses the importance of breathing in art, as do such ubiquitous comments as "the audience held their breath," "they were left breathless," and "it took my breath away." I feel that one of the greatest challenges in orchestrating music for wind ensemble is that so many of its performers make their sound by exhaling, and as an audience member at a band concert I often miss a sense of music's other task, which is to inhale.

There are two solutions. First, I try to carefully pace the instruments that exhibit varying degrees of blowing—from oboe (which blows so little, there's often air left over after several measures of playing!) at one extreme to unmuted, cylindrical brass instruments such as trumpets and trombones that can both blow forcefully and focus the column of air. Another solution is to rely heavily on percussion: the marimba, for example, gives me the sense of "pulling in" the sound rather than blowing out. Of course, much of this is instinctive to an orchestrator, but I think being sensitive to breathing tendencies can help.

Technical questions asked by band directors frequently have to do with doubling and instrumental substitution. While the power of the band often comes from having so many players on one part, subtlety is often sacrificed in the slow or exposed sections. Unlike with strings, where adding more to a part can increase the sound's richness, adding a number of wind instruments (with overtone structures less complex than those of strings) to a part can sound "less than rich." Therefore, having the third clarinet part played by five performers may be less desirable than having three performers play it. However, the difference usually has to be weighed against the pedagogical advantage of involving all five performers, so I feel it should be up to the conductor to make that decision.

I feel similarly about instrument substitution, such as having saxophones replace French horns when necessary. The score may have been written with the horn color and expressive capacity in mind, but if there aren't enough horns and there's an overabundance of saxophones, the substitution usually makes sense. There is, in fact, a long history of substitution for practical reasons, dating at least from the Baroque and perhaps from the beginning of music making.

At the same time, conductors should be aware of the context. If, for example, the score has a dialogue between the horns and saxes, that dialogue is lost in the horn-to-saxophone substitution, so other instruments should be used for the substitution, at least at that point in the music. And sometimes the orchestration of a work is so basic to its explication that perhaps the piece should be saved until a time when the ensemble has all of the requested performers. Again, I feel conductors should make this decision because they fully understand the trade-offs involved in such decisions.

D. Views from the Composer to the Conductor Pertaining to Score Study and Preparation

First of all, I find wind ensemble and band conductors to be wonderful in their approach to the conductor/composer collaboration. They often call with questions, and they are open to suggestions in rehearsals and flexible in their conception. I also appreciate the networking that goes on when a conductor discovers a good piece. The current generation of conductors grew up with wind ensembles as well as bands and most understand the aesthetic and practical concerns of both.

As for score study, it seems crucial to remember that pieces are like stories. Each has its own plot line and style and sometimes its own aural universe. I would urge conductors to identify what specific elements draw them to the work, then become acquainted with its characters and find its voice and narrative. Finally, the conductor must strive in rehearsals and performances to illuminate and intensify those, thereby releasing the drama. Only then will the piece come to life and contribute to the concert as a whole.

Titles can help in this discovery. While sometimes rather arbitrary, they can often serve as a gateway to a work. Conductors should research the titles and explain them to the ensemble. Particularly abstruse titles or titles in languages other than English provide a rich opportunity to broaden a performer's experience with a piece. When this is done, it will become clearer to the performer why the conductor asks for a certain color or style of playing. These nuances are crucial to the success of the performance.

Conductors should also discuss unusual elements of the work or its title with the audience, even if they are mentioned in the program notes. Such an introduction allows the audience to make a smoother transition from a previously performed work, sets up the sound world or mood of the piece, and helps the audience know the conductor's thoughts about the work and its interpretation.

On a more technical level, I would urge conductors to seek out musical connections that may not be obvious, particularly within each section. For example, given the standard score placement of instruments—with the oboe near the top of the page, tenor saxophone in the middle, and marimba near the bottom—a composite line that moves from the oboe through the marimba to the saxophone may not be readily apparent. It is my experience that this is the aspect of the score most often missed by conductors, even if the nature of the material, register, and dynamics makes it clear.

Regarding preparation after score study, one concern I have is that conductors usually separate warm-ups from working on the piece in rehearsals. I would urge conductors to explore and practice difficult elements as part of the rehearsal warm-up session *before* they encounter them in the piece. For example, I sometimes employ the octatonic scale (alternating whole and half steps), which can create tricky finger patterns. This scale could be practiced in warm-ups alongside major and minor scales. Actual pitch motives or patterns from the piece (but devoid of complex rhythms) could be introduced in this way as well. It helps the ear and the fingers, and in so doing, the piece is actually rehearsed.

This can also be done with rhythmic figures. A particularly challenging syncopation, for example, can be taught aurally at first in a "call-and-response" relationship. Then it can be written on the board along with other patterns, and they can be performed on an agreed-upon pitch or chord. Each pattern can be performed as pointed to. Over a few rehearsals, an entire passage can be practiced in this way. By the time the players come to the passage in the piece, it will be virtually sight-readable.

This is nothing new, of course, but I have sat through many rehearsals where the conductor rehearses a passage over and over because of the scalar and rhythmic challenges. This grinds down the piece and deprives those not involved with that particular passage of the opportunity to benefit from the material. Furthermore, the call-and-response approach can be great fun, including pitch, rhythm, dynamics, and articulation as a form of ear training. Individual students can be selected to play the call, either reading the patterns or improvising.

This process can even lead to a composition improvised on the spot by the ensemble. The call could become an ostinato pattern (maintained, for example, in the low brass and percussion) and then other complementary patterns could be layered above. This process works at all proficiency levels and with all age groups, provided it is introduced incrementally. It can even become a "piece" on the concert. The process teaches players about listening, responding, improvising, and structuring. In this way the conductor gives the students a sense of the compositional process, which in turn can also refresh their approach to notated music. (To learn more in a related vein, you may wish to read my article "Guidelines for Coaching Student Composers" in *Music Educators Journal*, July 2001, devoted to "Special Focus: Composition and Improvisation.")

E. The Relationship Between the Composer and the Commissioning Party

Obviously, the commissioning of art has profoundly nurtured Western culture. It is what allowed Michelangelo to pay someone else to paint his house so that he could paint the Sistine Chapel. But commissioning serves other functions as well. In an age when we tend to revere icons who have been dead for centuries (was not always that way!), this reminds us that art is a living and interactive process that can involve an entire community. Furthermore, because a concert is a ritual whereby we are nurtured and refreshed, commissioning and performing a new work are key to maintaining the vitality of the concert experience.

Selecting a composer should begin with your excitement about his or her other music. Then, if possible, talk with others who have commissioned this composer to learn about their experiences. Did the composer deliver the piece in a timely manner? What was it like to work with the composer through-out the process? The amount to be paid depends on several factors, including the composer's status, length of the proposed piece, and funding available. I prefer to have someone interested in commissioning a work propose an amount, and we can discuss our options from there.

The process of commissioning that has worked well for me includes the following guidelines:

1. Provide plenty of lead time, both in approaching a com-poser and applying for grants to support the commission. Depending on the availability of the composer, this can take one to several years.

2. Be clear in your mind and your communications with the composer as to the purpose of the commission and any thoughts you may have regarding the nature of the proposed piece. The requirements shouldn't be too restrictive, but if a piece is meant to celebrate the opening of a new building, you (and the composer) may want it to be very different than if it is to be a memorial to someone. Once the agreement has been made with the composer, no further requests regarding the piece's nature should be made.

3. A contract should be signed by both the commissioner and composer (both should keep copies) that indicates the precise instrumentation, approximate length, and due date of the score. It should also indicate whether the generation of parts is included in the commissioning fee and when they are due. Finally, it should specify the payment schedule for the commission—often a small portion at the signing of the contract with the balance due when the score and parts are received.

4. An agreement should be made about whether the composer will attend the final rehearsals and the premiere. This should be separate from the contract because premiere dates can shift when conceived a few years in advance, and there is no point in nullifying the commission agreement. The composer's attendance (including travel, accommodations, and meals) should be funded by the commissioner, and this money should be planned for from the start of the process.

5. The commissioner is entitled to give the first performance with no additional publishing or performance costs. The commissioner may also request a certain reasonable time

period thereafter during which the ensemble has exclusive performance rights (for example, in order to perform the piece at a festival at year's end) and/or recording rights. The copyright and publishing rights remain with the composer. An inscription recognizing the commissioning body is often included in the published score.

6. Consortia are a fine way to commission a work. Get together a few conductors of ensembles similar in nature and ability to yours, have them each contribute a portion of the commissioning fee, and guarantee them each "premieres." (If you initiate the commission, you're entitled to give the very first performance.) Everyone wins; several ensembles are involved in the birth process of a piece at a fraction of the cost and logistical effort, and the composer is guaranteed at least several performances of the new work.

F. Views on the Teaching of Composition and How to Mentor the Young Composer

Western civilization has been built from the tension between traditional values and innovation, usually favoring the latter in the name of progress. The history of Western art, including music, has reflected the evolution of cultures that have believed in and nurtured that progress. (The term "harmonic progression," for example, refers to a musical element that is forward-pushing and teleological.) Composers have frequently pushed against or disavowed the principles established during previous periods, embracing innovation as an expression of greater compositional "freedom."

This is no longer the case. Ever since composers of the 1960s lit pianos on fire and threw them off roofs, there has been little point in trying to push the envelope. Composers have had to pull back and reexamine materials and ideas that have been around for millennia to discover which best match their own sensibilities. This includes art music, but also music of so-called folk traditions as well as music in cultures that Westerners barely acknowledged 50 years ago. It makes teaching composition a great challenge in that one student may be interested in jazz, another in the European avant-garde (though there's no longer anything "avant" about it), another in the downtown Manhattan scene, another in Indian *ragas*. All of these draw upon different cultural roots and aesthetics.

What is shared by pieces influenced by these various traditions is a need for boundaries, for parameters. I feel this is true because, generally speaking, as human beings we need boundaries in order to find value in something. For example, small children will go outside to play with a ball, but very soon they will literally draw boundaries to make the game more interesting. Adults get bored playing tennis if there is no net, even though it's much more difficult to play with the net up. The point is to create a challenge and then try to meet it.

There are at least five roles that I try to play in mentoring young composers. One is to help students discover what principles are at work in their pieces and to help them erect boundaries by means of limiting motives and vocabulary, suggesting a formal design, and the like. Then the student can fight against these boundaries, creating energy. Somewhere in this process the piece begins to generate its own energy, and I hope that, in turn, this lends a sense of excitement to the process.

A second role involves identifying elements in the students' compositions that prevent their music from effectively accomplishing what they set out to do in the piece. I may feel the piece is too sectional or doesn't breathe, the climax comes too soon or too late, or that what is meant to be meditative is simply uninteresting.

Third, I try to act as both a cheerleader and a fan club. Composing is difficult, growth is glacial, the process is isolating, and the social rewards are usually limited (other than that, it's a lot of fun!), so such support is often necessary. Fourth, I try to be open to all of their ideas in the hope, not just that I'll better understand their music but that they will also remain open to ideas as they mature.

And, finally, I try to prepare students for what they may face as professional musicians. They must know about competitions, graduate school, and ways to make a living either as a composer or in other fields in which their talents may be valued.

Of course, mentoring is a subjective process, and I always sense varying degrees of success at both honing in on the issues and making an impact. It certainly is worthwhile to try, however, and generally it is extremely gratifying. At the same time, it helps me to remember what a pitching coach once said: "You can teach accuracy, but you can't teach speed." In music composition, a teacher can help develop craft, illuminate connections, and provide support, but ultimately the student must supply the vital musical ideas and the desire to keep coming back to them until they blossom into a work of art.

G. Individuals Who Have Been Especially Influential on My Development and Career

My childhood musical experience included piano lessons, singing in church choirs, and listening to my mother sing and my father improvise at the piano—always in E-flat! In middle school, I played piano in a jazz octet. In high school, I played in various jazz and rock groups—the former to explore the music, and the latter to have fun and try to impress girls. The most influential people to me musically during this period were my peers.

Besides John Mehegan, the great jazz pedagogue with whom I studied briefly, the next most influential musician in my life was Sam Adler, professor of composition at Eastman. I had been modestly prepared as a composer, but his boundless energy, great spirit, and enthusiasm were contagious. Sam had strong opinions about music and musicians but rarely shared his true opinions about my music; instead, he got excited about the *possibilities* of my music, and this, in turn, got me excited. My challenge then was to maintain that excitement for as much of the rest of the writing week as possible. Often when I compose I can still feel him sitting next to me making suggestions. When I teach, I try to find those places in the students' pieces that will get me excited about their possibilities.

The next group of influential people has been my colleagues in the School of Music at Ithaca College. Not only have they been eager to perform my music, they have always been willing to answer patiently my technical questions about their instruments. Through them and wonderful performers around the country and in various parts of the world, I've learned that a crucial part of composing is learning what excites your players. From conductors I've also learned so much about line, balance, and dramatic shape. I shall be forever indebted to each of them.

H. Ten Works I Believe All Band Conductors at All Levels Should Study;
and
I. Ten Composers Whose Music Overall Speaks to Me in Especially Meaningful Ways

I am combining these categories because I tend to like specific works and have few "favorite" composers across the board. I trust that conductors know many of the works in the Western "canon" and constantly return to works they love in order to be renewed. Therefore, I'll limit my list to works that have strongly affected the way I think about music, yet may not be known by everyone.

To me, great music is usually the vernacular made artful. There is something deeply profound about the process of tapping into ancient ideas, fears, hopes, and dramas and transforming them into a personal statement. (The term "profound," after all, is a combination of two words that mean "forward" and "bottom.") Most of all, I'm drawn to composers who don't journey far from their roots, in the spirit of Stravinsky, Bartók, and Shostakovich. Here are some pieces, in no particular order, that excite me anew each time I hear them.

- Cello Concerto by Witold Lutoslawski—such simple music expanded so far and driven so deep.
- Piano Etudes by György Ligeti—daring, flamboyant, exciting, yet always under supreme control.

- Symphony no. 1 by Christopher Rouse—persistent longing that is transformed into meditative power.
- *Music for Prague* by Karel Husa—able to maintain breath-taking intensity from beginning to end.
- *Black, Brown, and Beige* by Duke Ellington—elemental, lyrical, and passionately human.
- *Tehillim* by Steve Reich—a religious journey that spins the listener into a contemplative vortex.
- The obsessive searching of almost any John Coltrane solo, but also his tender lyricism in "Naima."
- *...and the mountains rising nowhere* by Joseph Schwantner, which is able, like few other pieces, to swallow you into its unique sound world and keep you there rapturously.
- *Ketjak*, the Ramayana Monkey Chant from Bali, a ritual that releases unbelievable power through the human voice as part of an intense communal rite.
- Japanese *Shakuhachi* music—sounds from another world and another time that are tranquil and intense at the same moment.

J. The Future of the Wind Band

Bands are both cursed and blessed by their current role in society. On the one hand, they are generally protected and supported by academic institutions. This frees them up artistically and logistically and accounts for their many new commissions, innovative programming, and substantial amounts of rehearsal time. On the other hand, the educational role of these pieces can limit their reach. Every fall a new ensemble has to be "made." Balance and even excellence are sometimes sacrificed in the service of giving more performers the experience. Also, band music's long-standing association with the military and the Fourth of July can create expectations in the concertgoer.

While few experiences equal the power and majesty of a large band, the wind ensemble has been a wonderful development in terms of agility, clarity, and balance. It has been a major factor in attracting fine composers to write for bands and has helped to attract better performers to play wind literature.

There have also been forces afoot that blur the distinction between wind bands and orchestras. Over the past century, orchestral conception has changed, such that the role of winds and percussion has increased. Debussy relied largely on winds for his main ideas, and Stravinsky often went so far as to relegate strings to almost exclusively accompanimental roles. American culture is so steeped in bands (marching, concert, and jazz) that as more and more contemporary American composers draw upon these roots, even in writing orchestral works, they, too, often focus primarily on winds and percussion. Furthermore, particularly to capture vernacular styles, pieces for both band and orchestra often feature such instruments as saxophone, electric bass, drum set, and percussion from various folk traditions. Finally, today first-rate composers write for both ensembles and turn increasingly to bands for extensive rehearsals, multiple performances, and fine playing. These composers bring their musical depth to the medium with a sophisticated approach to sonority and breadth of experience.

All of these qualities suggest that the wind band will flourish in the future as long as there is flexibility in both size and instrumentation. Another ability will be required, however, of all performing ensembles: they must provide something that an audience member clearly cannot receive by staying home and listening to compact discs or watching DVDs. Live concerts must be special events. Of course, the quality of music making comes first, and one could argue that nothing can replace the excitement of music performed in "real time." I feel, however, that we all must do more. For example, why do most band concerts involve only works for the full ensemble? Why do they all take place center stage? Why is the inclusion of a few strings or voices so unusual? Why are lighting, dancers, paintings, readings, film, and spatial dimensions rarely employed? Why don't more programs reflect the multicultural layers that generate our country's vitality?

Another element that may play an increasing role in the wind band's future is the interactive nature of recent technology. The computer and synthesizer have become great tools in allowing very young people to compose and immediately hear their efforts "performed." All of this can be done without first having to learn notation, copy parts, recruit performers who can perform the music effectively, or generate rehearsals and performances. As a result, this has attracted many students to become involved in composing who would not otherwise have access or interest. As they gain confidence in their skills, the school band or other group may increasingly become the link between the MIDI version and the "real" world. Already, many conductors encourage young composers in this way. As the process refines itself, band rehearsals could become workshops to a greater degree, and the concert could transform into a vibrant venue for premieres. Besides the obvious benefit to composers, it also reminds performers and audiences that music making is a fluid and interactive process rather than a replication.

K. Other Facets of My Everyday Life

Composing and teaching take up much of a given week. My rather large and wonderful family has also taken a good deal of time and energy over the years, although less so now that the children are gradually going out into the world. My wife, Louise, is a fine singer as well as composer and professor, and it's a great pleasure spending more and more time together.

Otherwise, reading is a favorite activity for both Louise and me. We particularly value reading material centered around political and social justice. We also like to travel and often plan hikes or bicycle tours around performances. Finally, we enjoy being with our many good friends. I'm grateful for all of these joys in my life.

L. Comprehensive List of Works for Band

For a list of recordings, please see www.ithaca.edu/wilson.

Grade 4

Black Nightshade. Concerto for four percussionists and wind symphony, commissioned by Canandaigua Academy. (9:00, 2004, published by the composer)

the harder they fall... Commissioned by the Otsego County Music Educators Association. First performance in Cooperstown, New York. (5:00, 2004, published by the composer)

Io Rising for brass quintet, percussion, and large wind ensemble. Brass quintet is grade 6 level. Commissioned by the ensemble Rhythm and Brass. First performance at the Midwest Band and Orchestra Clinic, Chicago, December 1994. (7:00, 1994, published by the composer)

Sang! Commissioned by the Murchison Middle School, Texas. (4:30, 1994, Ludwig Music Publishers)

Shortcut Home. Commissioned by the Hillsborough (New Jersey) High School. (3:00, 1998, Boosey & Hawkes)

Uprising for large wind ensemble. Commissioned by Canandaigua Academy, New York. (6:00, 1995, published by the composer)

Grade 5

Concerto for Horn and Wind Ensemble (or Orchestra). Commissioned by Gail Williams (former associate principal horn with the Chicago Symphony). First performance of the wind version in 2002 with the Ithaca College Wind Ensemble at the Eastman celebration of the 50th anniversary of the wind ensemble. (19:00, 1997, published by the composer)

Concerto for Trumpet and Wind Symphony *(Leader Lieder)*. Commissioned by the International Trumpet Guild. First performance in Manchester, England, by James Thompson (formerly with Atlanta and Montreal Symphonies) and the Royal Northern College Wind Symphony. (15:00, 2002, published by the composer)

Evolution. Commissioned by the Washington, D.C., Air Force Band. First performance at the Virginia Music Educators Association convention in November 1999. (16:00, 1999, published by the composer)

Kah! (Out of Darkness). Commissioned by the University of Dayton in celebration of their sesquicentennial. First performance by the University of Dayton Symphonic Wind Ensemble. (9:30, 1999, published by the composer)

The Shifting Bands of Time for wind ensemble. Commissioned by Ohio University. (10:30, 1997, Ludwig Music Publishers)

Grade 6

Calling, Ever Calling. Concerto for oboe (or soprano saxophone) and wind ensemble (or orchestra) commissioned by the Mid-American Conference Band Directors Association. First performance by Michael Henoch (oboist with the Chicago Symphony) and the Central Michigan University Wind Symphony at the 50th anniversary convention of the CBDNA in Kansas City, Missouri. (21:00, 1990, published by the composer)

Clarion Call for brass and percussion. Commissioned by the Ithaca College Wind Ensemble with the first performance at the convention of the New York State School Music Association. (4:00, 1988, Ludwig Music Publishers)

Dance of the New World. Commissioned by Belmont (Massachusetts) High School. (9:30, 1992, Ludwig Music Publishers)

Last Ride to Solutré for orchestral brass and percussion. Commissioned by the Detroit Chamber Winds and Strings. (12:00, 1995, published by the composer)

Piece of Mind. Commissioned by the Ithaca College Wind Ensemble. First performance at Symphony Space in New York City. (21:00, 1987, Ludwig Music Publishers)

Shakata: Singing the World into Existence for wind ensemble. Commissioned by Phi Mu Alpha Sinfonia. First performance by the University of Texas Wind Ensemble at the College Band Directors' National Conference in Austin, Texas. (8:00, 1989, Ludwig Music Publishers)

Time Cries, Hoping Otherwise. Concerto for alto saxophone and wind ensemble, commissioned by the University of Northern Arizona. First performance by Laura Hunter (West Coast saxophonist) and the Northern Arizona Wind Symphony at the western conference of the North American Saxophone Alliance. (21:00, 1990, Ludwig Music)

Vortex—Concerto for piano and large wind ensemble. Commissioned by the Southeastern College Band Directors Consortium. First performance by the University of Tennessee Wind Symphony at the regional CBDNA conference, February 2000. (10:30, 2000, Boosey & Hawkes)

Winds on the Steppes for 16 winds, piano, and percussion. Commissioned by the University of Florida Friends of Music. First performances by the University of Florida Wind Ensemble in Gainesville, Florida, and by the American Chamber Winds at the conference of the World Association of Symphonic Bands and Ensembles in Manchester, England. (9:30, 1991, Ludwig Music Publishers)

Acknowledgements

Elizabeth Dallman Bentley

Susan Cline

Elizabeth Curtis

Lisa de Vries

Anthony Fiumara

Gary Green

Gregg Hanson

Alec Harris

Jerry F. Junkin

Debbie Kinder

Laurie La Plante

Ray C. Lichtenwalter

Hila Plitmann

Malcolm W. Rowell, Jr.

Stephen K. Steele

David Warble

Marguerite Wilder

Thomas M. Wubbenhorst